Tomart's Encyclopedia & Price Guide to
ACTION FIGURE
COLLECTIBLES

by Bill Sikora & T.N. Tumbusch

G.I. Joe — Star Trek

TOMART PUBLICATIONS
Division of Tomart Corporation
Dayton, Ohio

To the Toy Creators...

...who must battle a league of Monday-morning government regulators, consumer advocates, child protectionists, accountants, corporate politics, and the whims of retail chain buyers' wives to get an action figure line to market.

Acknowledgements

This encyclopedia has been a group effort from the beginning. Now in its third version, the list of contributors is ever-growing. Everyone listed here has played a role in making it the best it could be.

Thanks to Bill Jordan and Mike Markowski for their work early on for *G.I. Joe* and *Captain Action*.

We are deeply indebted to many consultants who have improved the accuracy of this book by taking the time to review the manuscript in whole or in part: Anthony Balasco, Raymond Castile, Dr. Jerry Harnish, Ellen Harnish, Jon and Karl Hartman, Mark Huckabone, Suzan Hufferd, G.F. Ridenour, Mike Stannard, Jerry and Joan Wesolowski. Their expertise in the field is an invaluable contribution. Of these, Mark Huckabone, especially, was always there to answer questions, help verify facts, or to provide photographic reference for rare or difficult-to-find figures.

Also contributing to the content were numerous collectors, dealers, and fans who have provided information and/or items for photography, including Rex Abrahams, Mike Blanchard, Steve Crouse, Steve Denny, Brian Doyle, Jim Gilcher, Barry Goodman, Charles Griffith, Chris and Erin Holzinger, Bill Jordan, Jeff Kilian, Israel "Lev" Levarek, Keith Meyer, Steve Miller, Darren & Kathy Murer, Scott Parrish, Karl Price, Deirdre Root, Daniel Rous, Steve Sansweet, David Secrist, Chris Shay, Jim Silva, David Sobliros, Mike VanPlew, Charles Welhelm, Dick Whittick, Andrew Williams, and the many dealers and collectors whose names we unfortunately failed to record. Thanks for all your help with facts and figures.

The cover photography was done with the help of Tom Schwartz and Terry Cavanaugh. Page Imaging was by Type One Graphics, printing by Central Printing and Carpenter Lithographing Company.

The enourmous tasks of photo imaging were completed with the assistance of Nathan Zwilling, Karin Buening, Chuck Jones, Kelly McLees, Chad Stewart, Rebecca Trissel, Denise Tudor, and Susan Tumbusch.

Tomart's Encyclopedia and Price Guide to Action Figure Collectibles is an outgrowth of *Tomart's Price Guide to Action Figure Collectibles*, first published in 1991; revised and updated in 1992.

FOREWORD

Tomart's Encyclopedia and Price Guide to Action Figure Collectibles is the most complete work on action figures ever assembled. The encyclopedia is comprised of three separate books. It represents the combined research efforts of the staffs of *Action Figure Digest* and *Action Figure News and Toy Review*, plus hundreds of dealers and collectors nationwide. Nearly ten years have gone into assembling the photos and information presented. It is a history of what has been done and the collector values of all major action figure lines produced from pre-*G.I. Joe* (1964) up to and including lines scheduled for Christmas 1996 release.

An effort has been made to maximize the number of figures shown in full color. It was more difficult to get listings on the same page as the photos...or even close in some cases, but the publisher felt the more pictures the better ... and the more pictures in color, even better yet! Be sure to review "How to Use This Book" below before trying to reference any specific figure.

The complete "Foreword" to *Tomart's Encyclopedia and Price Guide to Action Figure Collectibles* is found in Book One. It provides a quick-read education on collecting action figures. Read it and become an expert. The illustrated history is an invaluable overview to dating action figure collectibles and accessing the important factors which make one action figure more valuable than others.

The introductory material provides valuable collector information on how to get connected and find action figures of interest for your personal collection. Listed are publications, events, and other sources.

HOW TO USE THIS BOOK

Tomart's Encyclopedia and Price Guide to Action Figure Collectibles was designed to be an authoritative and easy-to-use reference guide. It utilizes an identification and classification system designed to create a standard identification number for each individual figure and associated item.

Try as we have, we have probably missed some figures which will be brought to the publisher's attention and added to future editions. This system contains the framework by which they can be catalogued.

The format is based on the name of the figure line found on the package. Code numbers were created based on the first two letters of the series title, with the exception of *Star Wars* (SW). *Masters of the Universe* figures, for example, are found at MA. The later *He-Man* line is found at HE. If the first word in the title is "The," then it is moved to the end of the title and set off by a comma. *The Adventures of Indiana Jones* is alphabetized as *Adventures of Indiana Jones, The*; and the first two letters used for the code are AD.

If, for example, you want to locate a *G.I. Joe* figure, flip through the book until you find classification numbers beginning with GI and read the alphabetical category heading until you reach "G.I. Joe." Classification numbers have been established based on the series name exactly as it appears on the original package, but cross-references have been placed throughout to assist you. Roger Rabbit figures, for example, are listed at the classification *Who Framed Roger Rabbit?*, but you will also find a cross-reference at "Roger Rabbit" which will direct you there.

If the figure is already out of the package and you know the line, it is a simple matter to match the figure to the thousands of photos provided. If you do not know the line, the job becomes much harder because you now have to compare it to each line licensed by the copyright owner molded somewhere on the figure. If there is no copyright in raised or depressed letters somewhere on the figure, it probably isn't worth anything anyway. The historical inforamtion describing each line usually mentions who licensed the figure. The best places to look for the copyright notice are on the legs, butt, or bottom of the shoe. Figures with cloth outfits are normally marked on the figure's back underneath the shirt, dress top, or coat.

Each item in the line has been assigned a reference code number consisting of two letters and four numbers. Use of these numbers in secondary market dealer and distributor ads and collector's correspondence is encouraged. Permission to use Tomart's I.D. numbers to buy, sell or trade action figures in lists, letters or ads is hereby granted. All rights for reporting values in newsletters, magazines, books, on-line, or advisory services are reserved. Written permission must be granted to use Tomart's copyrighted arrangement and identification system. Violators have and will be prosecuted.

The identity code numbers serve to match the correct listing to a nearby photo. Usually, there is a listing for every photo, but not all items listed are depicted. Some items in this three-volume encyclopedia have been previously listed in other publications by Tomart. This book utilizes a code system which is consistent with some, but not all Tomart guides.

THE VALUES IN THIS PRICE GUIDE

Price ranges in this book are divided into three categories: "Complete No Package," "Mint in Package," and "Mint in Mint Package."

Complete No Package (CNP) refers to loose items with all weapons, decals, and other items found in the original bubble pack or box. Figures, accessories, vehicles, playsets, etc. without all the original items are therefore worth less than the value listed for "loose" but complete items.

Mint in Package (MIP) means the unopened figure on a card or in a box which is at least in fine condition with no tears, prominent creases, battered corners, or price sticker damage. The figure will of course be mint, but collectors value the card or box as much, if not more, than the contents. Figures, vehicles, playsets and other accessories may have been opened, decals applied, and assembled — but still complete and undamaged — in a fine or better original box.

The phrase "Mint in Package" can be misleading. This is frequently interpreted by dealers to mean the item *inside* the package is mint, but the package itself could be re-glued, bent, faded, marred, or covered with adhesive tags which are difficult to remove without damage.

Mint in Mint Package (MMP) means the item is in perfect condition, just like it rolled from the manufacturer's assembly line. The highest values for action figures assume the figure is mint, and is complete in a mint package. No price sticker was ever applied, or if so, it was removed without marks or any trace of adhesive. Particular collectors even want the cardboard inserts in the hanger holes to be intact if they are to pay the top price. Boxed items are preferred factory sealed. Mint items were probably original stock, never in circulation, or not used.

The values in this guide are based on the experience of the authors and the national panel of dealers and collectors credited in the acknowledgements. The real value any particular item will bring depends on what a buyer is willing to pay. No more. No less. Prices constantly change — up and down.

Consult *Action Figure Digest's* world wide web page for periodic updates, or check the monthly price guide found in *Action Figure News and Toy Review* for the most accurate swings in the market month to month.

How to Subscribe to *Action Figure Digest*

Tomart's Encyclopedia and Price Guide to Action Figure Collectibles is updated with each issue of *Tomart's Action Figure Digest* magazine. Subscribe today by sending check or money order in the amount of $42.00 to Action Figure Digest, 3300 Encrete Lane, Dayton, OH 45439-1944.

G.I. JOE — A REAL AMERICAN HERO
(Hasbro) 1982-94

In 1982 when Hasbro released its first 9 new *G.I. Joe* figures, nobody would have guessed these figures would be the prelude of the arrival of the largest action figure line ever produced, and perhaps, the most challenging to action figure collectors. Unlike their predecessors, this new generation of *G.I. Joes* stood only 3¾" high and were named by their code name and classification rather than just *G.I. Joe*. The package illustrations were inspiring and the figures were authentically sculptured with versatile body design. Most of the figures came with a back pack and weapons. All figures came with a command dossier detailing the figure's personal data, military specialities, and a synopsis of each Joe's character. This was the foundation of *G.I. Joe*, "America's Mobile Strike Force." These new *G.I. Joes* were focused on defeating the forces of aggression...an enemy known as Cobra!

During the first years of production, the function or classification, such as Infantry, Ranger, or Commando, was the predominate name on the package. By the fifth year, the figure's code name became more dominant. There were more than 150 vehicles and accessories in the first 10 years of the line. Detailed blueprints on the construction and functionality were included in their packages, adding to the toy's realism. *G.I. Joe* attained additional support from the ongoing syndication of the TV series, Marvel's *G.I. Joe* comic book, and hundreds of other licensed products.

The first year, 11 carded figures were available, plus a mail-in premium for Cobra Commander; 4 vehicles with drivers; and 3 battlefield accessories. All of these products were strictly military and khaki green colored. The first 16 figures had straight arms with only the elbow joint in the arm. This limited the figure's flexibility and caused problems when posing with accessories. The second year figures were made with a swivel arm design which allowed the figure's arm to rotate 360°. This swivel joint was typically located where the figure's bare arm would meet a rolled-up sleeve.

Many unique drivers came with the bigger vehicles. Up to 4 figures were included in a box. These drivers were quite popular because they did not come carded and, in most cases, were only available with their vehicle. In following years, some of these figures were made accessible through Hasbro's mail-order company, Hasbro Direct Incorporated.

Each year Hasbro Direct had a promotion for a special *G.I. Joe* figure(s) — only available through the mail. "Flag points" printed on the back of packages, the promotion insert order form, and partial cash payment were required to obtain these mail-order figures. Most mail-order figures are scarce and hard to find. The first figure was the straight arm version of Cobra Commander. Other offers included the first version of Sgt. Slaughter, The Fridge (a military version of Chicago Bears football player, William Perry), and the Steel Brigade figure which kids could name and customize as their personalized *G.I. Joe* figure.

Among the few vehicle premiums Hasbro Direct made available were the Manta windsurfer and a bright white/black/red version of Sgt. Slaughter's Triple 'T' tank. Hasbro Direct has also offered unique posters, figure sets and various older vehicles over the years, but these came in plain brown boxes rather than the colorful original packages.

G.I. Joes have been offered in 2 separate cereal premium promotions. The first was for a Starduster figure with a Jet Pack (JUMP) made available through the *G.I. Joe* Action Stars cereal in 1986, and Kellogg's Rice Krispies offered a scaled down version of Lifeline in 1991.

Special Forces sets began with "Battle Force 2000" in 1987. "Battle Force 2000" and "Destro's Iron Grenadiers" introduced hi-tech auxiliary figures and vehicles. Product lines such as "Tiger Force," "Slaughter's Marauders", "Python Patrol" consisted of previously released figures and vehicles with uniforms and weapons in different colors. Other figures have been released with parachutes, sonic back packs, and even talking back packs. Special Forces gradually took over, and most new figures were part of the Battle Corps, Ninja Force, D.E.F., or similar group.

There were many special packaged items, such as a VAMP and HAL boxed set; a bright red and orange version of Tripwire with an audio cassette; 2 versions of the Crossfire radio-controlled jeep with Rumbler; and Rapid-Fire with a cartoon video tape.

Larger retailers capable of huge orders occasionally ordered exclusive products to attract customers to their stores. Sears offered unique products for Cobra, including a headquarters (1982), a motorized tank (1983), and 4 Dreadnok vehicles (1985) not sold in any other store. The Toys "Я" Us "Special Mission: Brazil" set (1986) included a cassette tape, 4 recolored figures, plus Claymore, and their weapons — a very popular set with *G.I. Joe* collectors. The "Night Force" line (1988-89), consisting of previous figures in covert black uniforms and vehicles with glow-in-the-dark decals, was also a Toys "Я" Us exclusive. Unique to Target were a version of Hit & Run with a parachute pack, a 2-pack of Muskrat and Voltar, and the first version of the 12" Hall of Fame *G.I. Joe*, Duke (see GI7335).

The *Real American Hero* line was planned to go on longer while larger sizes were tried, but two major retailers complained to Hasbro top management. The line was cancelled in favor of *Sgt. Savage and his Screaming Eagles*. This new line met with some resistance before it was issued, and the whole *G.I. Joe* creative staff was replaced by a new Kenner team as part of a major reorganization of the Hasbro Toy Group. The new team developed *G.I. Joe Extreme* for 1995 release. This line eliminated most of the articulation *G.I. Joe* had enjoyed since his introduction in 1964...without any dramatic sales increase.

A small number of unique foreign variations of *G.I. Joe* figures, vehicles, and accessories exist. Most are versions of previous figures painted differently. Many of these variations are desirable to collectors, but are difficult to procure in the U.S. As a result, many American collectors concentrate on American products, which sometimes can be just as hard to find.

Beware of strange and unusual 3¾" Joes. A small Phillips screwdriver allows parts to be interchanged to create a "special" Joe. Some entrepreneurs offer these to dealers as special mail-ins at a premium price. Needless to say, value is only harmed by customizing.

Special thanks to Charles Griffith for his help in compiling this section.

See page 168 of Book One for color photos of the First Series.

First Series, straight arm (1982)

GI5021

	CNP	MIP	MMP
GI5001 Grunt, infantry trooper	20	60	90
GI5003 Stalker, ranger	30	75	100
GI5005 Snake Eyes, commando	35	110	2000
GI5007 Short Fuze, mortar soldier	25	60	90
GI5009 Breaker, communications officer	25	60	90
GI5011 Rock 'N Roll, machine gunner	25	60	90
GI5013 Zap, bazooka soldier, 2-handle bazooka	30	80	140
GI5014 Zap, bazooka soldier, 1-handle bazooka	25	60	90
GI5015 Scarlett, counter intelligence	35	120	220
GI5017 Flash, laser rifle trooper	25	60	90
GI5019 Cobra Officer	25	90	130
GI5021 Cobra, the enemy	25	100	150

GI5023   **GI5024**

GI5023 Cobra Commander, mail-in (original Cobra emblem on chest)	50	–	150
GI5024 GI5023, regular emblem on chest	35	–	80
GI5051 Mobile Missile System (MMS) w/Hawk	50	100	150
GI5053 Heavy Artillery Laser (HAL) w/Grand Slam	60	110	160
GI5055 Attack Vehicle (VAMP) w/Clutch	70	120	180
GI5057 Motorized Battle Tank (MOBAT) w/Steeler, version 1 (see also: GI5200)	85	160	220
GI5059 Jet Pack (JUMP)	25	35	45
GI5061 Rapid Fire Motorcycle (RAM), 2 box sizes	25	40	50
GI5063 Attack Cannon (FLAK)	15	30	40
GI5065 Major Bludd, swivel arm, mail-in premium	20	50	60

GI5101   GI5103   GI5105   GI5107   GI5109

GI5111   GI5113   GI5115   GI5117   GI5119

GI5141

GI5159

GI5069	Cobra Missile Command Headquarters w/Cobra Officer, Cobra Commander (original or regular emblem on chest), & Cobra, all swivel arm (Sears exclusive)	220	480	750	GI5115	Scarlett	28	100	190	GI5151	Falcon Attack Glider w/Grunt	125	225	320

GI5115	Scarlett	28	100	190
GI5117	Flash	28	70	85
GI5119	Cobra Officer	22	80	110
GI5121	Cobra	25	85	140
GI5123	Doc, medic	25	60	75
GI5125	Torpedo	25	60	75
GI5127	Tripwire	25	60	75
GI5129	Gung-Ho	25	60	75
GI5131	Snow Job	25	60	75
GI5133	Airborne	25	60	75
GI5135	Cobra Commander	40	150	250
GI5137	Major Bludd, 2 file card versions	20	50	60
GI5139	Destro	35	100	140
GI5141	Duke, mail-in	15	–	50

GI5069	Cobra Missile Command Headquarters w/Cobra Officer, Cobra Commander (original or regular emblem on chest), & Cobra, all swivel arm (Sears exclusive)	220	480	750

Second Series, swivel arm (1983)

GI5101	Grunt	25	60	75
GI5103	Stalker	30	65	80
GI5105	Snake-Eyes	40	150	250
GI5107	Short-Fuze	25	60	75
GI5109	Breaker	25	60	75
GI5111	Rock 'N Roll	25	60	75
GI5113	Zap	25	60	75

GI5151	Falcon Attack Glider w/Grunt	125	225	320
GI5153	Viper Attack Glider w/Cobra Viper Pilot	150	275	350
GI5155	Assault Copter Dragonfly (XH-1), pivot & swivel nose guns w/Wild Bill	60	120	175
GI5157	GI5155, swivel nose guns only	50	80	120
GI5159	Combat Jet Skystriker (XP-14F), round nose gun w/o grid w/Ace	75	120	180
GI5160	Combat Jet Skystriker (XP-14F) w/Ace	75	120	180

CNP: Complete, no package, with all weapons and accessories; MIP: Mint in package; MMP: Mint item in Mint package. Values in U.S. dollars. See page 3 for details.

5

GI5151

GI5153

GI5155

GI5161

GI5163

GI5165

GI5166

GI5167

GI5173

GI5175

GI5177

GI5161	Cobra H.I.S.S.				GI5164	GI5163 w/o tow hook	60	100	140	GI5167	Flame Thrower (Pac/Rat)	7	25	30
	w/H.I.S.S. driver	40	80	95	GI5165	Battle Gear Accessory				GI5169	Machine Gun (Pac/Rat)	7	25	30
GI5163	Armored Missile Vehicle					Pack, G.I. Joe	20	35	40	GI5171	Missile Launcher			
	Wolverine w/Cover Girl				GI5166	GI5165, package reads					(Pac/Rat)	7	25	30
	w/tow hook	60	100	140		"Accessory Pack 1"	20	35	40	GI5173	Battle Armor S.N.A.K.E.	20	40	50

Grand Slam figures from GI5177 and GI5196

GI5196

GI5181

GI5183

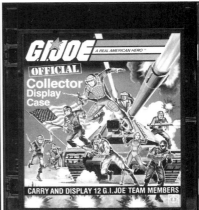

GI5190

GI5190, inside

GI5183

GI5198

GI5200

GI5185

GI5175	Twin Battle Gun, Whirlwind	25	50	75
GI5177	Jet Pack (J.U.M.P.) w/Grand Slam, silver pads	75	175	290
GI5179	Polar Battle Bear	20	35	40
GI5181	Cobra F.A.N.G.	20	30	35
GI5183	Amphibious Personnel Carrier (APC)	20	50	75
GI5185	G.I. Joe Headquarters Command Center	75	180	260
GI5190	Official Collector Display Case	20	35	40
GI5192	Pocket Patrol Pack	10	40	60
Re-issues with swivel-arm figures				
GI5194	Mobile Missile System (MMS) w/Hawk	55	85	135
GI5196	Heavy Artillery Laser (HAL) w/Grand Slam	60	95	145
GI5198	Attack Vehicle (VAMP) w/Clutch	65	110	170
GI5200	Motorized Battle Tank (MOBAT) w/Steeler,	60	130	180
Third Series (1984)				
GI5251	Scrap Iron	20	50	65
GI5253	Blowtorch	20	50	65
GI5255	Roadblock	35	65	85
GI5257	Spirit, tracker w/eagle, 2 file card versions	20	50	65
GI5259	Rip Cord	20	50	65
GI5261	Recondo	20	50	65
GI5263	Mutt & Junkyard	20	50	65
GI5265	Baroness, 2 file card versions	40	150	220
GI5267	Firefly	40	135	170
GI5269	Storm Shadow	40	145	185
GI5271	Duke	40	150	200
GI5273	Zartan w/Swamp Skier (Chameleon), version 1 file card	55	90	120

CNP: Complete, no package, with all weapons and accessories; MIP: Mint in package; MMP: Mint item in Mint package. Values in U.S. dollars. See page 3 for details.

GI5313	**GI5401**	**GI5403**		**GI5415**

GI5409

GI5417

GI5423	**GI5425**	

ID	Description			
GI5275	GI5273, version 2 file card	55	80	100
GI5277	Cobra Commander, (hooded) mail-in	20	30	40
GI5291	Attack Vehicle (VAMP Mark II) w/Clutch, tan uniform	45	120	160
GI5293	Cobra Night Attack 4-WD Stinger w/Stinger	40	75	85
GI5295	Flying Submarine (S.H.A.R.C.) w/Deep Six	30	70	85
GI5297	Cobra Water Moccasin w/driver, light green glove	50	75	85
GI5299	GI5297, dark green glove	65	105	150
GI5301	Hovercraft (Killer W.H.A.L.E.) w/Cutter	70	110	150
GI5303	Self-Propelled Cannon (Slugger) w/Thunder	40	70	90
GI5305	Sky Hawk	20	30	35
GI5307	Cobra Rattler w/Wild Weasel	75	150	220
GI5308	Attack Vehicle (VAMP) w/Heavy Artillery Laser (HAL) Sears exclusive	-	150	275
GI5309	Cobra A.S.P. (Assault System Pod)	15	25	35
GI5311	Cobra C.L.A.W. (Covert Light Aerial Weapon)	15	25	30
GI5313	Battle Gear 2, G.I. Joe	15	25	30
GI5315	Machine Gun Defense Unit	12	25	30
GI5317	Missile Defense Unit, Battlefield Accessories	12	25	30
GI5319	Mortar Defense Unit, Battlefield Accessories	12	25	30
GI5321	Bivouac, forward observation post battle station	15	25	40

ID	Description			
GI5323	Watch Tower	15	25	40
GI5325	Mountain Howitzer	15	25	40
GI5327	Battle Armor S.N.A.K.E., blue	40	80	120
GI5329	M.A.N.T.A. Windsurfer, mail-order	20	30	35
Fourth Series (1985)				
GI5351	Cobra's Sentry & Missile System (S.M.S.), Sears	75	120	200
GI5353	Footloose	15	35	45
GI5355	Quick Kick	15	35	45
GI5357	Lady Jaye	25	80	120
GI5359	Snake Eyes w/timberwolf	35	140	165
GI5361	Airtight	15	35	45
GI5363	Barbecue	15	35	45
GI5365	Bazooka	15	35	45
GI5367	Shipwreck w/parrot	25	70	110
GI5369	Flint	25	80	120
GI5371	Alpine	15	35	45
GI5373	Dusty	20	40	50
Dreadnoks GI5375-79 (2 file card versions each)				
GI5375	Torch	15	35	45
GI5377	Buzzer	15	35	45
GI5379	Ripper	15	35	45
GI5381	Crimson Guard, 2 file card versions	18	45	70
GI5383	Eels	25	50	75
GI5385	Snow Serpent	25	50	75
GI5387	Tele-Vipers	15	35	45
GI5389	Crimson Guard Commanders (Tomax, Xamot)	25	60	75
GI5401	Battle Gear Accessory Pack 3,	15	25	35
GI5403	A.W.E. Striker w/Crankcase	45	75	110
GI5405	Cobra Ferret	15	25	35
GI5407	Snow Cat w/Frostbite	40	70	90
GI5409	Cobra Hydrofoil (MORAY) w/Lamprey	40	75	85

ID	Description			
GI5411	Mauler M.B.T. Tank w/Heavy Metal	50	75	120
GI5413	Armadillo	15	25	30
GI5415	Silver Mirage cycle, 2 box sizes	20	35	40
GI5417	Transportable Tactical Battle Platform	30	65	100
GI5419	Bridge Layer w/Toll Booth	35	60	75
GI5421	Check Point	12	20	25
GI5423	Air Defense	12	20	25
GI5425	Cobra Bunker	12	20	25
GI5427	Forward Observer Unit	12	20	25
GI5429	Ammo Dump Unit	12	20	25
GI5431	Cobra Rifle Range Unit	12	20	25
GI5433	Cobra Flight Pod (Trubble Bubble)	20	25	35
GI5435	Weapon Transport	15	25	30
GI5437	Bomb Disposal	15	25	30
GI5439	Cobra Night Landing	15	25	30
GI5441	Aircraft Carrier U.S.S. Flagg w/Keel-Haul	175	400	700
GI5443	Listen 'n Fun w/Tripwire & Tape	15	25	35

GI5121

GI5123

GI5125

GI5127

GI5129

GI5131

GI5133

GI5135

GI5137

GI5139

GI5251

GI5253

GI5255

GI5257

GI5259

GI5261

GI5263

GI5265

GI5267

GI5269

GI5271 GI5353 GI5355 GI5357 GI5359

GI5361 GI5363 GI5365 GI5367 GI5369

GI5371 GI5373 GI5375 GI5377 GI5379

GI5381 GI5383 GI5385 GI5387 GI5389

GI5501

GI5503

GI5535

GI5537

GI5541

GI5543

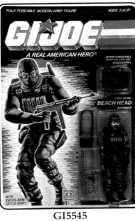
GI5545

GI5547

GI5549

GI5551

GI5553

GI5555

GI5557

GI5558

GI5560

GI5563

GI5565

GI5701

GI5703

GI5705

GI5707

GI5709

GI5711

GI5713

GI5715

GI5717

GI5719

GI5721

GI5725

GI5727

GI5729

GI5731

GI5733

GI5735

GI5770

GI5772

GI5776

GI5778

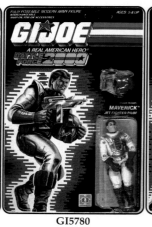
GI5780

GI5782

12

GI5875

GI5877

GI5880

GI5882

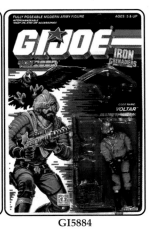

GI5884

GI5886

GI5888

GI5890

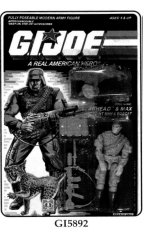

GI5892

GI5894

GI5896

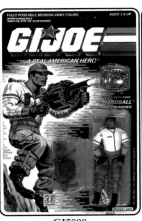

GI5898

GI5900

GI5902

GI5904

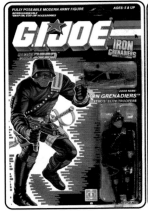

GI5906

GI5908

GI5910

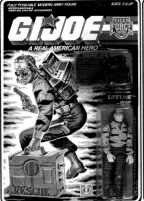

GI5974

GI5976

GI5273

GI5277

GI5291

GI5293

GI5295

GI5297

GI5301

GI5303

GI5305

GI5307

GI5308

GI5309

GI5321

GI5323

GI5325

14

GI5311

GI5315

GI5317

GI5319

GI5327

GI5329

GI5351

GI5405

GI5407

GI5411

GI5642

GI5644

15

GI5413

GI5419

GI5766

GI5768

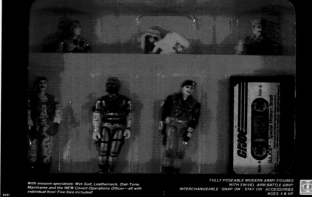

GI5634

GI5750

GI5630

GI5441

| GI5427 | GI5429 | GI5431 | GI5433 | GI5435 | GI5437 |

| GI5439 | GI5443 | GI5445 | GI5447 |

| GI5451 | GI5567 | GI5601 | GI5609 |

| GI5603 | GI5607 |

	GI5537	GI5539
GI5445	G.I. Joe Parachute Pack, mail-in	10	15	18
GI5447	Sgt. Slaughter, drill instructor	20	30	35
GI5451	(C.A.T) Motorized Crimson Attack Tank, (Sears exclusive)	65	140	175
Fifth Series (1986)				
GI5501	Iceberg	12	30	40
GI5503	Sci-Fi	12	30	40
GI5535	Zandar	10	25	35
GI5537	Zarana, version 1	30	50	80
GI5539	Zarana, version 2	10	25	35
GI5541	Leatherneck	12	30	40
GI5543	Dial-Tone	12	30	40

| GI5605 | GI5613 |

GI5545	Beachead	12	30	40
GI5547	Low-Light	12	30	40
GI5549	Lifeline	15	35	45
GI5551	Wet-Suit	20	45	55
GI5553	Roadblock	18	40	50
GI5555	Mainframe	12	30	40
GI5557	Hawk, G.I. Joe commander	20	45	55
GI5558	Viper	12	30	40
GI5559	Vipers	12	30	40

| GI5558 | GI5559 |

GI5611

GI5632

GI5754

GI5636

GI5638

GI5640

GI5646

GI5648

GI5650

GI5652

GI5654

GI5656

GI5752

GI5756

| GI5786 | GI5912 | GI6159 | GI6737 |

GI5560	B.A.T.	18	40	50	GI5601	Dreadnok Thunder-machine w/Thrasher	25	45	50	
GI5561	B.A.T.S.	18	40	50						
GI5563	Dr. Mindbender	12	30	40	GI5603	H.A.V.O.C. w/Cross Country	30	45	55	
GI5565	Monkeywrench	10	25	35						
GI5567	The Fridge, mail-order	15	25	30	GI5605	Conquest X-30 w/Slip Stream	30	45	55	

GI5607	Tomahawk w/Lift-Ticket	35	55	65
GI5609	Serpentor, Cobra Emperor w/Air Chariot	20	35	40
GI5611	Cobra STUN w/Motor-Viper	20	40	45

GI5758

GI5760

GI5762

GI5764

GI5788

GI5789

GI5784

GI5791

GI5793

GI5799

GI5803

GI5613	Cobra Night Raven SɜP, no landing gear notch, w/Strato-Viper	40	75	120
GI5614	GI5613 with landing gear notch	48	85	135
GI5630	Cobra Terror Drome w/Firebat & A.V.A.C.	65	130	175
GI5632	Sgt. Slaughter w/Triple 'T'	25	40	50
GI5634	Special Mission: Brazil w/Claymore, Dial-Tone, Leatherneck, Mainframe, Wet-Suit, Audio Tape (Toys "Я" Us)	120	180	280
GI5636	Cobra Hydro-sled	10	15	18
GI5638	Cobra Surveillance Port	10	15	18
GI5640	Devilfish	10	15	25

Dreadnok Ground & Air Assault Sets, Sears Exclusives GI5642-44

GI5642	Dreadnok Ground Assault Set w/Night Assault 4WD, Rapid Fire Motorcycle & trailer	75	135	180
GI5644	Dreadnok Air Assault Set w/Air Assault F.A.N.G. & VTOL	90	180	280
GI5646	Dreadnok: Swampfire	10	15	18
GI5648	Battle Gear Accessory Pack 4, Cobra	10	15	20
GI5650	Vehicle Gear Accessory Pack #1	7	10	12
GI5652	L.A.W. (Laser Artillery Weapon)	10	12	15

GI5654	L.C.V. Recon Sled (Low Crawl Vehicle)	10	20	25
GI5656	Outpost Defender	10	15	20

Sixth Series (1987)

GI5701	Law & Order	10	25	35
GI5703	Psyche-Out	10	25	35
GI5705	Falcon	15	35	45
GI5707	Outback	10	25	35
GI5709	Cobra Commander w/battle armor	20	40	50
GI5711	Crystal Ball	8	15	20
GI5713	Big Boa	10	25	35
GI5715	Jinx	12	30	40
GI5717	Tunnel Rat	12	30	40
GI5719	Chuckles	10	25	35
GI5721	Raptor w/falcon	10	20	30
GI5725	Crazylegs	10	25	35
GI5727	Fast Draw	15	30	35
GI5729	Sneak Peek	10	25	35
GI5731	Techno-Viper	10	25	35
GI5733	Croc Master w/crocodile	12	28	38
GI5735	Gung-Ho, marine dress blues	15	30	40
GI5750	Defiant: Space Vehicle Launch Complex w/Hardtop, Payload, Booster/Space Station, Space Shuttle, & Crawler/Gantry	240	550	1000
GI5752	Mobile Command Center w/Steam Roller	50	120	140
GI5754	Persuader w/Back Stop	25	35	45

GI5772		GI5774	

GI5756	Cobra Mamba w/Gyro-Viper	25	35	45
GI5758	Cobra MAGGOT w/W.O.R.M.S.	25	35	45
GI5760	Cobra Sea Ray w/Sea Slug	20	30	40
GI5762	Cobra WOLF w/Ice Viper	20	30	40
GI5764	Dreadnok: Zanzibar w/Air Skiff	18	28	35
GI5766	Sgt. Slaughter's Renegades: Mercer, Taurus, Red Dog	25	35	50
GI5768	Cobra-La Team: Golobulus, Nemesis Enforcer, Royal Guard	15	25	30

Battle Force 2000 GI5770-82

GI5770	Knockdown	10	25	40
GI5772	Blocker w/visor	25	45	60
GI5774	Blocker w/o visor	10	25	40
GI5776	Avalanche	10	25	40
GI5778	Blaster	10	25	40
GI5780	Maverick	10	25	40
GI5782	Dodger	10	25	40

| GI5807 | GI5709 | GI5813 | GI5815 | GI5819 |

| GI5795 | GI5797 | GI5801 | GI5805 |

| GI5811 | GI5817 | GI5821 | GI5843 |

| GI5841 | GI5845 | GI5847 | GI5849 |

GI5784	Starduster, version 1, 1984 on thigh, mail-order w/GI5261 torso, GI5059 jet pack (olive), GI5129 grenade launcher (gray)	25	35	45
GI5786	Steel Brigade, version 1, 1986 on thigh, mail-order w/GI5133 rifle (dark gray), GI5271 backpack (olive), Brigade patch & Bio certificate	20	25	35
GI5788	Radio-Controlled Crossfire Alpha 27 Hz w/Rumbler	35	60	90
GI5789	R/C Crossfire Delta 49 Hz w/Rumbler	35	60	90
GI5791	Action Pack, Anti-aircraft Gun, motorized	5	10	12
GI5793	Battle Gear Accessory Pack 5, G.I. Joe/Cobra	8	15	18
GI5795	Coastal Defender	10	15	18
GI5797	Cobra Buzz Boar	8	12	15
GI5799	Cobra Earth Borer	4	8	10
GI5801	Cobra Jet Pack	6	10	12
GI5803	Cobra Mountain Climber	4	8	10
GI5805	Cobra Pogo	8	12	15
GI5807	Cobra Pom-Pom Gun	4	8	10
GI5809	Cobra Rope Crosser	4	8	10
GI5811	Dreadnok Cycle	10	15	18
GI5813	G.I. Joe Helicopter	6	12	15
GI5815	G.I. Joe Radar Station	4	8	10
GI5817	Road Toad B.R.V.	6	10	12
GI5819	Rope Walker	4	8	10
GI5821	G.I. Joe S.L.A.M.	6	12	15
Battle Force 2000 Vehicles GI5841-51				
GI5841	Dominator	10	15	25
GI5843	Eliminator	10	15	25
GI5845	Marauder	10	15	25
GI5847	Skysweeper	10	15	25
GI5849	Vector	10	15	25
GI5851	Vindicator	10	15	25
Seventh Series (1988)				
GI5875	Shockwave	12	30	35
GI5877	Budo	12	30	35
GI5879	Charbroil, red eyes	8	20	25
GI5880	Charbroil, black eyes	8	20	25
GI5882	Muskrat	8	20	25
GI5884	Iron Grenadiers: Voltar w/condor	8	20	25
GI5886	G.I. Joe Ultimate Enemies: Muskrat w/Voltar, (Target exclusive)	20	65	110
GI5888	Hydro-Viper w/manta ray	8	20	25
GI5890	Dreadnok: Road Pig	12	30	35
GI5892	Spearhead & Max	8	20	25
GI5894	Hit & Run	12	30	35
GI5896	Lightfoot	8	20	25
GI5898	Hardball	8	20	25
GI5900	Astro Viper	8	20	25

GI5851

GI5916

GI5918

GI5920

GI5950

GI5952

GI5960

GI5954

GI5958

GI5956

GI5964

GI5968

GI5962

GI5966

CNP: Complete, no package, with all weapons and accessories; MIP: Mint in package; MMP: Mint item in Mint package. Values in U.S. dollars. See page 3 for details.

| GI5970 | | GI5972 | | GI5990 | | GI6025 |

| GI5978 | GI5980 | GI5982 | GI5984 | GI5986 |

GI5988

GI5992

GI5902	Toxo-Viper	8	20	25
GI5904	Blizzard	12	30	35
GI5906	Iron Grenadiers	8	20	25
GI5908	Storm Shadow	18	35	45
GI5910	Repeater	12	30	35
GI5912	Steel Brigade, version 2, 1987 on thigh, mail-order w/GI5381 rifle (dark gray), GI5271 backpack (olive), patch & certificate	17	27	33
GI5914	Starduster, version 2, 1988 on thigh, mail-order w/GI5127 torso, GI5059 jet pack (olive), GI5129 grenade launcher (gray), & GI5192 Pocket Patrol Pack	20	30	35
GI5915	Starduster, version 3, 1988 on thigh, mail-order w/GI5127 torso, GI5501 waist, GI5129 grenade launcher (gray), w/o GI5059 jetpack (olive), & w/GI5192 Pocket Patrol Pack	15	22	28

Battle Force 2000 Two-Packs GI5916-20

| GI5916 | Avalanche w/Blaster | 16 | 35 | 40 |
| GI5918 | Knockdown w/Dodger | 16 | 35 | 40 |

GI5920	Maverick w/Blocker w/o visor	16	35	40
GI5950	Rolling Thunder w/Armadillo	30	45	60
GI5952	Phantom X-19 Stealth Fighter w/Ghostrider	30	40	65
GI5954	Mean Dog w/Wild Card	25	35	40
GI5956	Warthog A.I.F.V. w/Sgt. Slaughter	25	35	40
GI5958	Skystorm X-Wing Chopper w/Windmill	20	30	35
GI5960	Desert Fox 6 W.D. w/Skid-Mark	20	30	35
GI5962	Cobra Bugg w/Secto-Viper	30	40	50
GI5964	Cobra Stellar Stiletto, 1-pc body w/Star-Viper	20	30	35
GI5965	GI5964, 2-pc body	25	35	45
GI5966	Iron Grenadiers: D.E.M.O.N. w/Ferret	22	30	35
GI5968	Iron Grenadiers: Destro's Despoiler w/Destro	20	25	35
GI5970	Iron Grenadiers: A.G.P. (Anti-Gravity Pod) w/Nullifier	20	25	30
GI5972	Super Trooper, mail-in	10	15	20

Tiger Force GI5974-92

| GI5974 | Lifeline | 10 | 15 | 25 |
| GI5976 | Duke | 15 | 25 | 35 |

GI5978	Dusty	12	18	28
GI5980	Roadblock	12	18	28
GI5982	Flint	12	18	28
GI5984	Bazooka	10	15	25
GI5986	Tripwire	10	15	25
GI5988	Tiger Fly w/Recondo	30	40	60
GI5990	Tiger Cat w/Frostbite	25	40	55
GI5992	Tiger Rat w/Skystriker	35	50	75

Night Force Two-Packs (Toys "Я" Us Exclusive) GI5994-98

GI5994	Sneak-Peek/Lt. Falcon	30	50	75
GI5996	Tunnel Rat/Psyche-Out	30	50	75
GI5998	Outback w/Crazylegs	30	50	75
GI6000	Airborne Assault Parachute Pack w/Hit & Run (Target)	25	75	120
GI6025	Cobra Adder	7	10	14
GI6027	G.I. Joe ATV	6	8	10
GI6029	Battle Gear Accessory Pack 6	5	10	12
GI6033	Cobra Battle Barge	6	9	12
GI6035	Cobra Gyrocopter	10	12	15
GI6037	Cobra IMP	8	12	15
GI6039	Cobra Rocket Sled	7	9	12
GI6041	G.I. Joe Double Machine Gun	5	8	12
GI6043	Dreadnok Battle Axe	5	8	12
GI6045	Cobra Machine Gun Nest	5	8	12
GI6047	G.I. Joe Mine Sweeper	5	8	12
GI6049	G.I. Joe Mortar Launcher	5	8	12

GI5994

GI5996

GI5998

GI6000

GI6027

GI6029

GI6033

GI6035

GI6039

GI6041

GI6043

GI6045

GI6047

GI6049

GI6037

GI6053

GI6055

GI6057

Night Force Vehicles (Toys "Я" Us Exclusive) GI6051-59			
GI6051 Night Blaster	25	40	55
GI6053 Night Raider	20	35	50
GI6055 Night Shade	20	35	50
GI6057 Night Storm	23	38	55
GI6059 Night Striker	30	45	60
GI6061 G.I. Joe R.P.V.	7	10	14

GI6063 G.I. Joe Scuba Pack	10	12	15
GI6065 Swampmasher	8	12	15
GI6067 G.I. Joe Tank Car	10	12	15
GI6069 Tiger Force: Tiger Paw	15	20	25
GI6071 Tiger Force: Tiger Shark	20	25	30
GI6073 Cobra Twin Missile Radar	5	8	12

Eighth Series (1989)

GI6101 Alley Viper	9	18	23
GI6103 Scoop	7	15	20
GI6105 Countdown	9	18	23
GI6107 Recoil	7	15	20
GI6109 Snake Eyes	20	35	45
GI6111 Iron Grenadiers: T.A.R.G.A.T.	9	18	23
GI6113 Rock & Roll	7	15	20

CNP: Complete, no package, with all weapons and accessories; MIP: Mint in package; MMP: Mint item in Mint package. Values in U.S. dollars. See page 3 for details.

GI6051

GI6059

GI6065

GI6063

GI6067

GI6069

GI6073

GI6101

GI6103

GI6105

GI6107

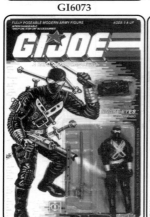

GI6109

GI6111

GI6113

GI6115

GI6117

GI6115	Battle Force 2000: Dee-Jay	7	15	20	GI6119	H.E.A.T. Viper		7	15	20	GI6125	Deep Six	7	15	20
GI6117	Dreadnok: Gnawgahyde				GI6121	Stalker		15	20	25	GI6127	Frag-Viper	7	15	20
	w/warthog	9	18	23	GI6123	Backblast		7	15	20	GI6129	Night-Viper	7	15	20

24

GI6131	Iron Grenadiers:				GI6142	Python Officer	7	12	18	GI6185	Darklon's Evader			
	Annihilator	7	15	20	GI6143	Python Crimson Guard	7	12	18		w/Darklon	20	25	30
GI6133	Downtown	7	15	20	GI6145	Python Trooper	7	12	18	GI6187	Crusader Space Shuttle			
Python Patrol GI6135-45					**Slaughter's Marauders GI6147-57**						w/Avenger Scout Craft			
GI6135	Python Tele-Viper	7	12	18	GI6147	Barbecue	10	15	22		& Payload	40	65	85
GI6137	Python Viper	7	12	18	GI6149	Footloose	10	15	22	GI6189	G.I. Joe Mudfighter			
GI6139	Python Copperhead	7	12	18	GI6151	Low-Light	10	15	22		w/Dogfight	15	20	25
					GI6153	Mutt w/Junkyard	10	15	22	GI6191	Arctic Blast w/Windchill	15	20	25
					GI6155	Sgt. Slaughter	10	15	22	GI6193	Destro's Razorback			
					GI6157	Spirit w/eagle	10	15	22		w/Wild Boar	20	25	35
					GI6158	Starduster, version 4,				GI6195	Raider w/Hot Seat	20	30	40
						1984 w/GI527 torso,				GI6197	Cobra Condor Z25			
						GI5501 waist, GI5129					w/Aero-Viper	35	45	60
						grenade launcher (gray),				GI6199	Thunderclap			
						w/GI5192 Pocket Pack	14	18	24		w/Long Range	30	45	60
					GI6159	Steel Brigade, version 3,				GI6201	Cobra H.I.S.S. II			
						1983 on thigh, mail-					w/Track Viper	18	25	35
						order w/GI5381 rifle				GI6203	Cobra H.I.S.S. II			
						(dark gray), GI5271					w/Mudfighter, Track			
						backpack (olive),					Viper, Dogfight, &			
						patch & certificate	10	18	23		2 misc. figures			
					GI6160	Keel-Haul, mail-order	5	10	15		(Bennie's exclusive)	50	75	110

GI6071

GI6119

GI6121

GI6123

GI6125

GI6127

GI6129

GI6131

GI6133

GI6135

GI6137

GI6139

GI6142

GI6143

GI6145

GI6147

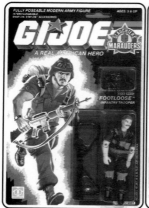

| GI6149 | GI6151 | GI6153 | GI6155 | GI6157 |

| GI6160 | GI6185 | GI6189 | GI6191 |

GI6187   GI6203

GI6193   GI6195

GI6207	Python STUN	10	15	20

Slaughter's Marauders Vehicles GI6209-13

GI6209	Equalizer	20	30	35
GI6211	Armadillo	10	15	20
GI6213	Lynx	15	25	30

Night Force Vehicles (Toys "Я" Us Exclusive) GI6221-25

GI6221	Night Scrambler	20	40	50
GI6223	Night Boomer	30	45	60
GI6225	Night Ray	25	45	55

Night Force Two-Packs (Toys "Я" Us Exclusive) GI6231-35

GI6231	Charbroil w/Repeater	25	40	60
GI6233	Lightfoot w/Shockwave	25	40	60
GI6235	Muskrat w/Spearhead & Max	25	40	60

Battlefield Robots GI6241-49

GI6241	Devastator	5	8	10
GI6245	Radar Rat	5	8	10
GI6247	Tri-Blaster	5	8	10

GI6249	Hovercraft	5	8	10
GI6275	Python Patrol: ASP	10	12	15
GI6277	Python Patrol: Conquest	20	25	30
GI6279	Battle Force 2000: Pulverizer	6	10	15
GI6281	Tiger Force: Tiger Sting	15	20	25
GI6283	Tiger Force: Tiger Fish	10	15	20
GI6285	Cobra FANG II	6	10	15

Ninth Series (1990)

GI6311	Capt. Grid-Iron	7	15	20

GI6197

GI6199

GI6201

GI6313	Night-Creeper	7	15	20	GI6321	Ambush	7	15	20	GI6349	Rapid-Fire w/Video	5	10	15

GI6313 Night-Creeper 7 15 20
GI6315 Rock-Viper 7 15 20
GI6317 Sub-Zero 7 15 20

GI6321 Ambush 7 15 20
GI6323 Free Fall 7 15 20
GI6324 Topside 7 15 20
GI6325 Laser-Viper 7 15 20
GI6327 Iron Grenadiers:
    Metal-Head 8 18 23
GI6329 Salvo 7 15 20
GI6331 S.A.W.-Viper 7 15 20
GI6333 Bullhorn 8 18 23
GI6335 Pathfinder 7 15 20
GI6337 Rampart 7 15 20
GI6339 Range-Vipers 7 15 20
GI6341 Stretcher 8 18 23
GI6343 Undertow w/barracuda 7 15 20

GI6349 Rapid-Fire w/Video 5 10 15
Sky Patrol GI6351-61
GI6351 Airborne w/Parachute
    Pack, gray 10 15 18
GI6353 Airwave w/PP, tan 10 15 18
GI6355 Altitude w/PP, green 10 15 18
GI6357 Drop Zone, brown 10 15 18
GI6359 Sky Dive w/PP, blue 10 15 18
GI6361 Static Line w/PP, white 10 15 18
GI6365 Steel Brigade, version 4,
    82-83 on butt, mail-order
    w/GI5381 rifle (dark
    gray), GI5271 backpack
    (olive), patch, certificate 8 15 20

GI6207

GI6209

GI6211

GI6213

GI6221

GI6225

GI6223

GI6231

GI6233

GI6235

GI6277

GI6241 GI6245 GI6247 GI6249

GI6275 GI6279 GI6281 GI6283

GI6285 GI6311 GI6313 GI6315

GI6317 GI6321 GI6323 GI6324 GI6325

GI6401	Avalanche w/Cold Front	25	45	60
GI6403	Overlord's Dictator w/Overlord	15	20	25
GI6405	General w/Major Storm, G.I. Joe Locust	60	95	150
GI6407	G.I. Joe Locust, brown/silver	20	30	40
GI6409	Cobra Hammerhead w/Decimator	35	65	95
GI6411	Hurricane V.T.O.L. w/Vapor	25	55	85
GI6413	Retaliator w/Updraft	25	55	85

Sonic Fighters GI6421-31

GI6421	Tunnel Rat	9	18	23
GI6423	Law	9	18	23
GI6425	Dial-Tone	9	18	23
GI6427	Dodger	9	18	23
GI6429	Viper	9	18	23
GI6431	Lampreys	9	18	23
GI6441	Iron Grenaiders: Destro's Dominator	10	15	18
GI6443	G.I. Joe Hammer	18	25	35
GI6445	Mobile Battle Bunker	10	15	20
GI6447	Cobra Piranha	5	10	12
GI6449	Cobra RAGE	10	15	20
GI6455	Sky Patrol: Sky Havoc	20	30	35
GI6457	Sky Patrol: Sky Hawk	10	12	15
GI6459	Sky Patrol: Sky Raven	25	40	60
GI6461	Sky Patrol: Sky Sharc	15	25	30

Tenth Series (1991)

GI6501	Dusty & Sandstorm	10	15	20
GI6503	General Hawk	12	18	23
GI6505	Crimson Guard Immortal	12	15	20
GI6507	Heavy Duty	10	15	20
GI6509	Sci-Fi	12	18	23
GI6511	Snow Serpent	12	18	23
GI6513	Low-Light	10	15	20
GI6515	Big Ben	12	18	23
GI6517	Desert Scorpion w/giant scorpion	12	18	23
GI6519	Incinerators	10	15	20
GI6521	Red Star	12	18	23
GI6523	Red Star, Cobra card	12	50	75
GI6525	Tracker	15	25	35
GI6527	Grunt	15	20	30
GI6529	B.A.T.	10	18	23
GI6531	Mercer	15	20	30
GI6533	Snake Eyes	15	20	35

GI6327 GI6329 GI6331 GI6333 GI6335

GI6337 GI6339 GI6341 GI6343 GI6349

GI6351 GI6353 GI6355 GI6357

GI6359 GI6361 GI6421 GI6423

CNP: Complete, no package, with all weapons and accessories; MIP: Mint in package; MMP: Mint item in Mint package. Values in U.S. dollars. See page 3 for details.

GI6425

GI6427

GI6429

GI6431

GI6401

GI6403

GI6407

GI6405

GI6409

GI6413

GI6445

GI6535	Cobra Commander, w/o eyebrows, clear red face plate	20	35	50
GI6536	GI6535, w/eyebrows	18	30	40

GI6537	Cobra Commander, w/o eyebrows, orange face plate (matches accessories)	18	30	40

GI6538	GI6537, w/eyebrows	15	25	35
GI6539	Rampage, mail order, Mauler M.B.T. driver	6	10	15

GI6441

GI6443

GI6447

GI6449

GI6455

GI6457

GI6461

GI6539

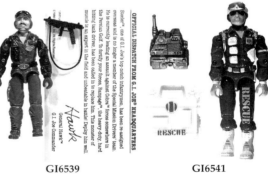

GI6541

GI6501

GI6503

GI6505

GI6507

GI6509

GI6575

GI6577

GI6579

GI6581

GI6511

GI6513

GI6515

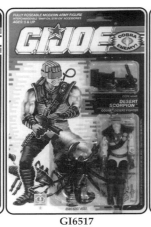

GI6517

GI6519

GI6521

GI6523

GI6525

GI6527

GI6529

GI6531

GI6533

GI6535

GI6583

GI6551

GI6553

GI6555

GI6557

32

GI6585

GI6591

GI6593

GI6595

GI6597

GI6620

GI6601

GI6603

GI6605

GI6607

GI6541	Lifeline, Kelloggs' Rice Krispies mail-order	6	10	14
GI6543	Steel Brigade, version 5, "MADE IN CHINA H-1" on butt, mail-order w/ GI5381 rifle (dark gray), GI5271 backpack (olive), patch & certificate	7	12	15
Talking Battle Commanders GI6551-57				
GI6551	General Hawk	6	8	12
GI6553	Stalker	6	8	12
GI6555	Cobra Commander (3)	6	8	12
GI6557	Overkill	6	8	12
GI6575	Badger	10	15	20

GI6577	Cobra Paralyzer	15	20	25
GI6579	Attack Cruiser	10	15	18
GI6581	Ice Sabre	10	15	18
GI6583	Brawler	15	20	25
GI6585	Battle Wagon	20	30	40
Air Commandos GI6591-97				
GI6591	G.I. Joe Glider w/Skymate	10	15	20
GI6593	G.I. Joe Glider w/Cloudburst	8	12	15
GI6595	Cobra Glider w/Night Vulture	8	12	15
GI6597	Cobra Glider w/Sky Ceeper	8	12	15

Eco-Warriors GI6601-20				
GI6601	Ozone	5	8	10
GI6603	Flint	5	8	10
GI6605	Cesspool	5	8	10
GI6607	Sludge Viper	5	8	10
GI6608	Sludge Viper, version 2	5	8	10
GI6609	Clean-Sweep	5	8	10
GI6611	Toxo-Viper	5	8	10
GI6620	Cobra Septic Tank	8	12	15
Battle Copters GI6550-52				
GI6650	G.I. Joe Battle Copter w/Major Altitude	10	15	20
GI6652	Cobra Battle Copter w/Interrogator	15	20	25

CNP: Complete, no package, with all weapons and accessories; MIP: Mint in package; MMP: Mint item in Mint package. Values in U.S. dollars. See page 3 for details.

GI6609

GI6611

GI6661

GI6663

GI6665

GI6667

GI6669

GI6671

GI6650

GI6652

GI6654

GI6701

GI6703

GI6705

GI6707

GI6709

GI6654 AH-74 Desert Apache	20	30	40		GI6663 Psyche-Out		6	9	12		GI6669 Major Bludd		6	9	12
Super Sonic Fighters GI6661-71					GI6665 Rock & Roll		6	9	12		GI6671 Dreadnok: Road Pig		6	9	12
GI6661 Lt. Falcon	6	9	12		GI6667 Zap		6	9	12						

GI6711   GI6713   GI6715   GI6717   GI6719

GI6721   GI6723   GI6725   GI6727   GI6735

GI6729   GI6731   GI6733   GI6734

Eleventh Series (1992)

GI6701 Duke (1)	8	10	12
GI6703 Wet-Suit (2)	6	8	10
GI6705 Roadblock (3)	60	80	160
GI6707 Big Bear (4)	4	7	9
GI6709 Destro (5)	8	10	12
GI6711 Flak-Viper (6)	4	7	9
GI6713 General Flagg (7)	4	7	9
GI6715 Gung-Ho (8)	4	7	9
GI6717 Barricade (9)	4	7	9
GI6719 Wild Bill (10)	4	7	9
GI6721 Firefly (11)	8	10	12
GI6723 Eel (12)	8	10	12
GI6724 Steel Brigade, version 6, "MADE IN CHINA H-1" on butt, mail-order w/ GI6107 rifle (dark gray), GI5271 backpack (olive), Brigade patch & Bio certificate	6	10	15

D.E.F. GI6725-34

GI6725 Bullet-Proof (1)	4	7	9
GI6727 Shockwave (2)	4	7	9
GI6729 Mutt & Junkyard (3)	4	7	9
GI6731 Headman (4)	4	7	9
GI6733 Cutter (5)	4	7	9
GI6734 Headhunters (6)	4	7	9
GI6735 Cobra Ninja Viper, mail-order	10	15	20
GI6737 Steel Brigade, version 7, same as GI6721, green & gold recoloring, mail-order w/GI6107 rifle (dark gray), GI5271 backpack (green), Brigade patch (green & gold), & recolored Bio certificate	5	9	12

Ninja Force GI6741-51

GI6741 Storm Shadow (1)	10	15	20
GI6743 Dojo (2)	7	10	15
GI6745 Nunchuk (3)	7	10	15
GI6747 T'Jbang (4)	7	10	15
GI6749 Slice (5)	7	10	15
GI6751 Dice (6)	7	10	15
GI6761 Air Commandos: Cobra Glider w/Air Devil	6	10	12
GI6763 Air Commandos: G.I. Joe Glider w/Spirit	6	10	12
GI6801 G.I. Joe Battle Copter w/Ace	8	10	15
GI6803 Cobra Battle Copter w/Heli-Viper	8	10	15
GI6805 Barracuda	8	10	15
GI6807 Patriot	6	10	15
GI6809 Storm Eagle	10	15	18
GI6813 Earthquake	10	15	18
GI6815 Liquidator	10	15	18
GI6817 Parasite	8	12	15
GI6819 Rat	6	9	12
GI6825 G.I. Joe Battle Figure Collector's Case	5	10	12

CNP: Complete, no package, with all weapons and accessories; MIP: Mint in package; MMP: Mint item in Mint package. Values in U.S. dollars. See page 3 for details.

| GI6741 | GI6743 | GI6745 | GI6747 | GI6749 | GI6751 |

| GI6761 | GI6763 | GI6801 | GI6805 |
| GI6803 | GI6807 |

| GI6809 | GI6815 | GI6825 |

| GI6813 | GI6840 |

GI6840	G.I. Joe Fort America	10	20	25	GI6853	Eco-Warriors: Barbecue	4	7	10	GI6856	Eco-Warriors: Eco Striker	6	10	12
GI6851	Eco-Warriors: Deep Six w/Finback	6	10	15	GI6854	Eco-Warriors: Toxo-Zombie	4	7	10	GI6858	Cobra Toxo-Lab	12	18	22

36

GI6817

GI6819

GI6856

GI6858

GI6866

GI6851

GI6853

GI6854

GI6901

GI6903

GI6905

GI6907

GI6909

GI6911

GI6913

GI6860	Sgt. Slaughter's Triple 'T', mail-order, new colors	10	15	20
GI6866	Headquarters	35	65	85

Twelfth Series – Battle Corps (1993)

GI6901	Bazooka (1)	4	7	9
GI6903	Cross-Country (2)	4	7	9
GI6905	Iceberg (3)	4	7	9
GI6907	Beach-Head (4)	4	7	9
GI6909	H.E.A.T. Viper (5)	4	7	9
GI6911	Alley Viper (6)	6	10	12
GI6913	Roadblock (7) (old colors)	4	7	9
GI6914	Roadblock (7) (new colors)	6	10	12
GI6915	Wet-Suit (8)	6	10	12
GI6917	Flak-Viper (9)	6	10	12
GI6919	Colonel Courage (10)	4	7	9
GI6921	Leatherneck (11)	4	7	9
GI6923	Snow Storm (12), orange and yellow trim	4	7	9

GI6915

GI6917

GI6919

GI6921

GI6923

GI6926

GI6927

GI6929

GI6931

GI6933

GI6935

GI6974

GI6976

GI6971

GI6973

GI6981

GI6983

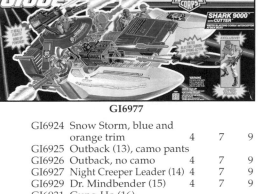

GI6977

GI6924	Snow Storm, blue and orange trim	4	7	9
GI6925	Outback (13), camo pants			
GI6926	Outback, no camo	4	7	9
GI6927	Night Creeper Leader (14)	4	7	9
GI6929	Dr. Mindbender (15)	4	7	9
GI6931	Gung-Ho (16), green w/tan	4	7	9

GI6985 GI6987 GI6989 GI6991 GI6993

GI6995 GI6997 GI6999

GI7025 GI7026 GI7027/GI7028 GI7032 GI7040

GI7041 GI7045 GI7047 GI7050 GI7055

CNP: Complete, no package, with all weapons and accessories; MIP: Mint in package; MMP: Mint item in Mint package. Values in U.S. dollars. See page 3 for details.

GI7056

GI7057

GI7058

GI7059

GI7060

GI7061

GI7062

GI7063

GI7070

GI7071

GI7073

GI7076

GI7077

GI7078

GI7087

GI7089

GI7092

GI7093

GI7096

GI7098

GI7080	GI7082		
		GI7106 GI7108 GI7105 GI7107	

GI7110   GI7113   GI7112   GI7111   GI7115   GI7116   GI7120

GI6932	Gung-Ho (16), maroon w/tan	5	8	10
GI6933	Barricade (17), blue w/gold	4	7	9
GI6934	Barricade (17), fushia w/gold	5	8	10
GI6935	Firefly (18), gray w/green	8	10	12
GI6936	Firefly (18), black w/green	5	8	10

Battle Corps Vehicles

GI6971	Mudbuster	10	12	18
GI6973	Ice Snake, Cobra	10	12	15
GI6974	Cobra Detonator w/Nitro-Viper	15	18	23
GI6976	Ghoststriker w/Ace	20	30	35
GI6977	Shark 9000 w/Cutter	18	25	30

Ninja Force

GI6981	Snake-Eyes (1)	10	12	18
GI6983	Zartan (2)	7	9	12
GI6985	Night Creeper (3)	7	9	12
GI6987	Scarlett (4)	10	12	15
GI6989	Banzai (5)	7	9	12
GI6991	Bushido (6)	7	9	12
GI6993	Slice (7)	7	9	12

Ninja Force Vehicles

GI6995	Ninja Lightning	7	10	12
GI6997	Pile Driver w/T'Gin-Zu	10	15	18
GI6999	Battle Ax w/Red Ninja	10	15	18

Twelfth Series (continued) Battle Corps (1993)

GI7025	Duke (19)	4	7	9
GI7026	Frostbite (20)	3	6	7
GI7027	Keel-Haul (21), w/small emblem on jacket back	5	8	10
GI7028	Keel-Haul, w/large emblem on jacket back	3	6	7
GI7029	Backblast (22), w/small emblem on chest	3	6	7
GI7032	Backblast (22), w/ large emblem on chest	5	8	10
GI7040	Crimson Guard Commander (23)	3	6	7
GI7041	Cobra Commander (24)	6	10	12
GI7044	Wild Bill (25) w/black pants, brown boots	3	6	7
GI7045	Wild Bill (25) w/white pants, brown boots	4	7	9
GI7046	General Flagg (26), brown jacket w/white trim	3	6	7

GI7084

GI7047	General Flagg (26), black jacket w/gray trim	4	7	9
GI7050	Cobra Eel (27), blue w/yellow	3	6	7
GI7051	Cobra Eel (27), purple w/yellow	4	7	9
GI7055	Law (28)	3	6	7
GI7056	Mace (29)	3	6	7
GI7057	Muskrat (30)	3	6	7
GI7058	Long Arm (31)	3	6	7
GI7059	Gristle (32)	3	6	7
GI7060	Headhunter Storm Trooper (33)	3	6	7
GI7061	Bulletproof (34), green & yellow camo	4	8	10
GI7062	Headhunters (35), black w/green	4	8	10
GI7063	Mutt & Junk Yard (36), blue/green w/pink vest	4	8	10

Star Brigade Armor Tech (1993)

GI7070	Robo-J.O.E. (1)	4	7	9
GI7071	Duke (2)	4	7	9
GI7072	Rock 'N Roll (3), w/purple weapons	5	10	12
GI7073	Rock 'N Roll (3), w/yellow weapons	5	10	12
GI7076	Heavy Duty (4)	4	7	9

GI7077	Destro (5)	4	7	9
GI7078	Cobra B.A.A.T. (6)	4	7	9
GI7080	Invader	8	10	12
GI7082	Starfighter w/Sci-Fi	12	18	25
GI7084	Armor-Bot w/Hawk	20	30	40

Star Brigade (1993)

GI7087	Payload (7), w/old style figure picture on file card	3	6	7
GI7088	Payload (7), w/new style figure picture on file card	8	10	12
GI7089	Countdown (8), w/brown launcher	3	6	7
GI7090	Countdown (8), w/black launcher	4	8	10
GI7092	Roadblock (9), white w/blue & red trim	3	6	7
GI7093	Ozone (10), gray shirt	3	6	7
GI7094	Ozone (10), tan shirt	3	6	7
GI7096	Astro Viper (11)	5	9	12
GI7098	T.A.R.G.A.T. (12)	5	9	12

Arctic Force (Mail-in) — **50** – **60**

GI7105	Sub-Zero	12	–	–
GI7106	Dee-Jay	12	–	–
GI7107	Stalker	12	–	–
GI7108	Snow Serpent	15	–	–

International Action Force — **45** – **50**

GI7110	Big Bear	10	–	–
GI7111	Big Ben	12	–	–
GI7112	Budo	12	–	–
GI7113	Spirit	10	–	–

Battle Pilots (Mail-in Set) — **25** – **30**

GI7115	Major Altitude	10	–	–
GI7116	Interrogator	15	–	–

Individual Mail-ins

GI7120	General Hawk w/ Supersonic Fighter Jet Pack	20	–	35
GI7122	Deep Six, yellow w/black	15	–	20
GI7123	Create a Cobra Figure	10	–	15
GI7124	Rapid Deployment Force w/bio card, GI5192 in black, GI5727, Repeater from GI6231, and Shockwave from GI6233, GI5547 gun GI5894 gun, & GI6525 gun (gold)	30	–	60
GI7125	G.I. Joe Collector's kit w/GI5277 and case	20	–	40

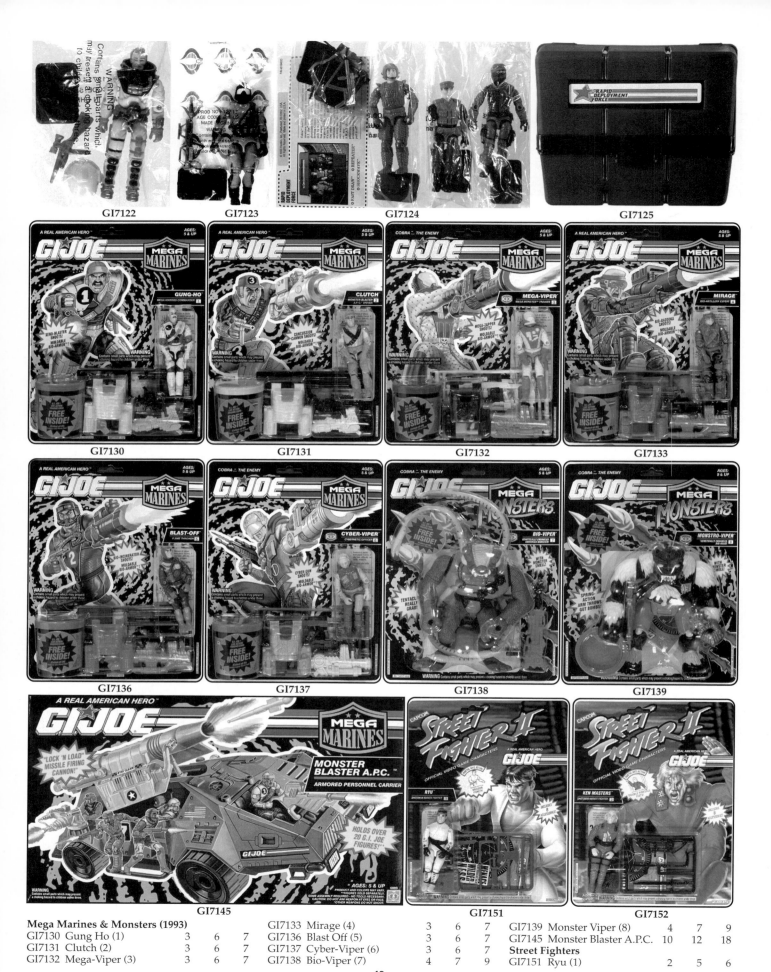

GI7122   GI7123   GI7124   GI7125

GI7130   GI7131   GI7132   GI7133

GI7136   GI7137   GI7138   GI7139

GI7145   GI7151   GI7152

Mega Marines & Monsters (1993)					GI7133	Mirage (4)	3	6	7	GI7139	Monster Viper (8)	4	7	9
GI7130	Gung Ho (1)	3	6	7	GI7136	Blast Off (5)	3	6	7	GI7145	Monster Blaster A.P.C.	10	12	18
GI7131	Clutch (2)	3	6	7	GI7137	Cyber-Viper (6)	3	6	7	**Street Fighters**				
GI7132	Mega-Viper (3)	3	6	7	GI7138	Bio-Viper (7)	4	7	9	GI7151	Ryu (1)	2	5	6

GI7153

GI7154

GI7155

GI7156

GI7157

GI7160

GI7161

GI7164

GI7165

GI7166

GI7167

GI7170

GI7171

GI7172

GI7173

GI7152	Ken Masters (2)	2	5	6
GI7153	Guile (3)	2	5	6
GI7154	Chun Li (4)	2	5	6
GI7155	Blanka (5)	2	5	6
GI7156	M. Bison (6) w/o shoulder guard	3	6	7
GI7157	M. Bison (6) w/ silver shoulder guard	2	5	6
GI7160	Edmond Honda (7)	2	5	6
GI7161	Dhalsim (8)	2	5	6
GI7164	Zangief (9)	2	5	6
GI7165	Vega (10)	3	6	7
GI7166	Balrog (11)	2	5	6

| GI7175 | GI7176 | GI7177 | GI7178 |

GI7180

GI7181

GI7182

GI7167	Sagat (12)	2	5	6
GI7170	Dragon Fortress w/KenMasters & Ryu	15	25	30
GI7171	Beast Blaster w/Blanka & Chun-Li	10	15	20
GI7172	Sonic Boom Tank w/Guile	8	12	15
GI7173	Crimson Cruiser w/ M. Bison w/o shoulder guard	8	12	15
GI7174	Crimson Cruiser w/ M. Bison w/ shoulder guard	15	20	25
GI7175	Guile 12"	10	15	20
GI7176	Blanka 12"	10	15	20
GI7177	M. Bison 12"	10	15	20

GI7178	Ryu 12"	10	15	20
Tonka Steel Brigade Vehicles				
GI7180	M.P. Pickup	8	10	15
GI7181	Military Combo (Dump-truck & Bulldozer)	15	25	35
GI7182	Striker (electronic)	10	15	20
Thirteenth Series Battle Corps (1994)				
8-13 Canadian Cards only GI7205-7210				
GI7190	Flint (1), black leg bands & weapons	4	6	7
GI7191	Flint (1), leg bands not painted	4	6	7
GI7192	Dial-Tone (2), green stripes on shoulders	4	6	7
GI7193	Dial-Tone (2), no stripes	4	6	7
GI7194	Shipwreck (3), black arm bands	4	6	7
GI7195	Shipwreck (3), arm bands not painted	4	6	7
GI7198	Metal-Head (4)	4	6	7
GI7199	Viper (5)	4	6	7
GI7202	Beach-Head (6)	4	6	7
GI7203	Alley Viper (7), orange stripe on legs	4	6	7
GI7204	Alley Viper (7), no stripes on legs	4	6	7

GI7205	Lifeline (8)	5	8	10
GI7206	Stalker (9)	5	8	10
GI7207	Ice Cream Soldier (10)	5	8	10
GI7208	Major Bludd (11)	5	8	10
GI7209	Snow Storm (12)	5	8	10
GI7210	Night Creeper Leader (13)	5	8	10

The last numbered series of 3¾" *G.I. Joe* figures is one of the most difficult to understand because it skipped numbers, produced card variations only distributed in Canada, and included two sub-series which were never produced. Numbers 1 thru 13 were released in an odd way. The line was introduced in the U.S. with figures numbered 8 thru 13 with 1 to 7 on new cards to follow. When the first six were ready, retailers wanted only higher numbers. Since Canadian distributing was running about 6 months behind the U.S., the first six figures on the new card design were sold only on bi-lingual cards. Only internal samples were produced on U.S. cards.

Card numbers 14 thru 20 were reserved for the proposed *Battle Ranger* series which was abandoned as *G.I. Joe* sales slumped. Cards 21 thru 27 are produced *Star Brigade* figures, and

| GI7191 | GI7192 | GI7194 | GI7198 | GI7199 |

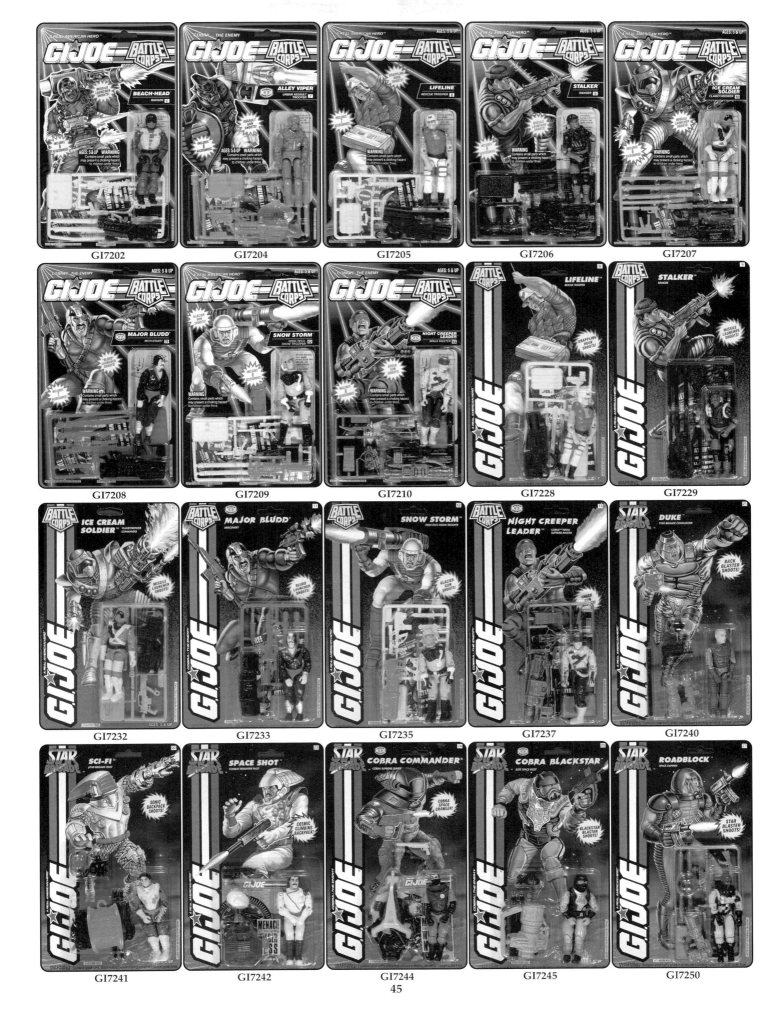

GI7202

GI7204

GI7205

GI7206

GI7207

GI7208

GI7209

GI7210

GI7228

GI7229

GI7232

GI7233

GI7235

GI7237

GI7240

GI7241

GI7242

GI7244

GI7245

GI7250

45

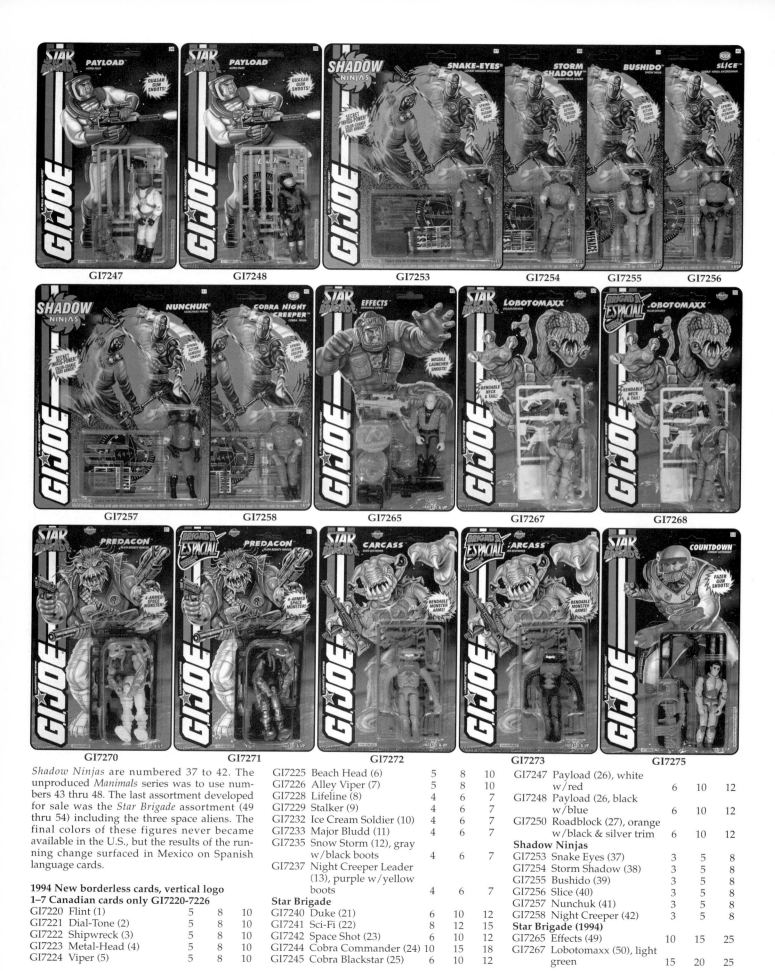

GI7247   GI7248   GI7253   GI7254   GI7255   GI7256

GI7257   GI7258   GI7265   GI7267   GI7268

GI7270   GI7271   GI7272   GI7273   GI7275

Shadow Ninjas are numbered 37 to 42. The unproduced *Manimals* series was to use numbers 43 thru 48. The last assortment developed for sale was the *Star Brigade* assortment (49 thru 54) including the three space aliens. The final colors of these figures never became available in the U.S., but the results of the running change surfaced in Mexico on Spanish language cards.

1994 New borderless cards, vertical logo
1–7 Canadian cards only GI7220-7226

GI7220	Flint (1)	5	8	10
GI7221	Dial-Tone (2)	5	8	10
GI7222	Shipwreck (3)	5	8	10
GI7223	Metal-Head (4)	5	8	10
GI7224	Viper (5)	5	8	10
GI7225	Beach Head (6)	5	8	10
GI7226	Alley Viper (7)	5	8	10
GI7228	Lifeline (8)	4	6	7
GI7229	Stalker (9)	4	6	7
GI7232	Ice Cream Soldier (10)	4	6	7
GI7233	Major Bludd (11)	4	6	7
GI7235	Snow Storm (12), gray w/black boots	4	6	7
GI7237	Night Creeper Leader (13), purple w/yellow boots	4	6	7

Star Brigade

GI7240	Duke (21)	6	10	12
GI7241	Sci-Fi (22)	8	12	15
GI7242	Space Shot (23)	6	10	12
GI7244	Cobra Commander (24)	10	15	18
GI7245	Cobra Blackstar (25)	6	10	12

GI7247	Payload (26), white w/red	6	10	12
GI7248	Payload (26, black w/blue	6	10	12
GI7250	Roadblock (27), orange w/black & silver trim	6	10	12

Shadow Ninjas

GI7253	Snake Eyes (37)	3	5	8
GI7254	Storm Shadow (38)	3	5	8
GI7255	Bushido (39)	3	5	8
GI7256	Slice (40)	3	5	8
GI7257	Nunchuk (41)	3	5	8
GI7258	Night Creeper (42)	3	5	8

Star Brigade (1994)

GI7265	Effects (49)	10	15	25
GI7267	Lobotomaxx (50), light green	15	20	25

GI7279

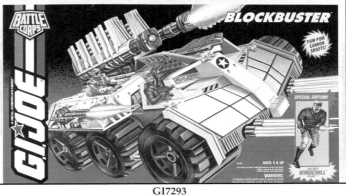

GI7293

GI7288

GI7289

GI7292

GI7276

GI7295

GI7296

GI7297

GI7298

GI7299

GI7305

GI7307

GI7268	Lobotomaxx (50), dark green w/silver overspray (Mexico)	25	30	35
GI7270	Predacon (51), blue	25	35	45
GI7271	Predacon (51), maroon/black/gold w/silver overspray (Mexico)	35	50	60
GI7272	Carcass (52), orange	20	30	40

GI7273	Carcass (52), red & black w/blue spray (Mexico)	30	40	50
GI7275	Countdown (53)	15	20	30
GI7276	Ozone (54)	15	20	30
GI7279	Dino-Hunters w/Low Light & Ambush (Toys "Я" Us exclusive)	20	40	50

Battle Corps Vehicles (1994)

GI7288	Manta-Ray	8	12	15

GI7289	Cobra Scorpion	8	12	15
GI7292	Razor-Blade	10	12	17
GI7293	Blockbuster w/ Windchill	15	20	30

30th Anniversary 3¾"

GI7295	Action Soldier	10	15	20
GI7296	Action Sailor	10	18	25
GI7297	Action Marine	10	15	20
GI7298	Action Pilot	10	20	28

GI7309	GI7312	GI7313	GI7314	GI7315

GI7320

GI7321

GI7299	Astronaut, Marine, Pilot (blue), Sailor (orange), Soldier & Space Capsule, display set	25	35	50
GI7305	Lt. Joseph Colton (mail-in)	6	10	12
GI7307	Lt. Joseph Colton (convention boxed)	15	25	35
GI7309	Fighter Pilot (black flightsuit) (convention boxed)	45	60	80

Florida F/X ShowBoxed 30th 3¾"

GI7312	Action Soldier	30	40	50
GI7313	Action Sailor	30	40	50
GI7314	Action Marine	30	40	50
GI7315	Action Pilot	30	40	50

Star Brigade Power Fighters

GI7320	Power Fighter w/Techno-Viper	10	15	20
GI7321	Power Fighter w/Gears, blue & silver w/green & silver helmet	8	15	20

GI7322	Power Fighter w/Gears, blue & green w/blue & green helmet	35	60	90

G.I. JOE HALL OF FAME (Hasbro) 1991-94

The *Hall of Fame* series was begun by Hasbro at the request of the Target store chain. The very first figure was a Target exclusive and was offered in September 1991. For the week of September 29 - October 5, 1991, a national flyer offered the first figure at the special price of $17.99 — the regular retail price being $21.95. Most stores were sold out of the figure within an hour of opening the doors.

The first 12" figure issued since 1976 was Duke. For the first time, Hasbro made a *G.I. Joe* figure with a specific name, naming him Duke after one of the characters from the *G.I. Joe — A Real American Hero* line. This figure used the Hasbro "Robb" body mold from the doll series *Maxie*, adding a new head with blond flocked hair made to look like the 3¾" Duke. Each came individually numbered with a sticker located on the back of the figure just above the waist. This figure was first issued in September 1991 and through the spring and summer of 1992.

GI7335

GI7336

GI7337

GI7338

GI7339

GI7340

GI7342

GI7343

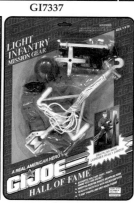

GI7345

GI7346

GI7347

GI7348 · GI7351 · GI7354 · GI7355 · GI7356 · GI7357
GI7358 · GI7360 · GI7361 · GI7362 · GI7363
GI7364 · GI7365 · GI7367 · GI7368 · GI7369

Duke was an unprecedented success, and Target's initial order of 30,000 was boosted to somewhere near 120,000. Other retailers quickly demanded a piece of the action, inspiring a limited return of the classic 12" *G.I. Joes*. A new version of Duke was created for the mass market, with a slightly different box design, a new head, modified hands (which enabled the figure to hold accessories better), and a camouflage cloth covering on the helmet. Cobra Commander, Snake Eyes, and Stalker were also available in the first year of the general release.

Collector response to the new 12" *Joes* was enthusiastic, but Hasbro continued to release large figures conservatively because of high production costs. "Basic Training" figures were an attempt to offset costs. They were sold with only a few accessories, and could be customized with assorted cloth and plastic accessory packs which were sold seperately.

GI7335	Duke, original Target release (6019)	10	25	35
GI7336	Duke, mass-market release (6826/6149)	10	20	25
GI7337	Cobra Commander (6827/6149)	10	20	30
GI7338	Snake Eyes (6828/6150)	12	25	35
GI7339	Stalker (6829/6150)	12	20	30
GI7340	Premium uniform from second *G.I. Joe* Convention, Limited to 600 pieces.	75	125	165
GI7342	Basic Training Grunt	8	15	18
GI7343	Basic Training Heavy Duty	8	15	18
Mission Gear Packs GI7345-48				
GI7345	Light Infantry	6	10	12
GI7346	S.W.A.T.	6	10	12
GI7347	Underwater Attack	6	10	12
GI7348	Arctic Assault	6	10	12
GI7351	Gung-Ho, Marine w/ gold sword	20	25	40
GI7352	Gung-Ho, Marine w/ silver sword	20	25	35
GI7354	Destro	25	30	40
GI7355	Ace	25	30	40
GI7356	Storm Shadow	20	25	35
GI7357	Flint, Green Beret	20	25	35
GI7358	Rock 'N Roll, green shirt w/side weapons, 2 versions of coloring exist on gatling gun, ammo pack & belt	50	75	100
GI7359	Rock 'N Roll, tan shirt w/o side weapons, 2 versions of coloring exist on gatling gun, ammo pack & belt	20	25	35
GI7360	Electronic Battle Command Duke	30	40	50
GI7361	Rapid Fire (Toys "Я" Us exclusive)	25	30	40
GI7362	Combat Camo Duke	15	20	25

CNP: Complete, no package, with all weapons and accessories; MIP: Mint in package; MMP: Mint item in Mint package. Values in U.S. dollars. See page 3 for details.

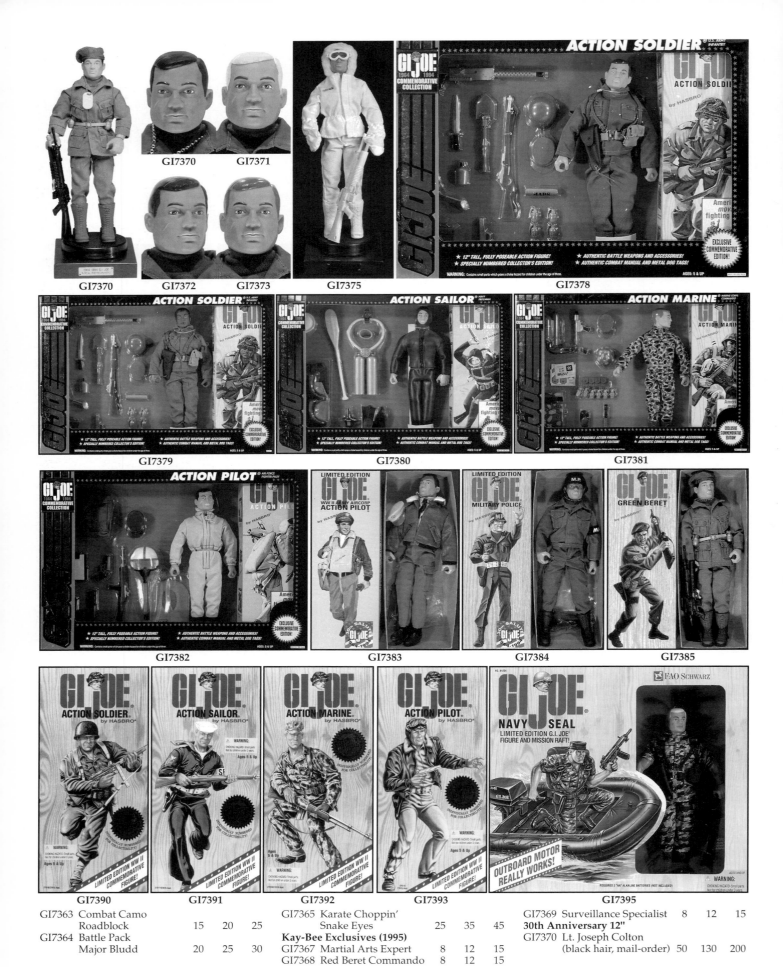

GI7370   GI7371

GI7370   GI7372   GI7373   GI7375   GI7378

ACTION SOLDIER
GI7379

ACTION SAILOR
GI7380

ACTION MARINE
GI7381

ACTION PILOT
GI7382

GI7383   GI7384   GI7385

GI7390   GI7391   GI7392   GI7393   GI7395

GI7363	Combat Camo			
	Roadblock	15	20	25
GI7364	Battle Pack			
	Major Bludd	20	25	30

GI7365	Karate Choppin'			
	Snake Eyes	25	35	45
Kay-Bee Exclusives (1995)				
GI7367	Martial Arts Expert	8	12	15
GI7368	Red Beret Commando	8	12	15

GI7369	Surveillance Specialist	8	12	15
30th Anniversary 12"				
GI7370	Lt. Joseph Colton			
	(black hair, mail-order)	50	130	200

50

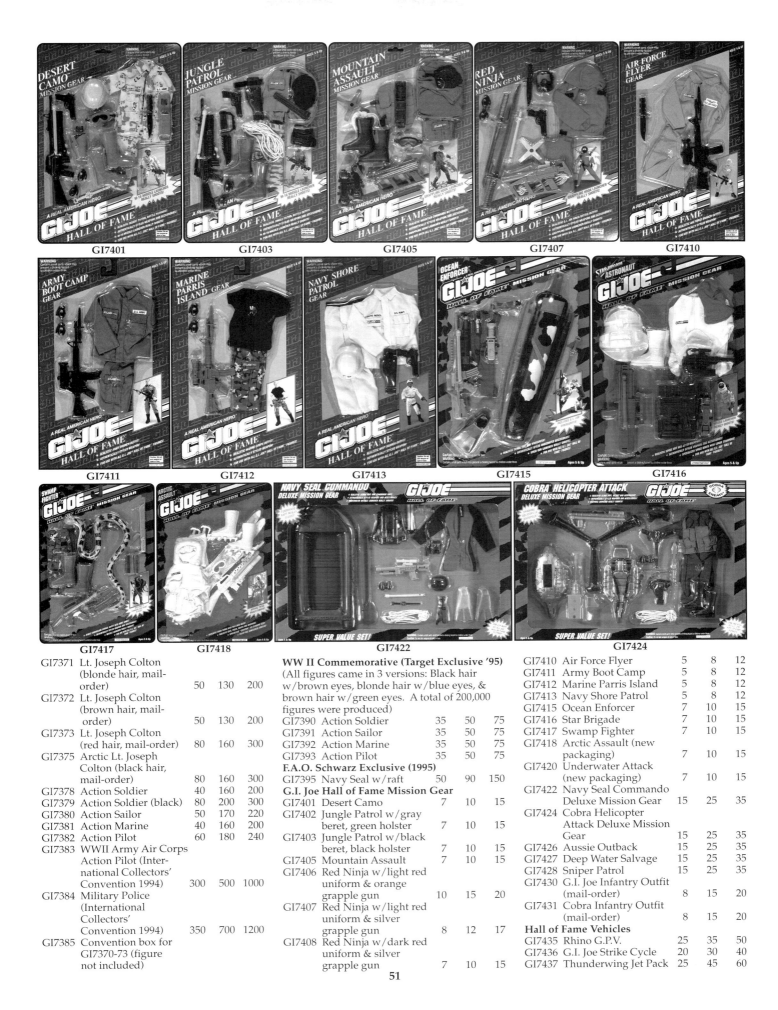

GI7401   GI7403   GI7405   GI7407   GI7410
GI7411   GI7412   GI7413   GI7415   GI7416
GI7417   GI7418   GI7422   GI7424

GI7371	Lt. Joseph Colton (blonde hair, mail-order)	50	130	200
GI7372	Lt. Joseph Colton (brown hair, mail-order)	50	130	200
GI7373	Lt. Joseph Colton (red hair, mail-order)	80	160	300
GI7375	Arctic Lt. Joseph Colton (black hair, mail-order)	80	160	300
GI7378	Action Soldier	40	160	200
GI7379	Action Soldier (black)	80	200	300
GI7380	Action Sailor	50	170	220
GI7381	Action Marine	40	160	200
GI7382	Action Pilot	60	180	240
GI7383	WWII Army Air Corps Action Pilot (International Collectors' Convention 1994)	300	500	1000
GI7384	Military Police (International Collectors' Convention 1994)	350	700	1200
GI7385	Convention box for GI7370-73 (figure not included)			

WW II Commemorative (Target Exclusive '95)
(All figures came in 3 versions: Black hair w/brown eyes, blonde hair w/blue eyes, & brown hair w/green eyes. A total of 200,000 figures were produced)

GI7390	Action Soldier	35	50	75
GI7391	Action Sailor	35	50	75
GI7392	Action Marine	35	50	75
GI7393	Action Pilot	35	50	75

F.A.O. Schwarz Exclusive (1995)

GI7395	Navy Seal w/raft	50	90	150

G.I. Joe Hall of Fame Mission Gear

GI7401	Desert Camo	7	10	15
GI7402	Jungle Patrol w/gray beret, green holster	7	10	15
GI7403	Jungle Patrol w/black beret, black holster	7	10	15
GI7405	Mountain Assault	7	10	15
GI7406	Red Ninja w/light red uniform & orange grapple gun	10	15	20
GI7407	Red Ninja w/light red uniform & silver grapple gun	8	12	17
GI7408	Red Ninja w/dark red uniform & silver grapple gun	7	10	15

GI7410	Air Force Flyer	5	8	12
GI7411	Army Boot Camp	5	8	12
GI7412	Marine Parris Island	5	8	12
GI7413	Navy Shore Patrol	5	8	12
GI7415	Ocean Enforcer	7	10	15
GI7416	Star Brigade	7	10	15
GI7417	Swamp Fighter	7	10	15
GI7418	Arctic Assault (new packaging)	7	10	15
GI7420	Underwater Attack (new packaging)	7	10	15
GI7422	Navy Seal Commando Deluxe Mission Gear	15	25	35
GI7424	Cobra Helicopter Attack Deluxe Mission Gear	15	25	35
GI7426	Aussie Outback	15	25	35
GI7427	Deep Water Salvage	15	25	35
GI7428	Sniper Patrol	15	25	35
GI7430	G.I. Joe Infantry Outfit (mail-order)	8	15	20
GI7431	Cobra Infantry Outfit (mail-order)	8	15	20

Hall of Fame Vehicles

GI7435	Rhino G.P.V.	25	35	50
GI7436	G.I. Joe Strike Cycle	20	30	40
GI7437	Thunderwing Jet Pack	25	45	60

GI7426   GI7427   GI7428   GI7437

GI7436

G.I.JOE
TOP SECRET

NAME
RANK
SERIAL NO.

GI7435   GI7445

GI7440   GI7441   GI7443   GI7448

Hall of Fame Accessories

GI7440	Smart Gun Blaster	10	15	20
GI7441	Backpack Missile Blaster	10	15	20
GI7443	Mobile Artillery Assault	12	18	22
GI7445	Official Footlocker	8	10	15
GI7446	J.C. Penny's Exclusive Footlocker, comes w/ GI7453 & sleeping bag	23	40	55
GI7448	Green Beret Weapons Arsenal, 2 versions	5	10	12
GI7450	Red Beret Weapons Arsenal, 2 versions	5	10	12
GI7453	The Utimate Arsenal	15	20	25
GI7454	High Caliber Weapons	5	10	12
GI7455	Urban SWAT Weapons	5	10	12
GI7457	Communications			
	Commando	10	20	35
GI7458	Martial Arts Training	10	20	35
GI7459	Medic Rescue	10	20	35

G.I. Joe — Sgt. Savage and his Screaming Eagles (Hasbro) (1994-95)

GI7475	Commando Sgt. Savage w/Video Tape (1)	6	8	12
GI7476	Combat Sgt. Savage (2)	4	6	8

52

GI7450

GI7453

GI7454

GI7455

GI7457

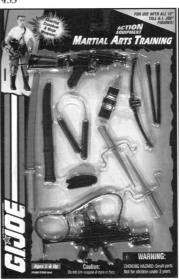

GI7458

GI7459

GI7475

GI7476

GI7477

GI7478

GI7477	D-Day (3)		4	6	8	**Sgt. Savage Battle Bunkers**		GI7498	I.R.O.N. Panther Tank	
GI7478	Dynamite (4)		4	6	8	GI7490	Battle Bunker w/		w/I.R.O.N. Anvil	18	23	28
GI7479	General Blitz (5)		4	6	8		Sgt. Savage	15	20	25	**Sgt. Savage 12"**	
GI7480	I.R.O.N. Stormtrooper (6)	5	7	9	GI7491	Enemy Battle Bunker		GI7499	Total Combat	
GI7482	Cryo-Freeze Sgt. Savage	8	12	15		w/General Blitz	15	20	25		Sgt. Savage	20	25	30
GI7483	Urban Assault Dynamite	8	12	15	**Sgt. Savage Vehicles**		**G.I. Joe Extreme**	
GI7484	Arctic Stormtrooper	15	20	25	GI7495	Grizzly SS-1		8	12	15	**First Series (1995)**	
GI7485	Jungle Camo D-Day	8	12	15	GI7496	P-40 Warhawk w/		GI7505	Ballistic		3	6	7
GI7488	Jet Pack Blitz	8	12	15		Fighter Pilot		GI7507	Freight		3	6	7
GI7489	Desert Camo Sgt.					Sgt. Savage	25	30	35	GI7509	Lt. Stone		3	6	7
	Savage (mail-in)		10	-	20					GI7511	Metalhead		3	6	7

GI7479

GI7480

GI7482

GI7483

GI7484

GI7485

GI7488

GI7489

GI7490

GI7491

GI7495

GI7496

GI7498

SGT. SAVAGE AND HIS SCREAMING EAGLES

TOTAL COMBAT SGT. SAVAGE

GI7499

with QUICK-DRAW COMBAT ACTION — GI7505

with STRONG-ARM BLOCKING POWER — GI7507

with SEMI-AUTOMATIC GATLING FIREPOWER — GI7509

with HEAVY METAL MISSILE LAUNCHER — GI7511

with POWER-LAUNCH CATAPULT — GI7513

IRON KLAW with BATTLE-ACTIVATED ASSAULT ROCKET — GI7515

INFERNO with FIREBOLT FLAMETHROWER — GI7517

BALLISTIC with ULTRA SLAM FIREPOWER — GI7519

LT. STONE with ULTRA SLAM FIREPOWER — GI7521

METALHEAD with ULTRA SLAM FIREPOWER — GI7523

IRON KLAW with ULTRA SLAM FIREPOWER — GI7525

GI7513 Sgt. Savage	3	6	7	GI7525 Iron Claw	4	8	10
GI7515 Iron Claw	3	6	7	GI7526 Lt. Stone/Iron			
GI7517 Inferno	3	6	7	Claw 2-pack	5	10	12
Deluxe Figures GI7519-25				**Vehicles**			
GI7519 Ballistic	4	8	10	GI7528 Road Bullet	5	7	10
GI7521 Lt. Stone	4	8	10	GI7529 Detonator			
GI7523 Metalhead	4	8	10	w/Sgt. Savage	10	15	17

Second Series (1996)

GI7531 Black Dragon	not determined
GI7533 Harpoon	not determined
GI7535 Mayday	not determined
GI7537 Quickstrike	not determined
GI7539 Rampage	not determined
GI7541 Wreckage	not determined

CNP: Complete, no package, with all weapons and accessories; MIP: Mint in package; MMP: Mint item in Mint package. Values in U.S. dollars. See page 3 for details.

GI7601   GI7602   GI7604   GI7606   GI7608   GI7610   GI7613

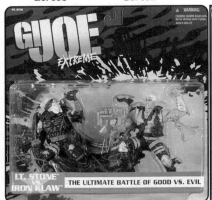

LT. STONE vs IRON KLAW™   THE ULTIMATE BATTLE OF GOOD VS. EVIL

GI7526

MISSILE-FIRING RAPID ASSAULT CYCLE!

ROAD BULLET ASSAULT CYCLE   WITH ULTRA SLAM FIREPOWER

GI7528

COMES WITH SGT. SAVAGE POWER-PUNCH ACTION FIGURE!

DETONATOR COMBAT CANNON   WITH ULTRA SLAM FIREPOWER

GI7529

GROUND TRACKER™ ASSORTMENT

TWO VEHICLES IN ONE!

SAND STRIKER ALL TERRAIN VEHICLE   WITH ULTRA SLAM FIREPOWER

GI7550

GROUND TRACKER™ ASSORTMENT

BATTLE DAMAGE™ ARMOR BREAKS AWAY UNDER HEAVY ATTACK!

BONE SPLITTER ARMORED TANK   WITH ULTRA SLAM FIREPOWER

GI7552

HEAVY ARTILLERY™ ASSORTMENT

COMES WITH INFERNO FIGURE AND BATTLE DAMAGE PLATFORM

SPITFIRE BATTLING PLATFORM   WITH ULTRA SLAM FIREPOWER

GI7556

SKY STALKER LONG DISTANCE ULTRA SLAM FIREPOWER

GI7554

ENEMY STRIKE UNLEASHES FREIGHT!

THUNDERIN' FURY LONG DISTANCE ULTRA SLAM FIREPOWER

GI7558

Deluxe

GI7543	Freight	not determined	
GI7545	Rampage	not determined	
Vehicles			
GI7550	Sand Striker	6 10 12	
GI7552	Bone Splitter	6 10 12	
GI7554	Sky Stalker	not determined	
GI7556	Spitfire w/Inferno	10 15 17	
GI7558	Thunderin' Fury w/Freight	not determined	

GI7560	Tiger Hawk	not determined
Playsets		
GI7565	Counterattack Tech Base	not determined
GI7566	Ice Station Zero	not determined
Accessories		
GI7570	Cybernetic Exo Armor	not determined
GI7572	Shadow Surveillance	not determined

GI7574	Alpine Enforcer	not determined
GI7576	Ammo Asst. Pack	not determined
GI7580	Extreme Collectors' Case	not determined
G.I. Joe Classic Collection (1996)		
GI7600	U.S. Army Infantry	not determined
GI7601	GI7600, black	not determined
GI7602	Australian O.D.F.	not determined

56

GO1028

GO1031

GO1036

GO1065

GO1086

GO1089

GO1098

GO1111

GO1260

GO1260

GI7603	GI7602, black	not determined
GI7604	U.S. Airborne Ranger HALO Parachutist	not determined
GI7605	GI7604, black	not determined
GI7606	British SAS	not determined
GI7607	GI7606, black	not determined
GI7608	U.S. Army M-1 Abrams Tank Commander	not determined
GI7609	GI7608, black	not determined
GI7610	French Foreign Legion Legionnaire	not determined
GI7611	GI7610, black	not determined
GI7612	U.S. Marine Corps Sniper	not determined
GI7613	GI7612, black	not determined

GOBOTS (Tonka) 1985-86

GoBots were small transforming robots created by Bandai and licensed for marketing in the U.S. to Tonka. They achieved their greatest fame along with Hasbro *Transformers* in the mid-1980s. All *GoBots* were vehicles which transformed to robots. As vehicles, they also had a pull-back and go action. Each one was numbered. Twelve different holograph stickers were packed with a couple different series. Towards the end of *GoBots'* success, "Power Suits" were sold to make them look like more powerful robots. below are the specific "characters" identified thus far. Close to a hundred different were produced. The Tonka Corporation was later acquired by Hasbro which produced additional *GoBots* in 1995 as part of its *Transformers: Generation 2* line.

GO1001	BuggyMan	2	5	8
GO1003	Cop-Tur	2	5	8
GO1006	Crain Brain	2	5	8
GO1009	Crasher	2	5	8
GO1012	Cy-Kill	2	5	8
GO1015	Dive-Dive	2	5	8

GO1018	Dozer	2	5	8
GO1025	Dumper	2	5	8
GO1028	Flip Top	2	5	8
GO1031	Good Knight	2	5	8
GO1034	Hans-Cuff	2	5	8
GO1036	Leader-1	2	5	8
GO1040	Night Ranger	2	5	8
GO1043	Pumper	2	5	8
GO1046	Rest-Q	2	5	8
GO1049	Road Ranger	2	5	8
GO1052	Scooter	2	5	8
GO1055	Scratch	2	5	8
GO1058	Screw Head	2	5	8
GO1060	Slicks	2	5	8
GO1065	Small Foot	2	5	8
GO1069	Spay-C	2	5	8
GO1074	Spoiler	2	5	8
GO1078	Spoons	2	5	8
GO1082	Stinger	2	5	8
GO1086	Street Heat	2	5	8
GO1089	Tank	2	5	8
GO1092	Turbo	2	5	8
GO1095	Tux	2	5	8
GO1098	Twin Spin	2	5	8
GO1099	Water Walk	2	5	8
GO1101	Zero	2	5	8

Monsterous GO1111-16

GO1111	Gore Jaw	1	5	10
GO1112	Fright Face	1	5	10
GO1113	Weird Wing	1	5	10
GO1114	Heart Attack	1	5	10
GO1115	South Claw	1	5	10
GO1116	Fangs	1	5	10
GO1260	Power suits, ea	1	3	4
GO1275	Collector's Case	3	5	7

See also: *Transformers*

GODDESS OF THE ULTRA COSMOS (Agglo) c. 1985

A knock-off of the *Golden Girl* and *Princess of Power* genre.

		CNP	MIP	MMP
GO3001	Goddess of Microlite	2	6	8
GO3002	Goddess of Gratonite	2	6	8
GO3003	Goddess of Stibnite	2	6	8
GO3004	Goddess of Scheelite	2	6	8
GO3005	Goddess of Sodalite	2	6	8
GO3006	Goddess of Bornite	2	6	8

GODZILLA (Mattel) 1977, (Imperial) 1985

Godzilla has been a mainstay of Japanese toys since the films first appeared. Hundreds of versions have been produced there, and some have been imported to the United States. Relatively few Godzilla toys have been made for the U.S. market. A large figure of Godzilla was produced in conjunction with Mattel's Shogun Warriors line. The figure had firing hands and a "flame" tongue. Imperial made a one-shot rubber figure.

		CNP	MIP	MMP
GO5001	Godzilla (Shogun)	50	120	180
GO5050	Godzilla, tagged	4	10	20
GO5051	Godzilla, carded	4	8	12

See also: *King Kong; Rodan; Shogun Warriors*

GODZILLA, KING OF THE MONSTERS (Trendmasters) 1994-95

Trendmasters brought back Godzilla and his classic monstrous adversaries in 1994-95, producing figures in various sizes.

4" Figures (carded)		CNP	MIP	MMP
GO5101	Godzilla	2	5	7
GO5102	Mecha-Godzilla	2	5	7
GO5103	Ghidora	2	5	7
GO5104	Mecha-Ghidorah	2	5	7
GO5105	Mothra	2	5	7
GO5106	Rodan	2	5	7

4" Electronic Figures (boxed) GO5111-16				
GO5111	Godzilla	3	8	10
GO5112	Mecha-Godzilla	3	8	10

CNP: Complete, no package, with all weapons and accessories; MIP: Mint in package; MMP: Mint item in Mint package. Values in U.S. dollars. See page 3 for details.

57

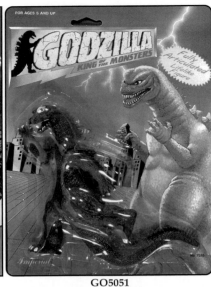

GO3001	GO3002	GO5001	GO5051

GO5101	GO5102	GO5103	GO5104	GO5105	GO5106

GO5111	GO5112	GO5114	GO5115	GO5116

		CNP	MIP	MMP
GO5123	Ghidora	5	12	15
GO5124	Mecha-Ghidorah	5	12	15
GO5125	Mothra	5	12	15
GO5126	Rodan	5	12	15
Godzilla Force				
GO5131	Pete Richards	2	5	8
GO5132	Michael Van Horn	2	5	8
GO5133	Margaret O'Brien	2	5	8
GO5134	David Easton	2	5	8
GO5136	Garuda Warship	5	10	15

GODZILLA WARS (Trendmasters) 1996

This was essentially a continuation of the *Godzilla, King of the Monsters* line. Old product was repackaged to kick-start the line. Snap-on armor and weapons were added in the "power-up" sets.

GO5118 image with caption:

GODZILLA KING OF THE MONSTERS 40th ANNIVERSARY COLLECTOR'S EDITION

SET INCLUDES: GODZILLA BATTRA MECHA-GODZILLA MECHA-GHIDORAH RODAN GIGAN GHIDORAH MOTHRA BIOLLANTE

GO5118

GO5113	Ghidora	3	8	10
GO5114	Mecha-Ghidorah	3	8	10
GO5115	Mothra	3	8	10
GO5116	Rodan	3	8	10

GO5118	40th Anniversary box	-	25	35
10" Figures				
GO5121	Godzilla	5	12	15
GO5122	Mecha-Godzilla	5	12	15

		CNP	MIP	MMP
GO5501	Godzilla	5	8	10
GO5503	Space Godzilla	5	8	10
GO5505	Biollante	5	8	10
GO5507	Battra	5	8	10
GO5509	Gigan	5	8	10

GO5121
GO5122
GO5126
GO5123
GO5125
GO5124
GO5136

GO5131
GO5132
GO5133
GO5134

GO5501
GO5503
GO5505
GO5507
GO5509

GO5511
GO5515
GO5517

GO5511	Moguera	5	8	10
GO5515	Power-Up Godzilla	6	9	12
GO5517	Power-Up Ghidorah	6	9	12

GODZILLA'S GANG (Mattel) c.1978

Articulated 6" vinyl dolls made by Popy of Japan were distributed by Mattel during the heyday of *Shogun Warriors*. Apart from Godzilla, all of the characters were actually derived from the Japanese TV series *Ultraman*.

| GO5801 | GO5804 | GO5807 | GO5809 | GO5806 | GO5805 |

| GO6001 | GO6002 | GO6003 | GO6004 | GO6005 |

| GO6006 | GO6007 | GO6008 | GO6009 | GO6010 |

		CNP	MIP	MMP
GO5801	Godzilla	20	65	75
GO5802	King Joe	12	40	50
GO5803	Gemustar	12	40	50
GO5804	Noko-Girin	12	40	50
GO5805	Micras	12	40	50
GO5806	Eleking	12	40	50
GO5807	Ikarusu-Planeteer	12	40	50
GO5809	Muruchi	12	40	50

GOLDEN FANTASY — See *Walt Disney Golden Fantasy*

GOLDEN GIRL AND THE GUARDIANS OF THE GEMSTONES (Galoob) 1984-87

The *Golden Girl* line seems to bridge the gap between dolls and action figures. While it is obviously a fantasy line with the usual accessories and playsets, doll-style clothing outfits were sold which often included purses for the figures. A fan club package was also offered.

		CNP	MIP	MMP
GO6001	Golden Girl	5	10	16
GO6002	Prince Kroma	10	20	25
GO6003	Onyx	5	10	16
GO6004	Jade	5	10	16
GO6005	Saphire	5	10	16
GO6006	Rubee	5	10	16
GO6007	Dragon Queen	5	10	16
GO6008	Ogra	9	18	22
GO6009	Vultura	5	10	16
GO6010	Wild One	8	17	20
GO6011	Moth Lady	5	10	16

Glorious Glitter Outfits GO6021-29

GO6021	Golden Girl	2	5	7
GO6022	Onyx	2	5	7
GO6023	Jade	2	5	7
GO6024	Saphire	2	5	7
GO6025	Rubee	2	5	7
GO6026	Dragon Queen	2	5	7
GO6027	Vultura	2	5	7
GO6028	Wild One	2	5	7
GO6029	Moth Lady	2	5	7

Forest Fantasy Outfits GO31-39

GO6031	Golden Girl	2	5	7
GO6032	Onyx	2	5	7
GO6033	Jade	2	5	7
GO6034	Saphire	2	5	7
GO6035	Rubee	2	5	7
GO6036	Dragon Queen	2	5	7

GO6011

GO6037

GO6047

GO6047

GO6100

GR2001

GR2011

GR2015

GR2016

GR2017

GO6037	Vultura	2	5	7
GO6038	Wild One	2	5	7
GO6039	Moth Lady	2	5	7
Festival Spirit Outfits GO6041-49				
GO6041	Golden Girl	2	5	7
GO6042	Onyx	2	5	7
GO6043	Jade	2	5	7
GO6044	Saphire	2	5	7
GO6045	Rubee	2	5	7
GO6046	Dragon Queen	2	5	7
GO6047	Vultura	2	5	7
GO6048	Wild One	2	5	7
GO6049	Moth Lady	2	5	7
Evening Enchantment Outfits GO6051-59				
GO6051	Golden Girl	2	5	7
GO6052	Onyx	2	5	7
GO6053	Jade	2	5	7
GO6054	Saphire	2	5	7
GO6055	Rubee	2	5	7
GO6056	Dragon Queen	2	5	7
GO6057	Vultura	2	5	7
GO6058	Wild One	2	5	7
GO6059	Moth Lady	2	5	7
GO6061	Olympia	5	20	30
GO6062	Olympia and Chariot	8	25	45
GO6065	Shadow	5	20	30

GO6066	Shadow and Chariot	8	25	45
GO6071-74	Dream Tents			
	four different, ea	2	6	10
GO6100	Palace of Gems	10	30	60

GREAT ADVENTURES (Fisher-Price) 1994-96

This series was aimed at younger audiences. The figures were articulated only at the arms, with special figures featuring battle action. Castle-oriented sets were produced in the first year, with pirates being added in late 1995.

Figures were initially available only with playsets. Extra figures were available in special packages starting in 1995.

		CNP	MIP	MMP
GR2001	Castle Playset	10	30	40
GR2011	Pirate Ship	10	30	40
GR2015	Knights (3 colors)	2	4	6
GR2016	Knights (gold)	2	4	6
GR2017	Knights (black)	2	4	6
GR2021	Dragon Set	2	4	6
GR2022	Bad Bones Pirates	2	4	6
GR2031	Jousting Knights	2	4	6
GR2032	Boulder Blaster	3	7	10
GR2033	Shark Raft	3	7	10
GR2034	Pirate Island	4	8	12

GR2035	"Ghost Knight" mail-in	3	7	10
GR2041	Claw Crew &			
	Yellow Jacks	3	5	7
GR2042	Fire Guard &			
	Ice Brigade	3	5	7
GR2043	Wizard Set	2	4	6
GR2044	Ghost Raiders	2	4	6
GR2045	Dragon Duel	2	4	6
GR2046	Mighty Mouth Whale	3	7	10

GREAT HEROES OF TIME (Toy Island) 1995

An educational series based on characters from history and the Bible. The David vs. Goliath set was carded two different ways for case packing purposes.

American Heroes		CNP	MIP	MMP
GR3001	Deerfield Massacre	2	8	10
GR3002	Yorktown	2	8	10
GR3003	Remember the Alamo	2	8	10
GR3004	Gettysburg	2	8	10
GR3005	Iwo Jima	2	8	10
Heroes of the World				
GR3101	Roman vs. Hannibal	2	8	10
GR3102	King Richard I			
	vs. Saladin	2	8	10

CNP: Complete, no package, with all weapons and accessories; MIP: Mint in package; MMP: Mint item in Mint package. Values in U.S. dollars. See page 3 for details.

Dragon Set
GR2021

Bad Bones Pirates
GR2022

Jousting Knights
GR2031

Boulder Blaster
GR2032

Shark Raft
GR2033

Pirate Island
GR2034

Claw Crew &
Yellow Jacks
GR2041

Fire Guard &
Ice Brigade
GR2042

Wizard Set
GR2043

Ghost Raiders
GR2044

Dragon Duel
GR2045

Mighty Mouth Whale
GR2046

GR2035

GR3001

GR3101

GR3204

GR3103	Kublai Khan			
	vs. Samurai	2	8	10
GR3104	Cortez			
	vs. Aztec Warrior	2	8	10
GR3105	WWI Fusilier			
	vs. Grenadier	2	8	10

Holyland Heroes

HO3201	Moses vs. Ramses II	2	8	10
HO3202	Joshua vs. Canaanite	2	8	10
HO3203	Samson vs. Phillistine	2	8	10
HO3204	David vs. Goliath			
	2 variations, ea	2	8	10

HO3206	Simon vs. Syrian	2	8	10

See also: *Bible Characters; Bible Greats*

GREATEST AMERICAN HERO (Mego) 1981

A one-shot Convertible "Bug" was produced with 2 3¾" action figures. Three 8" fig-

GR4501

GR4801

GR4803

GR4804

GR4901

GR2001

GR2003

GR2004

GU4004

GU5001

HA7001

HA7002

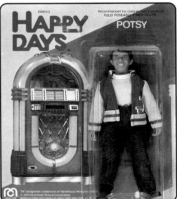
HA7003

HA7004

ures are advertised on the package back, but
were never produced.

	CNP	MIP	MMP
GR4501 Convertible "Bug"			
w/3¾" Ralph and Bill	75	125	175

GREMLINS (LJN) 1984
A few action figures produced in conjunction with other character toys for the 1984 film.

	CNP	MIP	MMP
GR4801 13" Stripe (boxed)	25	50	75
GR4803 Large Gizmo (boxed)	12	25	35
GR4804 Small Gizmo (carded)	8	12	20

GRIFFINS (Formative International Co.) 1995
An interchangeable knock-off of *Gargoyles*.

	CNP	MIP	MMP
GR4901 Griffins 2-packs, ea	2	4	6

GRIZZLY ADAMS (Mattel) 1978
These figures were each packaged in window boxes. Pressing a button on the back of a figure caused its right arm to move.

	CNP	MIP	MMP
GR5001 Grizzly Adams	15	25	45
GR5002 Ben	22	32	55
GR5003 Nakoma	15	25	45
GR5011 Grizzly Adams/Ben	-	55	75

GUMMI BEARS (Fisher-Price) 1985
Series based on the Disney cartoon TV show.

	CNP	MIP	MMP
GU4001 Zummi Gummi	1	4	6
GU4002 Sunni Gummi	1	4	6
GU4003 Cubbi Gummi	1	4	6
GU4004 Gruffi Gummi	1	4	6
GU4005 Tummi Gummi	1	4	6
GU4006 Grammi Gummi	1	4	6

GUNG-HO! (Lanard Toys) 1986
A series of generic military figures, designed to mix with the popular *G.I. Joe* toys.

	CNP	MIP	MMP
GU5001 John Eagle	2	6	8
GU5002 Hammer	2	6	8
GU5003 Flashfire	2	6	8
GU5004 Junkyard	2	6	8
GU5005 Gunner O' Grady	2	6	8
GU5006 Large Sarge	2	6	8
GU5007 Dragon Han	2	6	8
GU5008 Shark	2	6	8
GU5009 Tony Tanner	2	6	8
GU5010 Boomerang Billy	2	6	8
GU5011 Hiro Yamato	2	6	8
GU5012 Whispering Willie	2	6	8
See also: *Corps!, The*			

HA7011

HANNA-BARBERA — See *Dakin and Dakin-Style Figures; Pirates of Dark Water, The*

HAPPY DAYS (Mego) 1978
The Fonz figure was designed with "thumbs up" action which was controlled by a button in his back. Fonz figures were sold both on cards and in boxes.

	CNP	MIP	MMP
HA7000 Fonzie, boxed	18	35	50
HA7001 Fonzie, on card	18	35	50
HA7002 Ralph	20	40	60
HA7003 Potsy	20	32	58
HA7004 Richie	20	40	60
HA7010 Fonzie's Motorcycle	15	50	95
HA7011 Fonzie's Jalopy	20	50	95
HA7012 Fonzie Garage	35	75	125

CNP: Complete, no package, with all weapons and accessories; MIP: Mint in package; MMP: Mint item in Mint package. Values in U.S. dollars. See page 3 for details.

HARD CORPS (Drastic Plastic) 1992-1993

This line was not produced by a major toy company, but rather by a toy collector named David Reeves who attempted to form his own manufacturing operation. The *Hard Corps* were an organization of Space Marines formed to fight the Kray, conquering alien races found throughout the galaxies. *Hard Corps* was supported by SPACE (Space Project Advancement Center). Their spaceship was called the *Endeavor* and a whole universe was created for a Phase I group of 22 characters. The figures were delivered more than two years late, but to Reeves' credit, he lost big bucks to see the project completed.

Hard Corps was the first attempt to create a truly non-toy figure for collectors. The figures have sharp points and didn't conform to the rigid toy watchers' codes. They were innovative in other ways, particularly in poseability. The problems in delivering the product, however, brought the line to a premature end. The nine figures were sold as a set for $99 pre-production and $200 once they began shipping. Less than 1,000 sets were made. Tomart is not aware of any sales on the secondary market and cannot quote any value other the original sales prices stated above.

		CNP	MIP	MMP
HA1801	Major John Striker	undetermined		
HA1802	Sgt. Mike Ross	undetermined		
HA1803	Corp. Akira Oki	undetermined		
HA1804	C.H.R.I.S.	undetermined		
HA1815	Psyfid	undetermined		
HA1816	Killjoy	undetermined		
HA1817	Crygstor	undetermined		
HA1818	Trick'd	undetermined		
HA1819	Alien Encounter	undetermined		

HARDY BOYS, THE (Kenner) 1979

Based on the successful live-action TV show which alternated with *Nancy Drew*. Figures were 12" with cloth outfits, and used the same body as 12" *Star Wars* figures.

		CNP	MIP	MMP
HA8001	Joe Hardy	15	25	42
HA8002	Frank Hardy	15	25	42

HE-MAN (Mattel) 1990-91

Continuing the popularity of the *Masters of the Universe* line, this was a new series which re-introduced He-Man. While the previous series had been oriented toward heroic fantasy, the *He-Man* line gave the characters a science fiction look. Four new vehicles were added in 1991.

		CNP	MIP	MMP
HE1001	He-Man	3	6	8
HE1002	Flipshot	3	6	8
HE1003	Hydron	3	6	8
HE1004	Skeletor	3	6	8
HE1005	Kalamarr	4	8	10
HE1006	Flogg	3	6	8
HE1008	He-Man/Evil Mutant	6	14	18

HE1008

HA7012

Box for set of HA1801-HA1819

HA8001

HA8002

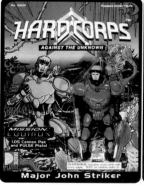
HA1801

HA1802

HA1803

HA1804

HA1815

HA1816

HA1817

HA1818

HA1819

HE1001	HE1002	HE1003	HE1004	HE1005
HE1006	HE1010	HE1011	HE1012	HE1013
HE1014	HE1015	HE1016	HE1017	HE1018
HE1019	HE1021	HE1022	HE1023	HE1024

HE1009	He-Man/Skeletor	6	14	18	HE1019	Lizorr		4	8	10	HE1091	Astrosub	4	8	10
HE1010	Brakk	4	8	10	HE1021	Spinwit		4	8	10	HE1092	Bolajet	3	5	7
HE1011	Battle-Punch He-Man	3	6	8	HE1022	Tuskador		4	8	10	HE1093	Shuttle Pod	4	8	10
HE1012	Nocturna	3	6	8	HE1023	Artilla		4	8	10	HE1094	Terroclaw	6	13	15
HE1013	Vizar	3	6	8	HE1024	Staghorn		4	8	10	HE1100	Starship Eternia	15	35	55
HE1014	Disks of Doom Skeletor	3	6	8	HE1025	Butthead		4	8	10	HE1101	Doom Copter	5	10	14
HE1015	Karatti	3	6	8	HE1026	Quakke		4	8	10	HE1102	Sagitar vehicle	3	7	9
HE1016	Hoove	3	6	8	HE1027	Spin-Fist Hydron		3	7	8	HE1103	Terrotread vehicle	3	7	9
HE1017	Kayo	3	6	8	HE1030	Thunder Punch He-Man		4	8	10	HE1104	Battle Bird vehicle	6	12	15
HE1018	Optikk	3	6	8	HE1031	Battle Blade Skeletor		4	8	10	See also: *Masters of the Universe*				

CNP: Complete, no package, with all weapons and accessories; MIP: Mint in package; MMP: Mint item in Mint package. Values in U.S. dollars. See page 3 for details.

HE1025

HE1026

HE1027

HE1030

HE1031

HE1091

HE1093

HE1101

HE1092

HE1102

HE1100

HE1094

HE1102

HEARTS OF DARKNESS (Toy Biz) 1996

A special three-pack with repainted figures of the Punisher, Ghost Rider, and Wolverine, sold exclusively by FAO Schwarz. Only 6,000 sets were produced.

	CNP	MIP	MMP
HE1501 Hearts of Darkness, boxed set of three	12	30	45

HE1104

HE1103

HE1501

| HE1401 | HE1402 | HE1403 | HE1404 | HE1405 |

| HE1406 | HE1407 | HE1415 | HE1439 | HE1437 |

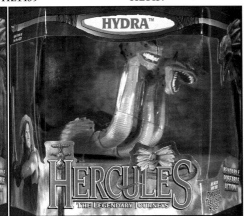

| HE1411 | HE1412 | HE1413 |

HERCULES — THE LEGENDARY JOURNEYS (Toy Biz) 1995-96

The *Hercules* and *Xena, the Warrior Princess* TV shows inspired this line of figures.

Assortment I HE1401-07	CNP	MIP	MMP
HE1401 Hercules I	3	5	7
HE1402 Hercules II	3	5	7
HE1403 Hercules III	3	5	7
HE1404 Ares	3	5	7
HE1405 Iolaus	3	5	7
HE1406 Minotaur	3	5	7
HE1407 Xena	6	10	15

Monster Assortment I HE1411-13			
HE1411 Cerebus	3	8	12
HE1412 Echidna	3	8	12
HE1413 Hydra	3	8	12
HE1415 Deluxe 10" Hercules	7	10	15

Assorment II HE1421-29			
HE1421 Hercules w/chain-breaking strength		not determined	

HE1423 Swashbuckling Hercules	not determined
HE1425 Mole-Man	not determined
HE1427 She-Demon	not determined
HE1429 Centaur	not determined

Monster Assortment II HE1431-35	
HE1431 Graegus	not determined
HE1433 Symphalian Bird	not determined
HE1435 Labyrinth Snake	not determined
HE1437 HE1415, 2nd version	not determined
HE1439 Deluxe 10" Xena	not determined
HE1441 Tower of Power	not determined

HEROES OF THE AMERICAN REVOLUTION (manufactured for S.S. Kresge Co.) ?

A set of 8" Mego-style figures made for S.S. Kresge Co.

		CNP	MIP	MMP
HE1701 John Paul Jones		8	15	20
HE1702 Marquis De Lafayette		8	15	20
HE1703 Nathan Hale		8	15	20
HE1704 Daniel Boone		8	15	20
HE1705 Benjamin Franklin		8	15	20
HE1706 Patrick Henry		8	15	20
HE1707 Paul Revere		8	15	20
HE1708 Thomas Jefferson		8	15	20

HI-5 SPORT STARS (TPI Distributing) 1993-94

A set of black sports figures sold at doller stores and closeout shops. The figures have generic bodies and pink accessories.

		CNP	MIP	MMP
HI2001 Mr. Basketball		1	3	5
HI2002 Mr. Baseball		1	3	5
HI2003 Mr. Football		1	3	5
HI2004 Mr. Track and Field		1	3	5
HI2005 Mr. Wrestler		1	3	5
HI2006 The Champ (boxer)		1	3	5

HOBO JOE RESTAURANTS — See *Dakin and Dakin-Style Figures*

HE1425   HE1421   HE1427   HE1423   HE1429

HE1431   HE1433   HE1435   HE1441

HO3001   HO3004   HO3005   HO3006   HO3007

HO3010   HO3011   HO3501

HOLLYWOOD MICKEY (ARCO) 1989

A series of Disney figures released in conjunction with the opening of the Disney/MGM studio tour. The figures came in two sizes: 5" PVC and 12" w/cloth costumes.

		CNP	MIP	MMP					
HO3001	Director Mickey	1	3	5	HO3005	Mickey Star, 12"	2	8	12
HO3002	Movie Star Mickey	1	3	5	HO3006	Minnie Star, 12"	2	8	12
HO3003	Donald	1	3	5	HO3007	Mickey, director, 12"	2	8	12
HO3004	Hollywood Minnie	1	3	5	HO3010	Trio Collection			
						(HO3002-04)	-	10	15

HO3011	Movie Star Collection		
	(HO3001-04)	- 12 20	

See also: *Disney; Mickey Mouse*

HOME ALONE (THQ) 1992
A single figure of Kevin was produced.

HO3501	Screaming Kevin	7	12	18

HONEY WEST (Gilbert) 1965
Based on the British-made TV series.

		CNP	MIP	MMP
HO4001	Honey West Figure	85	175	300
Outfits HO5011-13				
HO4011	Secret Agent	20	35	45
HO4012	Karate	20	35	45
HO4013	Formal	20	35	45
HO4015	Pet Set	15	25	40
HO4016	Spy Compact Set	15	25	40
HO4017	Equipment Set	15	25	40
HO4018	Spy Accessory Set	15	25	40

HOOK (Mattel) 1991-93
A clever series of figures based on the Steven Spielberg film. Second-series and deluxe figures saw very limited release.

		CNP	MIP	MMP
HO4501	Swashbuckling Peter Pan	3	5	8
HO4502	Air Attack Peter Pan	3	5	8
HO4503	Multi-Blade Captain Hook	3	5	8
HO4504	Tall Terror Captain Hook	3	5	8
HO4505	Lost Boy Ace	3	5	8
HO4506	Lost Boy Rufio	3	5	8
HO4507	Pirate Bill Jukes	3	5	8
HO4520	Lost Boy Attack Raft	5	12	14
HO4521	Lost Boy Strike Tank	5	13	18

Second Series figures

HO4531	Battle Swing Peter Pan	3	8	10
HO4532	Food-Fighting Pan	3	8	10
HO4533	Lost Boy Thudd Butt	4	10	15
HO4534	Swiss Army Hook	3	8	10
HO4535	Pirate Smee	not determined		

Deluxe Figures

HO4541	Learn-To-Fly Pan	8	15	20
HO4542	Lost Boy Attack Croc	10	18	22
HO4543	Skull Armor Hook	8	15	20

		CNP	MIP	MMP
HO5001	Zeb Macahan	15	25	40
HO5002	Lone Wolf	15	25	40
HO5011	Dakota	15	25	40
HO5019	Zeb Macahan/Dakota	-	70	90

HO4001

HO4017

HOW THE WEST WAS WON (Mattel) 1978
These figures were each packaged in window boxes. Pressing a button on the back of a figure caused its right arm to move.

HO4018

HO4501

HO4502

HO4503

HO4504

HO4505

HO4506

HO4507

HO4520

HO4533

HO4534

HO4541

HO4542

HO4543

| HO5001 | HU5051 | HU5053 | HU5055 | HU5057 |

| HU5059 | HU5061 | I-1040 | I-1000 | I-1051 |

| IN1501 | IN1503 | IN1505 | IN1507 | IN1509 |

HUNCHBACK OF NOTRE DAME, THE (Arco/Mattel) 1996

Figures based on the Disney version of the classic Victor Hugo tale.

5" scale figures		CNP	MIP	MMP
HU5001	Quasimodo	2	4	6
HU5003	Esmeralda	2	4	6
HU5005	Phoebus	2	4	6
HU5007	The Gargoyles	2	4	6
HU5009	Frollo	2	4	6
HU5011	Clopin	2	4	6
HU5021	Esmeralda w/horse	7	10	15
HU5022	Phoebus w/horse	7	10	15
HU5025	Quasimodo box set	8	12	16
HU5027	Esmeralda box set	8	12	16
HU5030	Gypsy Wagon	8	12	16
HU5035	Notre Dame			
	Adventure Playset	10	20	30
12" scale figures				
HU5051	Magic View			
	Quasimodo	9	15	20
HU5053	Esmeralda	7	10	15
HU5055	Phoebus	7	10	15
HU5057	True Hearts gift set	12	22	28
HU5059	Gypsy Dancing			
	Esmeralda	9	12	18
HU5061	Gypsy Magic Horse	9	12	18

See also: *Lincoln International Monsters; Real Ghostbusters, The*

HYPNOS — See *Pulsar*

I DREAM OF JEANNIE (Remco) 1978, (Trendmasters) 1996

Based on the TV show of the same name.

Remco		CNP	MIP	MMP
I-1000	Jeannie	25	45	65
I-1001-36	Outfits for I-1000, ea	5	8	15
I-1040	Bottle playset	55	155	225
Trendmasters				
I-1051	12" Talking Jeannie		not determined	

ICE AGE — See *Dino-Riders*

INCREDIBLE CRASH DUMMIES, THE (TYCO) 1991-94

TYCO succeeded where many have failed by creating an educational figure line that appealed to kids. Initially based on the Department of Transportation's (DOT) famous TV mascots Vince and Larry, the line's message of seat belt safety was enhanced by figures and accessories which "exploded" on impact.

Complaints about small parts prompted DOT to withdraw its support after the first six months, but the line was a big seller. TYCO executives were no dummies, and buckled up for 2½ years of steady production. The main characters were re-named "Slick" and "Spin," and given new paint jobs. All of the original cards were reprinted to remove references to Vince, Larry, and DOT, immediately increasing the collectibility of the original cards.

The next year introduced the Junkbots, a Dummy gone bad and his henchmen built from scrap auto parts. The "good" Dummies were given "Pro-Tek" suits (new paint jobs). TYCO solicited figures with new action features for a third year, but lack of buyer interest killed the line...including Darlene, who was seen on card backs but not produced.

		CNP	MIP	MMP
IN1501	Vince	5	10	15
IN1503	Larry	5	10	15
IN1505	Slick	2	7	10
IN1507	Spin	2	7	10
IN1509	Daryl, original card	2	7	10
IN1511	Daryl, revised card	2	7	10
IN1513	Spare Tire, original	2	7	10
IN1515	Spare Tire, revised	2	7	10
IN1517	Skid the Kid, original	2	7	10
IN1519	Skid the Kid, revised	2	7	10
IN1521	Hubcat/Bumper	3	8	12
IN1523	IN1521, revised card	3	8	12
IN1541	Crash Car w/Dash	12	18	20
IN1543	Student Driver Crash			
	Car w/Axel	12	18	20

IN1513   IN1517   IN1519   IN1521   IN1523

IN1541   IN1543   IN1545   IN1547

IN1549   IN1551   IN1553   IN1560

IN1565   IN1567   IN1571   IN1581

IN1562   IN1628

IN1545	Crash Cycle	5	8	10	IN1562	Crash Test Center	12	20	28	IN1581	Citgo edition Slick &		
IN1547	Crash Chopper	5	8	10	IN1565	Crash 'N Dash Chopper	5	8	10		Spin, set of 2, mail-in	12	18	20
IN1549	Crash ATV w/Flip	5	8	10	IN1566	Slam Cycle	5	8	10	IN1585	Pitstop (Canadian		
IN1551	Crash Lawn Mower				IN1567	Crash Plane	8	18	22		Tire promo)	6	10	15
	w/Wack	5	8	10	IN1569	Dummy Derby Car	6	14	20	**"Pro-Tek Suit" repaints IN1591-96**		
IN1553	Crash Go Kart w/J.R.	5	8	10	IN1570	Bash 'N Bomber Car	6	14	20	IN1591	Slick (repaint)	2	7	10
IN1560	Crash 'N Bash Chair	5	8	10	IN1571	Crash Cab	6	14	20	IN1592	Spin (repaint)	2	7	10

CNP: Complete, no package, with all weapons and accessories; MIP: Mint in package; MMP: Mint item in Mint package. Values in U.S. dollars. See page 3 for details.

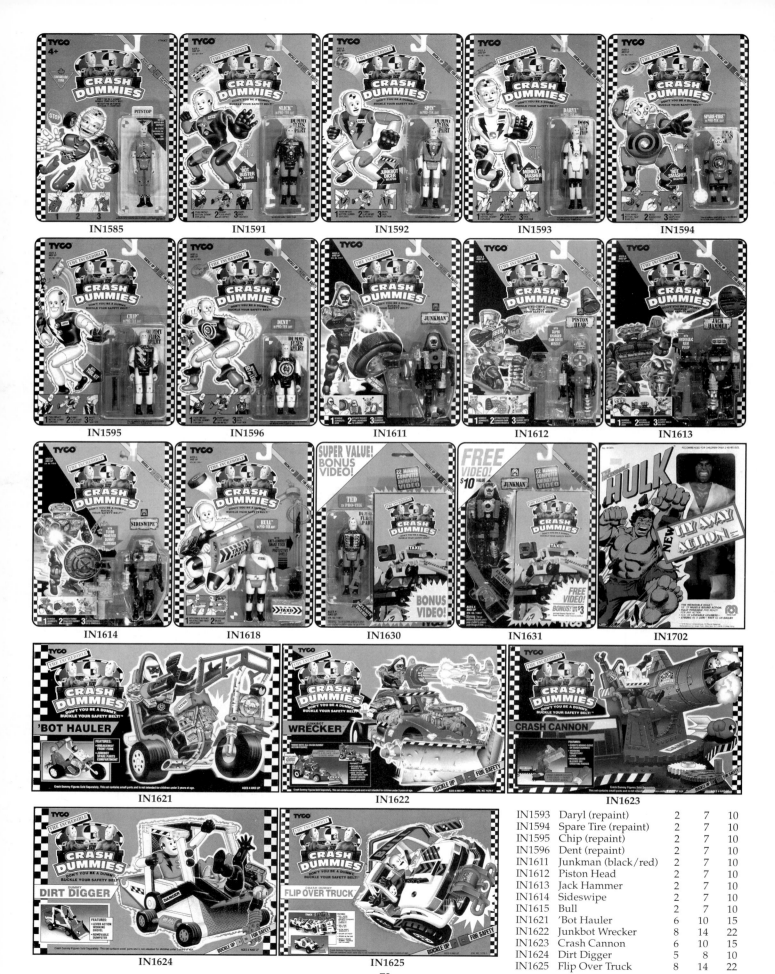

IN1585 IN1591 IN1592 IN1593 IN1594
IN1595 IN1596 IN1611 IN1612 IN1613
IN1614 IN1618 IN1630 IN1631 IN1702
IN1621 IN1622 IN1623
IN1624 IN1625

IN1593	Daryl (repaint)	2	7	10
IN1594	Spare Tire (repaint)	2	7	10
IN1595	Chip (repaint)	2	7	10
IN1596	Dent (repaint)	2	7	10
IN1611	Junkman (black/red)	2	7	10
IN1612	Piston Head	2	7	10
IN1613	Jack Hammer	2	7	10
IN1614	Sideswipe	2	7	10
IN1615	Bull	2	7	10
IN1621	'Bot Hauler	6	10	15
IN1622	Junkbot Wrecker	8	14	22
IN1623	Crash Cannon	6	10	15
IN1624	Dirt Digger	5	8	10
IN1625	Flip Over Truck	8	14	22

IN1710   IN1712   IN1714   IN1718   IN1720

IN1801

IN1901

IN1902

IN1903

IN2001

IN2002

IN2003

IN3002

IN3004

IN3006

IN3008

IN3012

IN3010

IN3011

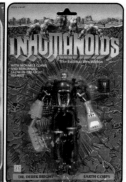

IN6001

IN6002

IN6004

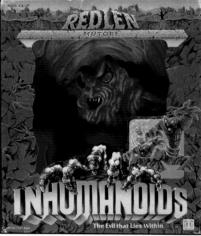

IN6021

IN6030

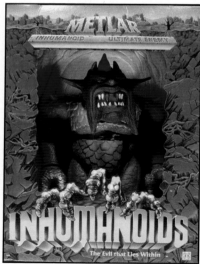

IN6040

IN6051

IN7000

IN7001

IN7002

IN7003

IN7004

IN7005

IN7006

IN7007

IN7008

IN7008 face

IN7009

IN7015

IN7016

IN7021

IN8023   IN8031   IN8032   IN8013

IN8021   IN8012   IN8015   IN8017

IN8002   IN8011

IN8001   IN8025   IN8022   IN8024   IN8026

IN8001

IN8013

IN8701

IN8702

IN8704

IR7001

IR7003

IR7005

IR7007

IR7009

IR7011

IR7013

IR7031

IR7033

IR7035

IR7037

IR7039

IR7021

IR7022

IR7023

IR7045

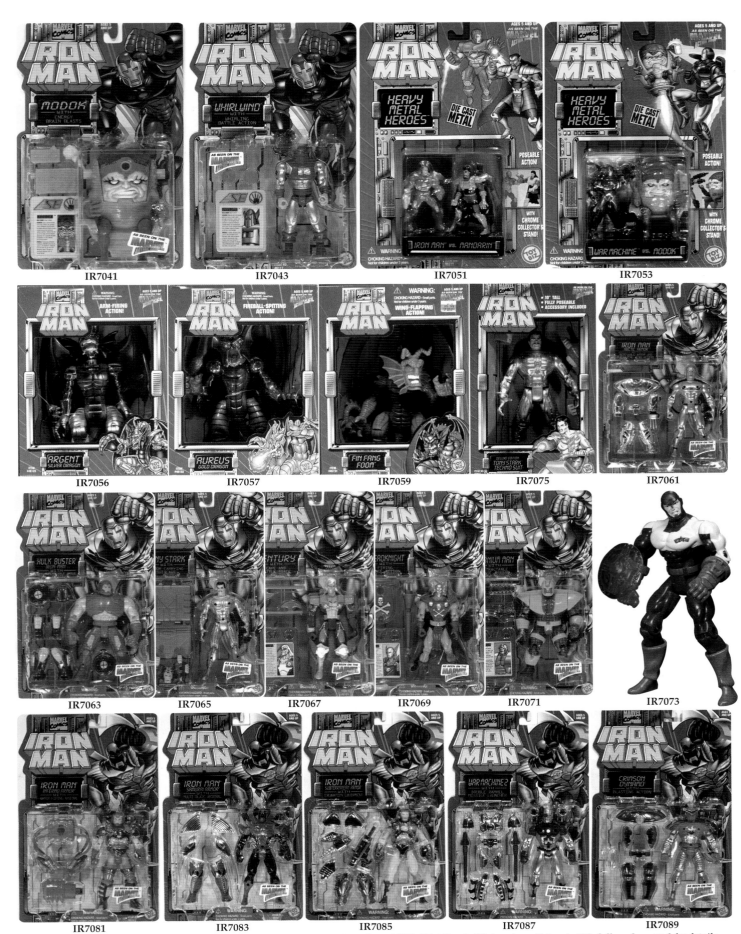

IR7041   IR7043   IR7051   IR7053

IR7056   IR7057   IR7059   IR7075   IR7061

IR7063   IR7065   IR7067   IR7069   IR7071   IR7073

IR7081   IR7083   IR7085   IR7087   IR7089

CNP: Complete, no package, with all weapons and accessories; MIP: Mint in package; MMP: Mint item in Mint package. Values in U.S. dollars. See page 3 for details.

IR7107   IR7101   IR7103   IR7109   IR7105   IR7111   IR7113

J-2000   J-2005   J-2010

JA5101   JA5102   JA5501   JA5502

JA5503   JA5504   JA5505   JA5506   JA5511

JA5521   JA5522   JA5523

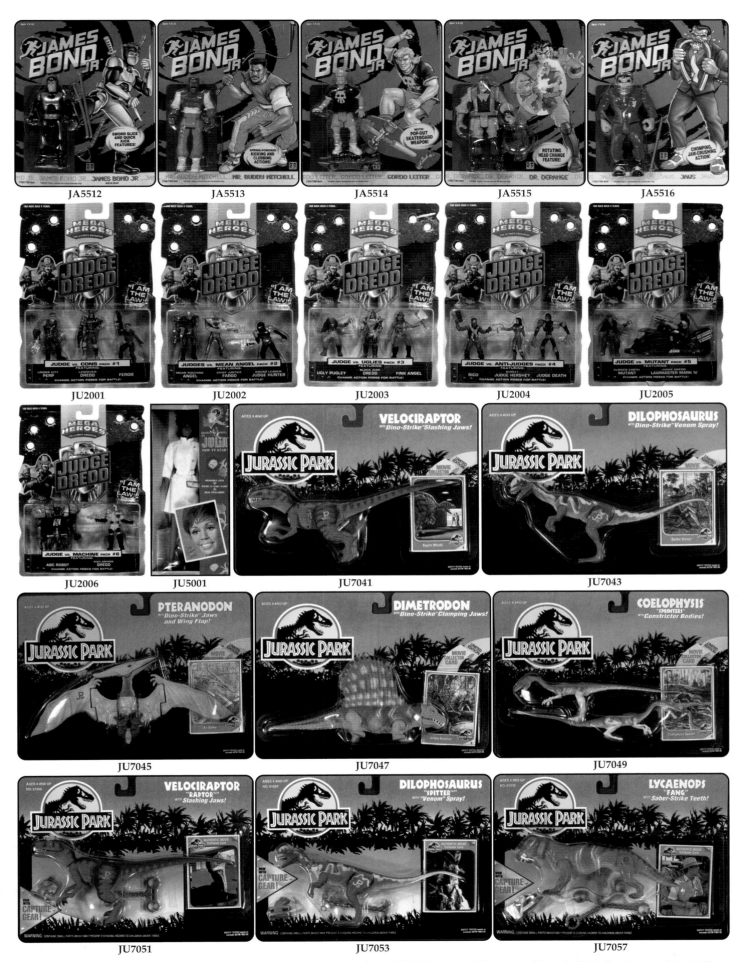

JA5512	JA5513	JA5514	JA5515	JA5516
JU2001	JU2002	JU2003	JU2004	JU2005
JU2006	JU5001	JU7041		JU7043
JU7045	JU7047	JU7049		
JU7051	JU7053	JU7057		

CNP: Complete, no package, with all weapons and accessories; MIP: Mint in package; MMP: Mint item in Mint package. Values in U.S. dollars. See page 3 for details.

JU7059

JU7071

JU7073

JU7075

JU7077

JU7081

JU7083

JU7085

JU7091

JU7087

JU7093

JU7094

IN1628	Junkyard Playset	5	12	18
IN1630	Ted w/video tape	4	8	12
IN1631	Junkman (purple/black)			
	w/video tape	4	8	12
IN1635	Skid the Kid (repaint)	3	9	11

INCREDIBLE HULK, THE (Mego) 1978-79, (Toy Biz) 1996

Mego made a 12½" figure of the Incredible Hulk in 1978. The following year, the same figure was sold with a fly-away action attach-

ment. Hulk figures which were made as part of a series appear elsewhere in the appropriate sections.

The 6" Toy Biz figures were issued to celebrate the return of the live-action TV series to the Sci-Fi Channel, and guest appearances on the Marvel Action Hour.

Mego		CNP	MIP	MMP
IN1701	The Incredible Hulk	25	40	60
IN1702	w/fly-away action	25	40	60

Toy Biz
IN1710	Abomination	2	5	7
IN1712	Leader	2	5	7
IN1714	Savage Hulk (2 figures)	2	5	7
IN1718	She-Hulk	2	5	7
IN1720	Grey Hulk			
	Battle-Damaged	2	5	7

See also: *Comic Action Heroes; Die Cast Super Heroes; Marvel Super Heroes; Official World's Greatest Super Heroes; Pocket Super Heroes*

INDIANA JONES (Kenner) 1982-83, (Star Toys) 1987

Kenner made a 12" figure of Indiana Jones in conjunction with the *Adventures of Indiana Jones* line (see AD3001-24). Star Toys later made a smaller Indiana Jones figure, which was packaged three different ways. Although it is a foreign item, numerous U.S. collectors have shown an interest in it.

See color photos on page 73.

Kenner IN1801	CNP	MIP	MMP
IN1801 12" Indiana Jones	110	175	235
Star Toys IN1901-03			
IN1901 Indiana Jones	25	55	95
IN1902 Jones w/snake	25	55	95
IN1903 Jones w/alligator	25	55	95

See also: *Adventures of Indiana Jones, The; Indiana Jones and the Temple of Doom*

INDIANA JONES AND THE TEMPLE OF DOOM (LJN) 1984

This was a very short-lived set. Figures of Indiana Jones, Mola Ram, and Giant Thugee are known to exist. Short Round and Willie Scott are advertised on the back of the blister cards, but the figures were never produced.

See color photos on page 73.

		CNP	MIP	MMP
IN2001	Indiana Jones	40	90	115
IN2002	Mola Ram	15	35	50
IN2003	Giant Thugee	15	35	50
IN2004	Short Round		not produced	
IN2005	Willie Scott		not produced	

See also: *Adventures of Indiana Jones, The; Indiana Jones*

INFACEABLES, THE (Galoob) 1985

The gimmick behind *Infaceables* is "vacuum action." When the legs are pulled, the air is sucked out of the figure's face, causing it to shrivel over a preformed shape underneath.

See color photos on pages 73-74.

		CNP	MIP	MMP
IN3001	Iron Lion	3	10	15
IN3002	Sphinx	3	10	15
IN3003	War Dog	5	12	18
IN3004	Robash	3	10	15
IN3005	Brainor	5	12	18
IN3006	Tembo	3	10	15
IN3007	Tuskus	3	10	15
IN3008	Torto the Claw	3	10	15
IN3010	Incredible Thrasher	8	15	25
IN3011	Horrible Hammer	8	15	25
IN3012	Crusher Cruiser	8	15	25

INHUMANOIDS (Hasbro) 1986

The Earth Corps scientists from *Inhumanoids* are 6½" figures of humans in exploration suits. Only the helmets, which "glow-in-the-light," are removable. Each figure has an excavation tool such as a grappling hook, moveable claws, an auger drill, or a liquid-firing backpack. The Granites could be taken apart to hide as a pile of rocks, the Redwoods were collapsible, and the Magnokor could be separated into two figures. Metlar, Tendril, and D. Compose were 14" figures with glowing fangs. A small merchandise catalog was included with each item.

See color photos on page 74.

		CNP	MIP	MMP
IN6001	Dr. Derek Bright	5	12	15
IN6002	Auger	5	12	15
IN6003	Herc Armstrong	5	12	15
IN6004	Liquidator	5	12	15
IN6010	The Granites	8	15	20
IN6011	Granok	8	15	20
IN6020	The Redwoods	8	15	20
IN6021	Redlen	8	15	20
IN6022	Redsun	8	15	20
IN6030	Magnokor	10	17	25
IN6040	Metlar	12	30	35
IN6041	Tendril	15	35	40
IN6042	D. Compose	15	35	40
IN6050	Trappeur Vehicle	10	17	25
IN6051	Terrascout Vehicle	7	12	16

INSPECTOR GADGET (Galoob) 1984-86, (Tiger) 1992-94

Derived from the European cartoon series, Galoob produced a large *Inspector Gadget* action figure when the show was first syndicated in the United States. It included an umbrella, an oversized hammer, a pair of handcuffs, and two accessories which attached to the figure's hat: a gyrocopter and a mechanical hand. The figure's neck, left hand, and legs were extendable, and the right hand was a spring-loaded missile. It was sold in a window box.

Tiger Toys later produced a line of 5¼" figures. The face of the villainous Dr. Claw, never seen on the TV show, was revealed for the first time.

See color photos on pages 74-75.

Galoob		CNP	MIP	MMP
IN7000	Inspector Gadget	25	45	75
Tiger				
Go Go Gadget figures IN7001-06				
IN7001	w/Snap-open Hat	5	8	12
IN7002	w/Expanding Arms	5	8	12
IN7003	w/Fumble Gadgets	5	8	12
IN7004	w/Expanding Legs	5	8	12
IN7005	w/Squirting Water	5	8	12
IN7006	w/Telescopic Neck	5	7	10
IN7007	Penny and the Brain	6	9	14
IN7008	Dr. Claw/M.A.D. Cat	5	10	20
IN7009	M.A.D. Agent	5	8	12
IN7015	Gadget Windsurfer	5	10	15
IN7016	Gadget w/Copter Pack	5	10	15
IN7021	Gadget Mobile	8	15	25

INTER-CHANGEABLES, THE (Hourtoy) 1982

The *Inter-Changeables* were a re-issue of Mego's *Micronauts* line. Hourtoy licensed the molds from Takara when Mego folded in 1982. Most of the items are identical, and were even sold in similar packaging.

Numbers in parentheses indicate the original *Micronauts* product which a given item is similar to. Several items were produced in assorted colors, and numerous color variations exist between the *Inter-changeables* and the original line.

See color photos on page 75.

		CNP	MIP	MMP
IN8001	Cosmo-Man (MI3001)	2	4	5
IN8002	Cosmic Warp Chamber (MI3007)	2	4	6
IN8011	Amphi-Copter (MI3011)	3	5	8
IN8012	Cosmobot (MI3020)	3	5	8
IN8013	C.A.R.P. (MI3021)	3	5	8
IN8015	C.I.T.S. (MI3022)	5	10	15
IN8017	C.E.D.M. (MI3023)	3	5	8
IN8021	Captain Cosmo (MI3032)	3	5	8
IN8022	Cosmo Steed (MI3032)	3	5	8
IN8023	Count Magno (MI3033)	3	5	8
IN8024	Magna Steed (MI3034)	3	5	8
IN8025	Lord Meto	5	10	15
IN8026	Metallion	5	10	15
IN8031	C.I.R.E.S. (MI3041)	3	5	8
IN8032	C.I.E.L. (MI3111)	5	8	10

See also: *Micronauts*

INVADING INSECT V WORLD (Leader Shine Entertainment Co.) 1994

Brightly-colored transforming insect/robots found mainly at K-mart. Marketed at the time Hasbro's *Transformers: Generation 2* was released.

See color photos on page 76.

		CNP	MIP	MMP
IN8701	Fly (A)	1	3	5
IN8702	Mosquito (B)	1	3	5
IN8703	Hornet (C)	1	3	5
IN8704	Moth (D)	1	3	5

IRON MAN (Toy Biz) 1995-96

Toy Biz introduced the *Iron Man* line in conjunction with the Marvel Action Hour television show. Each assortment featured revised card art showing a different suit of the Iron Man armor. Some figures came with snap-on armor pieces and shooting weapons. The mold for Spider-Woman was later re-used to create a temporary Invisible Woman for the *Fantastic Four* line.

U.S. Agent was cancelled when retailers began demanding smaller case assortments. The molds for the figure were modified to produce a different character, but approximately 100 bagged figures were produced. Most of these were given to Toy Biz employees, and one was donated for an *Action Figure Digest* contest prize. A number of these have since made their way into the hands of collectors.

This section includes only those figures which were sold under the name *Iron Man*. Related figures which were sold as part of another series appear elsewhere in the appropriate sections.

See color photos on pages 76-78.

Assortment I		CNP	MIP	MMP
(Classic Armor cards) IR7001-13				
IR7001	Iron Man	5	10	15
IR7003	Iron Man Hydro Armor	5	10	15
IR7005	War Machine	5	10	15
IR7007	Mandarin	5	10	15
IR7009	Blacklash	5	10	15
IR7011	Spider-Woman	5	10	15
IR7013	Grey Gargoyle	5	10	15
IR7021	10" Iron Man	7	12	18
IR7022	10" War Machine	7	12	18
IR7023	10" Mandarin	7	12	18
Assortment II (Stealth Armor Cards) IR7031-43				
IR7031	Iron Man Hologram Armor	5	10	15
IR7033	Iron Man Space Armor	5	10	15
IR7035	Iron Man Stealth Armor	5	10	15
IR7037	Blizzard	5	10	15
IR7039	Hawkeye	5	10	15
IR7041	Modok	5	10	15
IR7043	Whirlwind	5	10	15
IR7045	10" Iron Man Space Armor	7	12	18
Heavy Metal Heroes IR7051-52				
IR7051	Iron Man vs. Mandarin	2	4	8
IR7053	War Machine vs. Modok	2	4	8
Dragons IR7056-58				
IR7056	Argent	8	15	20
IR7057	Areus	8	15	20
IR7059	Fin Fang Foom	8	15	20
Assortment III (Arctic Armor Cards) IR7061-71				
IR7061	Iron Man Arctic Armor	5	10	15
IR7063	Hulk Buster Iron Man	5	10	15
IR7065	Tony Stark	5	10	15
IR7067	Century	5	10	15
IR7069	Dreadknight	5	10	15
IR7071	Titanium Man	5	10	15
IR7073	U.S. Agent	600	-	-
IR7075	10" Tony Stark	7	12	18

CNP: Complete, no package, with all weapons and accessories; MIP: Mint in package; MMP: Mint item in Mint package. Values in U.S. dollars. See page 3 for details.

| JU7001 | JU7002 | JU7003 | JU7004 | JU7005 |

Assortment IV (Samurai Armor Cards)
IR7081-89

IR7081	Inferno Iron Man	5	10	15
IR7083	Samurai Iron Man	5	10	15
IR7085	Subterranean			
	Iron Man	5	10	15
IR7087	War Machine II	5	10	15
IR7089	Crimson Dynamo	5	10	15

Assorment V IR7101-09

IR7101	Radiation Armor		not produced
IR7103	Lava Armor		not produced
IR7105	Magnetic Armor		not produced
IR7107	Dark Aegis		not produced
IR7109	Living Laser		not produced

9" Mega Armor IR7111-13

IR7111	Iron Man		not produced
IR7113	War Machine		not produced

See also: *Fantastic Four; Fantastic Four/Iron Man Collectors Edition; Marvel Super Heroes; Marvel Super Heroes Secret Wars; Official World's Greatest Super Heroes; Projectors*

J.J. ARMES (Ideal) 1976-77
Billed as the "World's Greatest Investigator," J.J. Armes came with "bio-kinetic" (interchangeable) hands.
See color photos on page 78.

		CNP	MIP	MMP
J-2000	J.J. Armes	16	35	50
J-2005	Mobile Investigation			
	Unit	15	32	40
J-2010	C.A.M.P. Playset	15	32	45

JAMES BOND (Gilbert) 1965-66
A 12" James Bond figure came with a cap-firing gun triggered by a spring-action arm. Oddjob came packed in two different costumes, a martial arts robe or a much rarer suit complete with his top hat weapon. Numerous outfits and adventure packs were available.
See color photos on page 78.

		CNP	MIP	MMP
JA5100	James Bond in tux	250	800	1200
JA5101	James Bond in coat	100	225	275
JA5102	Oddjob w/robe	125	300	400
JA5103	Oddjob w/suit	225	750	950
JA5110	Disguise Kit	45	60	80
JA5111	Disguise Kit #2	30	50	70
JA5112	Thunderball set	30	55	75
JA5113	Deluxe Scuba Outfit	35	57	75
JA5114	Scuba Outfit #2	30	45	60
JA5115	Scuba Outfit #3	30	45	60
JA5116	Scuba Outfit #4	30	45	60

See also: *Moonraker*

JAMES BOND JR. (Hasbro) 1992-93
James Bond Jr. was Hasbro's only domestic 1992 action figure line other than *G.I. Joe*. The figures were based on a TV cartoon series of the same name. James Jr., the nephew of the original Bond, was a young adventurer constantly struggling against the evil intentions of S.C.U.M. (Saboteurs and Criminals United in Mayhem). Naturally, James Bond Jr. was well-prepared with numerous outrageous gadgets.

Two waves of six figures were released before the cancellation of the TV show killed the line. James Bond Jr. in Flight Gear was initially delayed by engineering problems.
See color photos on pages 78-79.

		CNP	MIP	MMP
JA5501	James Bond Jr.			
	(Street Gear)	5	8	12
JA5502	JBJ Scuba Gear	5	8	12
JA5503	I.Q.	5	8	12
JA5504	Odd Job	5	8	12
JA5505	Captain Walker			
	D. Plank	5	8	12
JA5506	Dr. No	5	8	12
JA5511	JBJ Flight Gear	5	8	12
JA5512	JBJ Ninja Gear	5	8	12
JA5513	Buddy Mitchell	5	8	12
JA5514	Gordo Leiter	5	8	12
JA5515	Dr. Derange	5	8	12
JA5516	Jaws	5	8	12
JA5521	Subcycle	6	8	12
JA5522	S.C.U.M. Shark	8	12	14
JA5523	Sports Car	10	16	20

JOHNNY WEST — See *Best of the West*

JUDGE DREDD (Mattel) 1995
Mattel attempted to introduce a new action figure size with this movie tie-in line. Each pack contained two or three figures with limited articulation, and retailed for around $5. The figure packs were numbered to encourage collectors. A few playsets were planned, but never produced.
See color photos on page 79.

		CNP	MIP	MMP
JU2001	Judge vs. Cons (1)	5	8	10
JU2002	Judges vs.			
	Mean Angel (2)	5	8	10
JU2003	Judge vs. Uglies (3)	5	8	10
JU2004	Judge vs.			
	Anti-Judges (4)	5	8	10
JU2005	Judge vs. Mutant (5)	5	8	10
JU2006	Judge vs. Machine (6)	5	8	10

JULIA (Mattel) 1969
Character doll of actress Diahann Carroll who starred in the prime-time TV series of the same name.
See color photo on page 79.

		CNP	MIP	MMP
JU5001	Julia	50	150	200

JURASSIC PARK (Kenner) 1993-94
Jurassic Park was the smash hit film of 1993. Anticipating the many knock-offs the line would generate, Kenner stamped each character and dinosaur with a "brand" to indicate their official status. Packages warned "if it's not Jurassic Park™, it's extinct!"

But it was the quality of the dinosaur figures which actually ensured the line's success. Kenner created detailed toys that the knock-off companies couldn't beat. They could roar, stomp, spit, bite, and be bitten. Major dinosaurs featured rubber "skin" over a plastic framework, with all action mechanisms and joints concealed. Kids, as always, knew the difference between these cool toys and the cheap wanna-bees…and demanded the real thing.

The human figures were less interesting, and originally bore no reseamblance to the actors from the film. Each was packaged with a trading card, a baby dinosaur PVC, and the usual Kenner mini-bazooka. Series II repaints of the original five figures were given new heads which looked more like the original characters. After the first year, stills from the film replaced drawings on the trading cards…the only consistent packaging variation. "Dino Trackers" and "Evil Raiders" were added to give the dinos more to chew on. Later releases of some of the dinosaur figures were repainted and repackaged with "capture gear" to freshen the line. The scientific names of the dinosaurs seem to have been a source of confusion, so nicknames like "Fang" and "Spitter" were added to later packages.

"Dino-Damage" added an extra element of play value to the line, allowing villain characters (who presumably deserved it), some dinosaurs, and accessories to be "wounded" or ripped apart. Appropriate bits of bone, guts, machinery or whatever were revealed.
See color photos on pages 79-80.

		CNP	MIP	MMP
JU7001	Alan Grant	5	8	10
JU7002	Ellie Sattler	5	8	10
JU7003	Tim Murphy	5	8	10
JU7004	Robert Muldoon	5	8	10
JU7005	Dennis Nedry	5	8	10
Series II figures				
JU7006	Alan Grant			
	w/Aerial Net Trap	5	8	10
JU7007	Alan Grant			
	w/Bola Launcher	5	8	10
JU7008	Ellie Sattler	5	8	10
JU7009	Tim Murphy	5	8	10
JU7010	Robert Muldoon	5	8	10
JU7011	Dennis Nedry	5	8	10
JU7012	Ian Malcolm	5	9	12
Dino-Trackers				
JU7021	"Harpoon" Harrison	5	8	10
JU7022	"Jaws" Jackson	5	8	10
JU7023	Sgt. "T-Rex" Turner	5	8	10
Evil Raiders				
JU7031	Dr. Snare	5	8	10
JU7032	Scrap Davis	5	8	10
JU7033	Skinner	5	8	10

JU7006 JU7007 JU7008 JU7009 JU7010

JU7011 JU7012 JU7021 JU7022 JU7023

JU7031 JU7033 JU7105

JU7101 JU7103 JU7111

Small carded dinosaurs

JU7041	Velociraptor	6	12	16
JU7043	Dilophosaurus	6	12	16
JU7045	Pteranodon	8	14	18
JU7047	Dimetrodon	6	12	16
JU7049	Coelophysis (2-pack)	9	15	20

Small carded dinosaurs with "Capture Gear"

JU7051	Velociraptor "Raptor"	8	14	18
JU7053	Dilophosaurus "Spitter"	8	14	18

JU7055	Lycaenops "Fang"	9	15	20
JU7057	Pachycephalosaurus "Ram Head"	9	15	20
JU7059	Tanystropheus "Cobra"	9	15	20
JU7061	Estemmenosuchus "Devil Horn"			undetermined
JU7063	Ornithosuchus "Slash"			undetermined
JU7065	Scutosaurus "Plateface"			undetermined

Carded "Dino Screams" electronic dinosaurs

JU7071	Velociraptor	9	12	16

JU7073	Dilophosaurus	9	12	16
JU7075	Baryonyx "Snapper"	12	16	20
JU7077	Gallimimus "Speeder"	12	16	20

Large boxed dinosaurs

JU7081	Young T-Rex	10	20	35
JU7083	Stegosaurus	10	20	35
JU7085	Triceratops	10	20	35
JU7087	Tyrannosaurus Rex	15	35	50
JU7091	JU7081, repaint w/capture gear	15	25	45

CNP: Complete, no package, with all weapons and accessories; MIP: Mint in package; MMP: Mint item in Mint package. Values in U.S. dollars. See page 3 for details.

JU7113

JU7115

		CNP	MIP	MMP
JU7093	Carnotaurus "Demon"	10	25	40
JU7094	Quetzalcoatlus			
	"Fire Beak"	15	25	45
Accessories				
JU7101	Bush Devil Tracker	10	15	20
JU7103	Jungle Explorer	10	20	28
JU7105	Capture Copter	10	20	28
JU7111	Jungle Runner	8	10	18
JU7113	Strike Cycle	8	10	15
JU7115	Capture Cruiser	8	12	18
JU7121	Command Compound	20	60	90

KARATE KID, THE (Remco) 1986

Each figure had three "karate" features, including a moving arm, a spring-action waist, and a kicking leg. They were packaged on cards with break-away accessories and a "secrets of Miyagi" scroll.

		CNP	MIP	MMP
KA6001	Daniel	5	15	20
KA6002	Miyagi	5	15	20
KA6003	Sato	5	15	20
KA6004	Kreese	5	15	20
KA6005	Chozen	5	15	20
KA6006	Johnny	6	16	22
KA6011	Attack Alley and Training Center	15	30	60
KA6012	Sato's Cannery	12	20	30
KA6013	Competition Center w/Referee	12	20	30
KA6014	Corner Challenge	10	18	25

KING ARTHUR AND THE KNIGHTS OF JUSTICE (Mattel) 1992

This short-lived series transported members of the New England Knights football team to the days of King Arthur.

		CNP	MIP	MMP
KI3501	King Arthur	2	6	8
KI3502	Sir Lancelot	2	6	8
KI3503	Sir Darren	2	6	8
KI3504	Warlord Viper	2	6	8

JU7121

KI3505	Warlord Slasher	2	6	8
KI3511	Valor the Warhorse	6	10	12
KI3512	Boulder Basher set	8	12	18
KI3513	Slime Pit set	undetermined		

KING KONG (AHI) 1977, (Imperial) 1985

		CNP	MIP	MMP
KI5001	King Kong (AHI)	15	50	60
KI5050	King Kong (Imperial)	5	-	12

See also: *Godzilla*

KNIGHT OF DARKNESS — See *Star Team*

KNIGHT RIDER (Kenner) 1983-86

Kenner's Knight 2000 Voice car included an articulated figure of Michael Knight. The figure was also sold seperately on a card.

KA6001

KA6002

KA6003

KA6004

KA6005

KA6006

KA6011

KA6012

KA6013

KA6014

KI3511

KI3512

| KI3501 | KI3502 | KI3503 | KI3504 | KI3505 | KI5050 |

| KN2000 | KN2001 | KO5001 | KO5005 |

| KO5010 | LA4001 | LA4002 | LA4003 |

| LA4004 | LA4005 | LA4006 | LA4007 | LA4008 |

		CNP	MIP	MMP
KN2000	Knight 2000 Car w/			
	Michael Knight	35	75	125
KN2001	Michael Knight, card	15	25	35

KOJAK (Excel Toy Corp.) 1976
A Mego-style figure based on the TV series.

		CNP	MIP	MMP
KO5001	Kojak	35	50	75
KO5005	Police Emergency Set	25	50	95
KO5010	Kojak's Headquarters			
	Playset (Sears)	50	125	180

LAND OF THE LOST (Tiger) 1992-93
The Krofft Entertainment animated series provided the inspiration for this line. "Talking" figures were repaints of the original figures with electronic backpacks, plus a few modifications to eliminate the original action features.

LA4001	Tom Porter	5	8	12
LA4002	Kevin Porter	5	8	12
LA4003	Annie Porter	5	8	12
LA4004	Christa	5	8	12
LA4005	Stink	5	8	12
LA4006	Tasha	5	8	12

LA4007	Shung	5	8	12
LA4008	Nim	5	8	12
LA4011	Talking Kevin	6	11	15
LA4012	Talking Annie	6	11	15
LA4013	Talking Christa	6	11	15
LA4014	Talking Stink	6	11	15
LA4015	Talking Shung	undetermined		
LA4016	Dinosaur 2-pack	6	11	15
LA4021	Scarface (T-Rex)	7	12	18
LA4022	Princess (Triceratops)	undetermined		
LA4023	Pterodactyl Glider	6	12	18
LA4031	Boulder Bomber	4	10	15
LA4032	S.S. Frisco	8	10	12

LA4011

LA4012

LA4013

LA4014

LA4016

LA4021

LA4031

LA4032

LA4035

LA4023

LA4036

LA6000 (Sears packaging)

LA4033

LA6010

LA6401

LA6402

LA6403

| LA6404 | LA6405 | LA6406 | LA6407 | LA6408 |

| LA6415 | LA8001 |

| LA6411 | LA6416 | LA8002 |

LA4033	Land Master	10	15	22
LA4035	Shung's Lair	12	18	25
LA4036	Porter's Treehouse	15	25	35

LASSIE (Gabriel) 1976

Lassie came alone or packaged with an 8½" boy, a non-articulate puppy, and a basket. The farm was sold seperately.

		CNP	MIP	MMP
LA6000	Lassie	8	12	24
LA6001	Lassie & her Friends	15	35	50
LA6010	Lassie's Farm	20	40	80

LAST ACTION HERO, THE (Mattel) 1993-94

The film was a "big mistake," but finding the entire toy line was no "piece of cake." Talking Jack Slater was only available through the J.C. Penney catalog. Evil Eye Benedict was released about two months after the rest of the series, and saw limited distribution before the remaining figures were closed out at Odd Lots stores. To further complicate matters, a running change was made in the figure's packaging to better display his briefcase. The Evil Eye

Roadster was even more limited...only a few thousand were produced.

		CNP	MIP	MMP
LA6401	Hook Launchin' Danny	5	8	12
LA6402	Dynamite Jack Slater	5	8	12
LA6403	Heat Packin' Jack	5	8	12
LA6404	Skull Attack Jack	5	8	12
LA6405	Undercover Jack	5	8	12
LA6406	Axe Swingin' Ripper	5	8	12
LA6407	Evil Eye Benedict (closed briefcase)	8	15	25
LA6408	Evil Eye Benedict (open briefcase)	8	15	25
LA6411	Talking Jack Slater	25	50	75
LA6415	Slater's Convertible	10	20	30
LA6416	Evil Eye Roadster	20	35	50
Generic-Pack Sets (white boxes)				
LA6421	Jack w/Convertible	-	20	35
LA6422	Evil Eye Benedict w/Evil Eye Roadster	-	20	35

LAUREL AND HARDY — See *Dakin and Dakin-Style Figures*

| LE0501 | LE0502 |

LAVERNE AND SHIRLEY (Mego) 1978

These 12" figures came in pairs, packed in window boxes.

		CNP	MIP	MMP
LA8001	Laverne and Shirley	45	85	115
LA8002	Lenny and Squiggy	55	95	130

LEGEND BRUCE LEE, THE (LarGo) 1983

Bruce Lee came packaged with two different weapons. The figures were identical.

		CNP	MIP	MMP
LE0501	Bruce w/nunchaku	10	18	30
LE0502	Bruce w/bo stick	10	18	30
LE0505	Bruce Lee 2-pack	20	30	45

LEGEND OF THE LONE RANGER, THE (Gabriel) 1982

The Lone Ranger film inspired both 3¾" and 9½" figures. Figures and horses (3¾") were sold separately or together on cards. The Western Town playset was a premium, earned by sending four character names cut from figure or horse packages as a proof-of-purchase. The larger figures and horses were re-issues of 1979 toys by Gabriel. They were sold together in window boxes.

3¾" Figures LE1001-05		CNP	MIP	MMP
LE1001	The Lone Ranger	4	10	15
LE1002	Tonto	4	10	15
LE1003	Butch Cavendish	4	10	15
LE1004	Buffalo Bill Cody	4	10	15
LE1005	General George Custer	4	10	15
3¾" Horses LE1011-13				
LE1011	Silver	8	15	20
LE1012	Scout	8	15	20
LE1013	Smoke	8	15	20
3¾" Figure Combinations LE1021-23				
LE1021	Lone Ranger & Silver	-	25	35
LE1022	Tonto & Scout	-	25	35
LE1023	Butch Cavendish & Smoke	-	25	35
LE1025	Western Town playset	20	35	55
9½" Figures LE1030-31				
LE1030	Lone Ranger & Silver (re-issue of LO3021)	25	40	50
LE1031	Tonto & Scout (re-issue of LO3022)	25	40	50

See also: *Captain Action; Lone Ranger, The*

LEGENDS OF BATMAN (Kenner) 1994-96

Inspired by DC's *Elseworlds* comics and other alternative incarnations of the Dark Knight, this collection features more muscular and detailed figures than other Kenner *Batman* lines. As usual, villains were produced in much lower quantities. Repainted *Legends* figures packaged on special *Batman* cards were sold exclusively at Warner Bros. Studio stores.

LE2001	Cyborg Batman	3	6	8
LE2003	Crusader Batman	3	6	8
LE2005	Power Guardian	3	6	8
LE2007	Future Batman, no bat-symbol on wing unit	3	10	12
LE2008	LE2007 w/bat-symbol on wing unit	3	6	8
LE2011	Knightquest Batman	3	6	8
LE2013	Nightwing	3	6	8
LE2015	Joker	3	8	10
LE2017	Catwoman	4	9	15
LE2021	Batcycle	5	7	10
LE2023	Dark Rider Batman	6	10	12
LE2025	Batmobile	8	12	20
LE2031	Knightsend Batman	3	6	8
LE2033	Samurai Batman	3	6	8
LE2035	Viking Batman	3	6	8
LE2037	Riddler	4	9	15
LE2041	Silver Knight Batman	5	10	12
LE2043	Flightpak Batman	5	10	12
LE2045	Desert Knight Batman	5	10	12
LE2051	Dark Warrior Batman	3	6	8
LE2053	Long Bow Batman	3	6	8
LE2055	Crusader Robin	3	6	8
LE2057	Ultra Armor Batman	3	6	8
LE2061	Buccaneer Batman	5	10	12
LE2063	First Mate Robin	5	10	12
LE2065	Laughing Man Joker	5	10	12
LE2067	Peg-Leg Riddler w/ Crusader Batman	10	12	14

Warner Bros. Studio Stores exclusive repaints
LE2301	Cyborg Batman	10	20	30
LE2303	Crusader Batman	10	20	30
LE2305	Power Guardian B-man	10	20	30
LE2308	Future Batman	10	20	30
LE2311	Knightquest Batman	10	20	30
LE2313	Nightwing	10	20	30

LEGENDS OF KNIGHTS AND DRAGONS (Imperial) 1992

The Knights of the Round Table ride again in this set. Each pack included a knight, mount, and several accessories.

		CNP	MIP	MMP
LE2601	King Arthur	3	6	8
LE2602	Merlin	3	6	8
LE2603	Sir Gawain	3	6	8
LE2604	Sir Lancelot	3	6	8
LE2605	Sir Galahad	3	6	8
LE2606	Sir Tristram	3	6	8

LEGENDS OF THE WEST (Excel Toy Corp.) 1973, (Empire Toys) 1978

Two lines of Western figures, using public domain historical characters as subjects. Excel figures were 9½" tall, and came packaged in window boxes with cloth and plastic accessories. The Empire line of 4" figures came blister carded with removable hats, guns, and belts. They were fully articulated, except at the elbow joint. Two different single-design cards were used, each of which included a brief biographical sketch.

Excel Toy Corp., 1973		CNP	MIP	MMP
LE2951	Jesse James	8	15	20
LE2953	Buffalo Bill Cody	8	15	20
LE2955	Cochise	8	15	20
LE2957	Wyatt Earp	8	15	20
LE2959	Wild Bill Hickok	8	15	20
LE2961	Davy Crockett	8	15	20
Empire Toys, 1978				
LE3001	Bat Masterson	2	5	7
LE3002	Jesse James	2	5	7
LE3003	Wild Bill Hicock	2	5	7
LE3004	Calvary Scout	2	5	7
LE3005	Wyatt Earp	2	5	7
LE3006	General Custer	2	5	7
LE3007	Deadwood Dick	2	5	7
LE3008	Billy the Kid	2	5	7
LE3009	Arrowhead	2	5	7
LE3010	Geronimo	2	5	7
LE3011	Cochise	2	5	7
LE3012	Davy Crockett	2	5	7
LE3013	General Santa Anna	2	5	7
LE3014	Buffalo Bill Cody	2	5	7
LE3021	Horse (Palomino)	3	6	10
LE3022	Horse (Pinto)	3	6	10
LE3030	Covered Wagon	10	20	25
LE3031	Stage Coach	10	20	25

LEGENDS OF THE WILD WEST (Imperial) 1991-93

Six western heroes were sold individually on cards, or in 2-packs with horses. A button hidden under each horse's saddle triggered a built-in sound chip. The two packs came carded or boxed.

		CNP	MIP	MMP
LE3501	General Custer	1	4	5
LE3502	Billy the Kid	1	4	5
LE3503	Wyatt Earp	1	4	5
LE3504	Sitting Bull	1	4	5
LE3505	Buffalo Bill	1	4	5
LE3506	Geronimo	1	4	5
"Action Play Sets" (boxed or carded)				
LE3511	General Custer/horse	3	6	8
LE3512	Billy the Kid w/horse	3	6	8
LE3513	Wyatt Earp w/horse	3	6	8
LE3514	Sitting Bull w/horse	3	6	8
LE3515	Buffalo Bill w/horse	3	6	8
LE3516	Geronimo w/horse	3	6	8

LI'L MISS JUSTRITE — See *Dakin and Dakin-Style Figures*

LINCOLN INTERNATIONAL MONSTERS (Lincoln) 1974-75

These figures were sold on personalized cards, but are grouped here for identification purposes. The Hunchback of Notre Dame and Phantom of the Opera were added in the second year, and are much harder to find.

		CNP	MIP	MMP
LI6011	Count Dracula	40	75	150
LI6012	Frankenstein	40	75	150
LI6013	Wolfman	40	75	150
LI6014	Mummy	40	75	150
LI6015	Hunchback of Notre Dame	60	100	175
LI6016	Phantom of the Opera	60	100	175

See also: *Classic Movie Monsters; Mad Monster Series, The; Maxx FX; Mini Monsters; Official World Famous Super Monsters; Real Ghostbusters, The; Universal Monsters*

LION KING, THE (Mattel/Arco) 1994

Mattel produced six carded sets of action figures and PVCs for Disney's *Lion King*. Most of the toys were also available in two larger gift sets. Shenzi was only sold in the gift sets. A spinoff line of *Jungle Friend Babies* was marketed for girls, combining articulated figures with squirting and PVC figures.

		CNP	MIP	MMP
LI6301	Rafiki/Young Simba	3	6	9
LI6302	Adult Simba	3	6	9
LI6303	Mufasa	3	6	9
LI6304	Scar	3	6	9
LI6305	Banzai/Zazu	3	6	9
LI6306	Pumbaa/Timon	3	6	9
LI6311	Gift Set w/Young Simba, Scar, Shenzi and Zazu	8	12	14
LI6312	Gift Set w/Adult Simba, Pumbaa, Rafiki, and Timon	8	12	14
LI6315	Pride Rock Playset	10	18	25
LI6317	Roaring Kings set	12	18	20
Jungle Friend Babies				
LI6321	Snacking Simba	4	8	12
LI6322	Sleeping Simba	4	8	12
LI6323	Naptime Nala	4	8	12
LI6324	Bedtime Pals	4	8	12
LI6325	Swingin' Pretty Zebra	4	8	12
LI6326	Squirt 'N splash Elephant	4	8	12
LI6327	Li'l Wetting Cheetah	4	8	12
LI6331	Jungle Playground	12	18	25

LITTLE DRACULA (DreamWorks) 1991

One of the better treats released in time for Halloween '91, *Little Dracula* was a high-quality series of imaginative figures. Action features included light-up eyes, removeable brains, and suction cups.

		CNP	MIP	MMP
LI6500	Little Dracula	4	8	12
LI6501	Drac Attack Little Dracula	5	12	18
LI6502	Igor	4	8	12
LI6503	Deadwood	4	8	12
LI6504	Werebunny	4	8	12
LI6505	Garlic Man	4	8	12
LI6506	Maggot	4	8	12
LI6507	The Man With No Eyes	5	9	14
LI6508	Twin Beaks	5	9	14
LI6520	Dracster vehicle	10	15	25
LI6521	Garlicmobile	10	15	25
LI6522	Coffin Car (UK only)	20	50	70

LE1001   LE1002   LE1003   LE1004   LE1005

LE1011   LE1012   LE1013   LE1021   LE1022

LE2001   LE2003   LE2005   LE2007   LE2007   LE2008

LE2011   LE2013   LE2015   LE2017   LE2021

CNP: Complete, no package, with all weapons and accessories; MIP: Mint in package; MMP: Mint item in Mint package. Values in U.S. dollars. See page 3 for details.

LE2023

LE2025

LE2031

LE2033

LE2035

LE2037

LE2041

LE2043

LE2045

LE2051

LE2053

LE2055

LE2057

LE2061

LE2063

LE2065

LE2067

90

LE2301 LE2303 LE2305 LE2308 LE2311

LE2313

LE2601

LE2955

LE2957

LE3002

LE3004

LE3009

LE3012

LE3013

LE3014

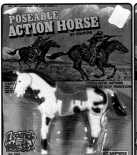
LE3021

LE3022

LE3030

LE3031

CNP: Complete, no package, with all weapons and accessories; MIP: Mint in package; MMP: Mint item in Mint package. Values in U.S. dollars. See page 3 for details.

LE3501

LE3512

LE3513

LI6011

LI6012

LI6013

LI6014

LI6015   LI6016

LI6301

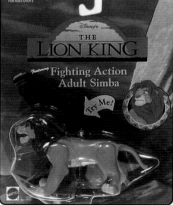

LI6302

LI6303

LI6304

LI6305

LI6306

LI6311

LI6312   LI6315   LI6317

LI6321   LI6323   LI6324   LI6325

LI6326   LI6327   LI6331

LI6500   LI6501   LI6502   LI6503   LI6504

LI6520   LI6521   LI65022

LI6505 LI6506 LI6507 LI6508 LI7001

LI7002 LI7005 LI7006 LI7008 LI7010 LI7012

LI7020 LI7021 LI7022 LI7025 LI7026 LI7027

LI7030 LI7031 LI7032 LI7034 LI7035 LI7036

LITTLE MERMAID, THE (TYCO) 1989-93, (Applause) 1989

Nicely-done boxed figures from the popular Disney feature of the same name. Eric was manufactured in smaller quantities, but demand for Ariel is much greater. The popu-

larity of the TYCO line continued until 1993, inspiring new figure variations and outfits.

Applause made a single figure of Ariel on a rock. The figure was removeable, and was only sold unpackaged.

		CNP	MIP	MMP
LI7001	Ariel	10	15	20
LI7002	Eric	25	65	80
LI7005	Holiday Ariel	15	40	50
LI7006	Ariel (shell on package)	10	15	20
LI7008	Ariel and her Friends	15	25	35

LI7045

LI7047

LI7050

LI7110

LO3001

LO3002

LO3003

LO3004

LO3005

LO3006

LO3008

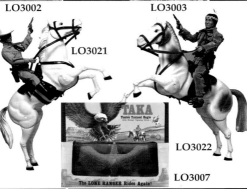
LO3021　LO3007　LO3022

SMOKE
LO3013

BANJO
LO3014

LO3031

LO3032
LO3034

LO3033

LO3035

LI7010	Eric (shell package)	15	25	35	LI7025	Undersea Party Ariel	4	8	12	LI7036	MerBabysitter Ariel	10	15	20
LI7012	Ariel the Beautiful Bride	12	30	55	LI7026	Tropical Ariel	9	12	15	LI7045	Cool Teen Shelly	4	8	12
					LI7027	Springtime Ariel	9	12	15	LI7047	Prince Eric (blue outfit w/gold trim)	8	15	20
LI7020	Ariel's Under-The-Sea Treasures	4	8	12	LI7030	Ariel's Sister Arista	9	12	15					
LI7021	Dinner at Eric's Palace	4	8	12	LI7031	Eric the Sailor	10	15	20	LI7048	Singing Ariel	8	15	20
LI7022	Ariel's Bedtime at the Palace	4	8	12	LI7032	Royal Princess Ariel	10	20	30	LI7050	Ariel's Undersea Hideaway	15	30	45
					LI7034	Beautiful Hair Ariel	10	20	30					
					LI7035	Whale of a Tale Ariel	12	18	26	LI7110	Ariel on rock (Applause)	20	-	-

The Hidden Rattler Adventure

LO3041

The Landslide Adventure

LO3042

The Blizzard Adventure

LO3043

The Adventure of The Hidden Silver Mine

LO3044

The Adventure of The Apache Buffalo Hunt

LO3045

The Adventure of The Carson City Bank Robbery

LO3046

The Adventure of The Tribal Powwow

LO3049

The Adventure of The Missing Mountain Climber

LO3050

The Adventure of The Red River Floodwaters

LO3051

The Adventure of The Lost Cavalry Patrol

LO3047

The Adventure of The Hopi Medicine Man

LO3048

The LONE RANGER Rides Again... in the adventure of The Bootleggers

LO3061

The LONE RANGER Rides Again... in the adventure of The Broken Horseshoe

LO3062

LONE RANGER RIDES AGAIN, THE (Gabriel) 1979

Each Lone Ranger item came back with a small comic book. Figures, horses and accessories came in four-color boxes, outfits for the figures came in wedge-shaped window boxes. Figures and horses were also available in sets.

The LONE RANGER Rides Again... in the adventure of The Crooked Gambler

LO3063

The LONE RANGER Rides Again... in the adventure of The Gun Runners

LO3064

The LONE RANGER Rides Again... in the adventure of The Indian War

LO3065

The LONE RANGER Rides Again... in the adventure of The Kidnappers

LO3066

		CNP	MIP	MMP
LO3001	The Lone Ranger	10	25	32
LO3002	Tonto	10	25	32
LO3003	Butch Cavendish	15	27	35
LO3004	Red Sleeves	15	27	35
LO3005	Dan Reid	15	27	35
LO3006	Little Bear w/Nama	15	27	35
LO3007	Taka			
LO3008	Tex Dawson (UK only)			
LO3011	Silver	18	28	32
LO3012	Scout	15	25	30
LO3013	Smoke	18	30	35
LO3014	Banjo	18	30	35

Figure and horse sets, boxed LO3021-23

LO3021	Lone Ranger & Silver	-	40	55
LO3022	Tonto & Scout	-	40	55
LO3023	Butch Cavendish & Smoke	-	40	55
LO3031	4 in one Prairie Wagon	15	25	35
LO3032	Solitary Trapper	12	25	30
LO3033	Carson City Playset	20	45	55
LO3034	Mysterious Prospector	25	45	55
LO3035	Tribal Tepee	5	12	15

Adventure Sets LO3041-50

LO3041	Hidden Rattler	8	12	15
LO3042	Landslide	8	12	15
LO3043	Blizzard	8	12	15
LO3044	Hidden Silver Mine	8	12	15
LO3045	Apache Buffalo Hunt	12	17	20
LO3046	Carson City Bank Robbery	12	17	20

LO3983

LO3984

LO3985

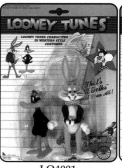

LO4001

LO4005

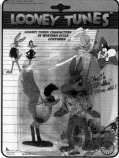

LO4011

LO4021   LO4022   LO4023

LO4051   LO4052   LO4053   LO4054   LO4055

LO4057   LO4058   LO4059   LO4086

LO3047	Lost Calvary Patrol	15	25	30
LO3048	Hopi Medicine Man	15	25	30
LO3049	Tribal Powwow	15	25	30
LO3050	Missing Mountain Climber	15	25	30

Additional Outfits (Marx, foreign release)

LO3061	Bootleggers	8	10	15
LO3062	Broken Horseshoe	8	10	15
LO3063	Crooked Gambler	8	10	15
LO3064	Gun Runners	8	10	15
LO3065	Indian War	8	10	15
LO3066	Kidnappers	8	10	15
LO3067	Last Chance Saloon	8	10	15
LO3068	Lazy Trapper	8	10	15
LO3069	Rebel Riders	8	10	15
LO3070	Secret Corral	8	10	15
LO3071	Stage Robbery	8	10	15
LO3072	Stolen Rifles	8	10	15

See also: *Captain Action; Legend of the Lone Ranger, The*

LOONEY TUNES (Lucky Bell) 1988-90, (TYCO) 1994-95, (Warner Bros. Stores) 1994+

Looney Tunes characters by Lucky Bell were sold singly and in pairs on blister cards. The characters were flocked and wore western-style costumes. Separate gift sets of Bugs Bunny were sold, each containing a figure of Bugs with three different outfits.

TYCO picked up the *Looney Tunes* license in 1994, producing regular and talking figures. About the same time, Dakin-style figures with limited articulation were made available exclusively at Warner Bros. Studio Stores. Most of these were jointed only at the head and arms.

Lucky Bell LO3981-4023		CNP	MIP	MMP
LO3981	Bugs Bunny	2	6	8
LO3982	Daffy Duck	2	6	8
LO3983	Tweety	2	6	8
LO3984	Sylvester	2	6	8
LO3985	Wile E. Coyote	2	6	8
LO3986	Road Runner	2	6	8
LO4001	Bugs Bunny/Daffy	4	8	12
LO4005	Tweety/Sylvester	4	8	12
LO4011	Wile E. Coyote/ Road Runner	4	8	12
Bugs Bunny Deluxe Gift Sets LO4021-23				
LO4021	Athlete set	4	8	10
LO4022	Medical set	4	8	10
LO4023	Beach set	4	8	10
TYCO				
LO4051	Bugs Bunny	1	4	6
LO4052	Wile E. Coyote	1	4	6
LO4053	Road Runner	1	4	6
LO4054	Tasmanian Devil	1	4	6
LO4055	Marvin the Martian	1	4	6
TYCO Talking Figures				
LO4057	Bugs Bunny	1	4	6
LO4058	Tasmanian Devil	1	4	6
LO4059	Marvin the Martian	1	4	6

LO4083   LO4082   LO4081   LO4084   LO4085

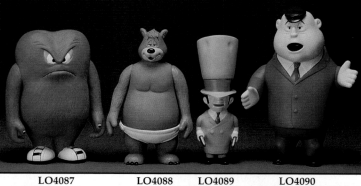

LO4087   LO4088   LO4089   LO4090

LO5001

LO5002

LO5003

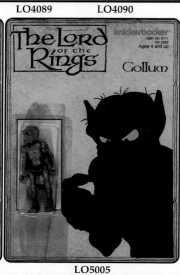

LO5005

LO5004

LO5006

LO5011

LO5012

LO6001

LO6002

LO6003

LO6004

LO6005

LO6006

Warner Bros. Studio Store exclusives

LO4081	Bugs Bunny	10	-	-	LO4084	Sylvester	10	-	-	LO4088	Baby Bear Junior	6	-	-
LO4082	Daffy Duck	10	-	-	LO4085	Tweety	10	-	-	LO4089	Bugsey	6	-	-
LO4083	Tasmanian Devil	15	-	-	LO4086	Marvin	8	-	-	LO4090	Mugsey	6	-	-
					LO4087	Gossamer	6	-	-	**See also:** *Dakin and Dakin-Style Figures*				

LO6041   LO6042   LO6043   LO6044   LO6045   LO6046

LO6049   LO6022   LO6023   LO6051

VICKI   CAPTAIN STUBING   "DOC"   "GOPHER"   "JULIE" JULIE   ISAAC

LO8001   LO8002   LO8003   LO8004   LO8005   LO8006

M-2005   M-7003   MA1201   MA1208

MA1010

MA1001-4

MA1210   MA1502   MI9031   MI9001   MI9003

MA1805

MA1806

MA1808

MA1811

MA1815

MA1817

MA1818

MA1822

MA1820

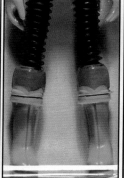

MA1820

MA1821

MA1821

MA1831

MA1832

MA1833

MA1834

MA1835

MA1836

MA1837

MA1839

MA1840

MA1845

MA1846

MA1847

MA1848

MA1850

MA1861 (top of box)

MA1861 (front of box)

MA1865

MA1867

MA1870 (front of box)

MA1871 (top of box)

MA1872

MA1875

MA1885

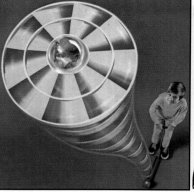

MA1890

MA1895

MA1896

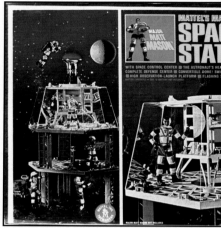

MA1900

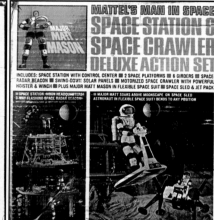

MA1903

MA1910

MA1912

MA1915

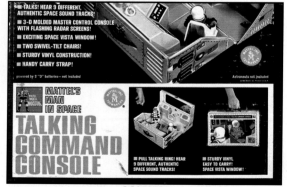

MA1920

MA1925

MA1926

LORD OF THE RINGS, THE (Knickerbocker) 1979

The Saul Zaentz animated film adaptation of J.R.R. Tolkien's classic tale was the basis for this rare figure line. The figures were based on film model sheets, with the exception of the Ringwraith and his charger. In the film, the Ringwraiths were mostly shadowy live-action images without much definition. For the figure line, Knickerbocker created a menacing dark rider every bit as fearful as the fluid images in the film...or better. The Ringwraith and his charger are easily the best two figures in the line, and the most sought-after by collectors.

The Lord of the Rings was not a successful licensing property, and had little retail support.

The figure line, however, is one of the rarest and most sought-after in all action figure collecting...as the value estimates below indicate.

See color photos on page 98.

	CNP	MIP	MMP
LO5001 Gandalf the Grey	25	85	140
LO5002 Aragorn	15	50	75

MA2001   MA2002   MA2013   MA4001   MA4002   MA4003

MA4801   MA4802   MA4803   MA4804   MA4805

MA4806   MA4807   MA4808   MA4813   MA4817

making pumpkin bombs and his terrifying cackling laugh, Green Goblin spreads doom, destruction and panic wherever he flies. When it comes to making Spider-Man's life miserable, nobody does it better than Green Goblin. What makes him so terrifying and so hard to capture is the fact that there's no rhyme or reason to Green Goblin's crime sprees. No one, not even Spider-Man, can predict what he'll do next!

The secret to launching those deadly pumpkin bombs is to simply raise Green Goblin's right arm, place one pumpkin bomb in his hand and push the button located on his back. Stand back and watch as Green Goblin continues in his evil crusade.

jet-powered Goblin, making pumpkin bombs and his terrifying cackling laugh, Green Goblin spreads doom, destruction and panic wherever he flies. When it comes to making Spider-Man's life miserable, nobody does it better than Green Goblin. What makes him so terrifying and so hard to capture is the fact that there's no rhyme or reason to Green Goblin's crime sprees. No one, not even Spider-Man, can predict what he'll do next!

The secret to launching those deadly pumpkin bombs is to simply raise Green Goblin's right arm, place one pumpkin bomb in his hand and release. Stand back and watch as Green Goblin continues in his evil crusade.

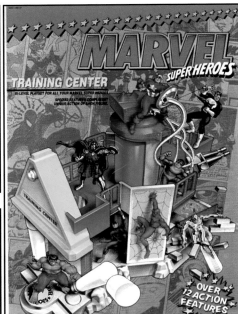

MA4815   MA4815   MA4816   MA4812

MA4809   MA4810

MA4819

MA4820

MA4822

MA4824

MA4825

MA4826

MA4828

MA4830

MA4832

MA4891

MA4893

MA4895

MA4897

MA4899

MA4901

MA4903

MA4905

MA4907

MA4909

LO5003	Frodo	15	50	75
LO5004	Samwise	25	85	125
LO5005	Gollum	15	50	75
LO5006	Ringwraith	60	125	165
LO5011	Frodo's Horse	25	85	200
LO5012	Charger of the Ringwraith	50	100	225

LOST WORLD OF THE WARLORD, THE/ WARRIOR BEASTS, THE (Remco) 1983-84

These figures were based on DC comics.

The Warlords LO6001-11		CNP	MIP	MMP
LO6001	Warlord	5	15	20
LO6002	Arak	5	12	20
LO6003	Hercules	5	12	20

LO6004	Mikola	5	12	20
LO6005	Deimos	5	12	20
LO6006	Machiste	5	12	20
LO6011	Warpult	5	12	20

War Team figure/horse sets LO6021-23				
LO6021	Warlord and stallion	10	20	30
LO6022	Machiste and stallion	10	20	30
LO6023	Mikola and stallion	10	20	30

		CNP	MIP	MMP
LO6025	Deimos and stallion	10	20	30
LO6030	Journey Thru Time (includes LO6001)	25	60	80

The Warrior Beasts

LO6041	Gecko	2	4	6
LO6042	Snakeman	2	4	6
LO6043	Craven	2	4	6
LO6044	Skullman	2	4	6
LO6045	Wolf Warrior	2	4	6
LO6046	Hydraz	2	4	6
LO6047	Ramar	2	4	6
LO6048	Guana	2	4	6
LO6049	Stegos	2	4	6
LO6050	Zardus	2	4	6
LO6051	Ramar/Fire Dragon	10	15	20
LO6052	Figure/War Beast	10	15	20
LO6053	Figure/War Beast	10	15	20

LOVE BOAT, THE (Mego) 1981

Based on the TV show.

		CNP	MIP	MMP
LO8001	Vicki	5	10	15
LO8002	Captain Stubing	6	12	18
LO8003	"Doc"	5	10	15
LO8004	"Gopher"	5	10	15
LO8005	Julie	5	10	15
LO8006	Isaac	5	10	15

M-FORCE (Marchon, Inc.) 1985

A generic combat series, probably a knock-off of *Rambo*.

		CNP	MIP	MMP
M-2001	Slam	2	4	5
M-2002	Snake	2	4	5
M-2003	Rizzo	2	4	5
M-2004	Zack	2	4	5
M-2005	Ace	2	4	5
M-2006	Mean Jo Ling	2	4	5

M-P.A.C.T. (Toymax) 1991

The Multi-National Police Against Crime and Turmoil came with sound-chip backpacks.

M-7001	Pete Tolmer	2	4	5
M-7002	Sir George Goodwill	2	4	5
M-7003	Lt. Col. Ivan Krinski	2	4	5
M-7004	William Sadler	2	4	5
M-7005	Tom Adams	2	4	5
M-7006	Sgt. Ken Knight	2	4	5
M-7007	Andrew Ness	2	4	5
M-7008	Daniel Lee Crane	2	4	5
M-7011	Varga Tolstoy	2	4	5
M-7012	Kelly Nightwing	2	4	5
M-7013	Victor Savage	2	4	5
M-7014	Dimitri Greco	2	4	5
M-7021	Air Avenger			undetermined
M-7022	Aero Scorpion			undetermined
M-7023	Global Force H.Q.			undetermined

MAD MONSTER SERIES, THE (Mego) 1974

A Mego series released as part of the *Official World's Greatest Super Heroes* line. Each figure has glow-in-the-dark hands and eyes. A few head variations are known to exist.

MA1001	Dracula	60	135	185
MA1002	Wolfman	40	100	150
MA1003	Frankenstein	25	65	100
MA1004	Mummy	25	65	100
MA1006	Dracula, red hair, different face	60	135	185
MA1007	Frankenstein, blue hair, different face	25	65	100
MA1010	Mad Monster Castle	125	450	600

MADBALLS (AmToy) 1986

Each *Madballs* figure had a ball-shaped head which pops off at the flip of a switch. The heads were interchangeable. Horn Head only came with the Mad RollerCycle.

		CNP	MIP	MMP
MA1201	Screamin' Meemie	4	7	9
MA1202	Oculus Orbus	4	7	9
MA1203	Dust Brain	4	7	9
MA1204	Skull Face	4	7	9
MA1205	Slobulus	4	7	9
MA1206	Lock Lips	4	7	9
MA1207	Wolf Breath	4	7	9
MA1208	Bruise Brother	4	7	9
MA1210	Mad RollerCycle w/Horn Head	6	15	20

MAGNUM P.I. (LJN) 1983

The figure of Don Magnum (Tom Selleck) was sold on a card or in a Ferrari boxed set.

MA1501	Magnum P.I.	5	20	40
MA1502	Ferrari w/Magnum	25	50	85

Major MATT MASON (Mattel) 1966-71

Major MATT MASON — Mattel's Man in Space was a popular toy during the NASA Gemini and Apollo manned space programs. The figures are wire-reinforced rubber flexies with accordion joints which made them functional as action figures. Matt and his crew were supported by a wide variety of space accessories, equipment, and playsets.

Precise dating of some *Major MATT MASON* items can be confusing, because all of the human figures are marked "©Copyright 1966 Mattel Inc." This is the year the mold was made. This space suit body was later re-used for all of the human figures, most of which were produced after the first year.

Matt was the only figure available during the first year. He was sold on a blister card with a set of accessories (later called the "Flight Set") or with a "Moon Suit." The Moon suit was also sold by itself on a blister card. The Space Crawler vehicle and Space Station playset were also sold during the first year, and continually produced until the end of the line. Deluxe sets were marketed with various combinations of figures and accessories. Matt's head mold was changed at some point to a larger version painted with a darker skin tone. Additionally, the straps on MATT's space suit can be found in blue or black.

Sgt. Storm was essentially a Matt Mason figure with a red suit and a new head. Major MATT and Sgt. Storm were both sold with a "Cat Trac," (later called a "Lunar Trac"). Sgt. Storm was also available with the Flight Set.

"Major MATT MASON's Friend From Outer Space" was Capt. Lazer, who has lights in his eyes, chest, and left arm. Three clear plastic accessories could be attached to the arm. The figure also came with a removable helmet and "space-tredder" boots. Capt. Lazer's molds were later cannibalized to produce the large *Battlestar Galactica* figures.

Doug Davis (orange suit) and Jeff Long (blue suit) were produced in 1969. Jeff Long is the most difficult of the human figures to find. Callisto, an alien, was made the same year. Its major accessory was a "Space Sensor" which could fire and retract a plastic line.

The alien Scorpio was produced in 1970. He came with a bellows-controlled vest which fired "search globes." The figure has removable arm and leg shields which are frequently missing, and the head has a small light inside.

Accessory "Paks" were sold mostly on bubble cards. In 1970, four of the Paks were repackaged in chip boxes. The Space Power Suit and Supernaut Power-Limbs were also sold together as the Super Power Set.

Mattel catalogues list several items which have not been confirmed, including a third alien figure, Or, which was to be sold only with an Orbitor vehicle. These are included in the list below. Special thanks to Mike Blanchard, Steve Crouse and Keith Meyer for their assistance in updating this section.

See color photos on pages 100-102.

Major MATT MASON figure MA1800-06

		CNP	MIP	MMP
MA1801	with Cat Trac	60	150	220
MA1803	with Flight Set	-	325	400
MA1805	with Moon Suit	-	400	525
MA1806	w/Space Power Suit	-	425	550
MA1808	Talking Major MATT	85	225	400
MA1810	Sgt. Storm w/Cat Trac	60	180	350
MA1811	Sgt. Storm w/Flight Set	-	400	600
MA1815	Capt. Lazer	75	225	500
MA1817	Doug Davis w/Cat Trac	45	175	275
MA1818	Jeff Long w/Cat Trac	75	275	375
MA1820	Callisto, high boots	70	275	350
MA1821	Callisto, low boots	70	275	350
MA1822	Scorpio	500	1100	1400
MA1825	Space Mission Team w/Major MATT, Doug Davis, Jeff Long, Callisto	-	700	800

Carded Space Paks MA1831-40

MA1831	Space Probe	35	60	90
MA1832	Rocket Launch	25	60	90
MA1833	Moon Suit	35	60	85
MA1834	Reconojet	25	50	75
MA1835	Space Shelter	25	50	75
MA1836	Satellite Launch	25	50	75
MA1837	Space Power Suit	25	50	75
MA1838	Gamma-Ray Gard	25	50	75
MA1839	Supernaut Power Limbs	15	35	50
MA1840	Space Travel	25	50	75

Boxed Space Paks MA1845-48

MA1845	Space Power Suit	25	75	100
MA1846	Supernaut Power Limbs	25	75	100
MA1847	Gamma Ray Gard	25	50	75
MA1848	Space Shelter Pak	25	75	100
MA1850	Super Power Set	-	300	500
MA1861	Space Crawler	35	75	150
MA1863	Space Crawler Action Set w/Major MATT	-	150	225
MA1865	Astro Trac	65	125	175
MA1867	Space Bubble	25	50	85
MA1870	Uni-Tred Space Hauler	35	75	115
MA1872	Uni-Tred & Space Bubble	-	125	180
MA1875	Firebolt Space Cannon	40	100	150
MA1877	Firebolt Space Cannon Action Set	-	175	250
MA1879	Firebolt Space Cannon Super Action Set	-	500	650
MA1882	Mobile Launch Pad	65	135	175
MA1885	Star Seeker	75	135	175
MA1890	Orbitor w/Or			not confirmed
MA1895	XRG-1 Reentry Glider	75	155	300
MA1897	MA1895 w/figure	-	300	500
MA1900	Space Station	65	120	175
MA1903	Space Station & Space Crawler Deluxe Set	-	200	275
MA1910	Space Discovery Set	-	400	550
MA1912	Lunar Base Command	-	600	750
MA1915	Astro Trac Missile Convoy Set (Sears)	-	700	900
MA1920	Talking Command Console	75	100	150
MA1925	Rocket Ship Case	100	150	200
MA1926	Satellite Locker	35	50	80
MA1932	56" Major MATT display figure	400	-	-

MAN FROM U.N.C.L.E., THE (Gilbert) 1965

The figures were sold in cardboard boxes, complete with U.N.C.L.E. pocket insignia and identification card. A cap-firing gun was included, which was triggered by releasing a spring-loaded arm.

See color photos on page 103.

CNP: *Complete, no package, with all weapons and accessories;* MIP: *Mint in package;* MMP: *Mint item in Mint package. Values in U.S. dollars. See page 3 for details.*

MA3505   MA3502

		CNP	MIP	MMP
MA2001	Napoleon Solo	75	100	250
MA2002	Illya Kuryakin	75	100	250
MA2011	Target Set	20	55	75
MA2012	Jumpsuit Set	20	55	75
MA2013	Armament Set	20	55	75
MA2014	Scuba Set	20	55	75
MA2015	Arsenal Set #1	15	35	45
MA2016	Arsenal Set #2	15	35	45
MA2017	Pistol Conversion Kit	15	35	45

MANTECH (Remco) 1984

ManTech was an interchangeable series of figures using 6mm holes and pegs with a rotating mechanism.

		CNP	MIP	MMP
MA3501	AquaTech	4	8	12
MA3502	SolarTech	4	8	12
MA3503	LaserTech	4	8	12
MA3504	NegaTech	4	8	12
MA3505	TerrorTech	4	8	12
MA3506	DoomTech	4	8	12
MA3511	Traxon LSA	8	12	14
MA3512	Terrorizer LSA	8	12	14
MA3521	Laser II Battlestation	10	20	30
MA3525	Combo Robot Warrior	5	10	15
MA3526	Spider Tech	5	10	15
MA3527	Eagle Tech	5	10	15
MA3528	Robot Tech	5	10	15
MA3529	Kong Tech	6	12	20
MA3534	Trundaxx	9	20	30

MARTIAN CHRONICLES, THE (Larami) 1974

Three Martian figures were made, based of the film adaptation of Ray Bradbury's anthology *The Martian Chronicles*. All three characters are shown on the card, but no names are given.
See color photos on page 103.

		CNP	MIP	MMP
MA4001	Orange/white robe	25	50	80
MA4002	Blue/white robe	25	50	80
MA4003	Pink/white robe	25	50	80

MARVEL SUPER HEROES (Toy Biz) 1990-94

Super heroes from the entire Marvel universe were included in the first Toy Biz line.

Venom figures (all sizes) were the toughest to find. The Venom with Living Slime Pores was replaced shortly after its release by a similar figure which squirted "alien liquid" (water). Supersize Punisher was availible by mail with proof-of-purchase symbols from the other three Supersize figures, but few were mailed because of the scarcity of Venom. Talking figures were released in November, 1991.

Though the figures were in heavy demand, Marvel was dissatisfied with the sculpting of the characters, and there were a number of shipping delays. Seeking to gain an expanded presence for Marvel characters on toy store shelves, the comic company ultimately solved the problem by investing approximately $7 million to acquire 46% ownership of Toy Biz. As a result, Marvel effectively gained control of Toy Biz, and figure quality was vastly improved. *Marvel Super Heroes* and its spinoff lines have produced a wide variety of figures, including minor characters which no other company would have considered.

The color-changing Invisible Woman saw very limited distribution, and for a time became one of the most infamous short-run figures ever produced. The same mold was re-used without color-changing paint in 1994, and a launcher mechanism was added.

No new figures were created in 1993, probably as a result of the Marvel investment. Four new figures were added in 1994, but all of these were based on existing molds. Toy Biz figures produced after this time were sold in more specialized lines.

See color photos on pages 103-104.

1990

		CNP	MIP	MMP
MA4801	Spider-Man w/web-suction hands	5	10	15
MA4802	Captain America	5	10	15
MA4803	Daredevil	20	40	60
MA4804	Dr. Doom	5	10	15
MA4805	Dr. Octopus	5	10	15
MA4806	The Incredible Hulk	5	10	15
MA4807	The Punisher	5	10	15
MA4808	Silver Surfer (grey)	6	15	20
MA4809	Spider-Man Dragster	10	15	25
MA4810	Captain America Turbo Coupe	10	15	25
MA4812	Training Center	12	20	50

1991

		CNP	MIP	MMP
MA4813	Web-Shooting Spider-Man	5	12	18
MA4814	Punisher w/sound	5	10	15
MA4815	Green Goblin, button-release arm	10	35	60
MA4816	MA4815, spring arm	5	10	15
MA4817	Iron Man/Tony Stark	8	12	20
MA4819	Thor, short hammer	15	30	50
MA4820	Thor, long hammer	5	10	18
MA4822	Web-Climbing Spider-Man	8	15	20
MA4824	Venom w/Living Slime Skin Pores	5	12	18
MA4825	Venom (squirting)	5	8	10
MA4826	Talking Spider-Man	5	10	15
MA4828	Talking Punisher	5	10	15

MA4830	Talking Hulk	5	10	15
MA4832	Talking Venom	6	12	18
MA4852	Punisher Van	10	30	50
MA4862	Attack Tower	7	15	25
MA4865	Hulk Rage Cage	8	20	35
MA4875	Supersize Spider-Man	10	20	30
MA4876	Supersize Hulk	10	20	30
MA4877	Supersize Venom	12	25	45
MA4878	Supersize Punisher	40	-	-

1992

MA4891	Spider-Man II (Multi-Jointed)	5	10	15
MA4893	Silver Surfer (chrome)	6	12	18
MA4895	Venom (tongue-flicking)	10	25	40
MA4897	Deathlok	5	8	12
MA4899	Spider-Man w/enemy Tracking Tracer	6	12	20
MA4901	Mr. Fantastic	10	15	25
MA4903	Thing	10	15	25
MA4905	Invisible Woman (color change)	50	150	200
MA4907	Human Torch	5	12	20
MA4909	Annihulus	5	12	20

1994

MA4921	Daredevil (red, black, & silver costume)	4	9	12
MA4923	Invisible Woman w/catapult launcher	4	9	12
MA4925	Punisher w/trenchcoat	4	5	10
MA4927	U.S. Agent	4	5	10

See also: *Amazing Spider-Man, The; Captain Action; Captain America; Comic Action Heroes; Die-Cast Super Heroes; Fantastic Four; Fantastic Four/Iron Man Collector's Edition; Incredible Hulk, The; Iron Man; Marvel Super Heroes Secret Wars; Maximum Carnage; Official World's Greatest Super Heroes; Pocket Super Heroes; Projectors; Uncanny X-Men, The*

MARVEL SUPER HEROES SECRET WARS (Mattel) 1984

Leading Marvel super heroes were suddenly transported to a remote planet by a being known only as "the Beyonder" to do battle with the most powerful supervillains of the day. This event was chronicled in a special 12-issue mini-series, and later in regular comics. These "Secret Wars" were widely merchandised in toys and other products.

MA4852

MA4865

MA4862

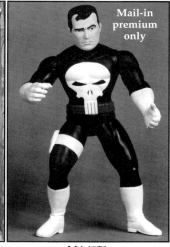

Mail-in premium only

MA4875	MA4876	MA4877	MA4878

MA4921	MA4923	MA4925	MA4927	MA5000

MA5001	MA5002	MA5004	MA5005	MA5006

Mattel, then riding the high of their *Masters of the Universe* action figure line, developed a sleeker, different look for these famous Marvel characters. It was also the first time Marvel had an action figure line based solely on its own characters. Spider-Man and Captain America appeared in Ideal's *Captain Action* line in 1967 and throughout the '70s in Mego's *Official World's Greatest Super Heroes* series. In both cases DC characters were also included.

The device common to each figure was a "secret shield" with four different lenticular card inserts. There were a total of 16 figures produced. They were packaged on English, Spanish, and French cards. Strangely, the bubble configuration varies with each language. Only 13 were sold on English cards in the United States. Iceman, Constrictor, and Electro were sold on French and Spanish cards in

Canada, Europe, and South America.

There were many packaging variations in an attempt by Mattel to supply "special" products to larger retailers. The Turbo Cycle and Doom Cycle came packaged with and without the figures of Captain America and Doctor Doom; as did the Turbocopter and Doom Chopper. A 3-pack of Captain America, Daredevil, and Spider-Man in black costume and a two-pack of Captain America and Doctor Doom were sold. Spider-Man and Iron Man were available with trucks in South America.

		CNP	MIP	MMP
MA5000	Captain America	5	15	20
MA5001	Spider-Man	10	25	35
MA5002	Iron Man	7	20	28
MA5003	Wolverine (black claws)	15	75	150
MA5004	MA5003, (silver claws)	10	30	50
MA5005	Doctor Doom	5	8	15
MA5006	Magneto	6	12	20
MA5007	Kang	4	7	12
MA5008	Doctor Octopus	5	12	20
MA5009	Spider-Man, black	15	40	60
MA5010	Daredevil	12	25	43
MA5011	Falcon	18	35	50
MA5012	Baron Zemo	10	25	40
MA5013	Hobgoblin	20	50	70
MA5015	Iceman	25	65	110
MA5016	Constrictor	25	65	110
MA5017	Electro	30	70	115
MA5020	Captain America/ Doctor Doom set	-	40	85
MA5021	Set w/MA5000, MA5009, MA5010	-	85	175
MA5030	Doom Roller vehicle	10	15	25
MA5031	Turbo Cycle	6	15	25
MA5032	Doom Cycle	6	15	25
MA5033	MA5032 w/MA5005	10	30	50

MA5007

MA5008

MA5009

MA5010

MA5011

MA5012

MA5013

MA5015

MA5016

MA5017

MA5021

MA5030

MA5031

MA5033

MA5034

MA5035

MA5036

		CNP	MIP	MMP
MA5034	Star Dart w/MA5009	15	30	50
MA5035	Doom Star w/MA5007	10	15	25
MA5036	Freedom Fighter	10	15	25
MA5037	Turbocopter	15	35	75
MA5038	Doom Chopper	15	35	75
MA5051	Tower of Doom	10	20	25

MARVEL TEAM-UP (Toy Biz) 1995

This pair of two-packs was a K-mart exclusive. Each pack included temporary tattoos. The Human Torch was the repainted Silver Surfer (see FA4006 and FA4021).

		CNP	MIP	MMP
MA5501	Human Torch/Web Racing Spider-Man	10	15	25
MA5502	The Thing/Web Shooter Spider-Man	10	15	25

See also: *Fantastic Four; Spider-Man*

M*A*S*H (Tri-Star International) 1970, 1982-83

Two sets of *M*A*S*H* figures were produced. In the small size, Hot Lips and Klinger wearing the dress were the hardest to find.

Large figures MA6001-03		CNP	MIP	MMP
MA6001	Hawkeye	15	24	35
MA6002	B.J.	15	24	35
MA6003	Hot Lips	15	24	35
3¾" figures MA6021-33				
MA6021	Hawkeye	5	10	15
MA6022	B.J.	5	10	15
MA6023	Hot Lips	6	16	20
MA6024	Winchester	5	10	15
MA6025	Col. Potter	5	10	15
MA6026	Father Malcahy	5	10	15
MA6027	Klinger in uniform	5	10	15

MA5038

MA5501

MA5502

MA5051

MA6003

MA6021

MA6022

MA6023   MA6024   MA6025   MA6026   MA6027   MA6028

MA6030

MA6032

MA6033

MA6028	Klinger in dress	15	25	40
MA6030	Four-pack	-	35	55
MA6031	Helicopter w/MA6021	15	25	35
MA6032	Jeep w/MA6021	8	20	30
MA6033	Ambulance w/MA6021	8	20	35
MA6040	Military Base playset	15	30	65

M.A.S.K. (Kenner) 1985-87

The Mobile Armored Strike Kommand (*M.A.S.K.*) is based on the allure of hidden weapons and action features. Each vehicle or playset included a mini-comic and one or more figures. A few characters were sold with more than one vehicle, but with different outfits and accessories. Figures were not sold separately until 1986. The nine original figures and Hondo Mac Lean came in two-packs, while new ones were sold individually with "adventure packs."

MA6031

MA6040

GATOR

MA7003

AFTERBURNER

MA7010

CONDOR

MA7001

SWITCHBLADE

MA7006

THE COLLECTOR

MA7009

FIREFLY

MA7012

SKYBOLT

MA7051

		CNP	MIP	MMP
MA7001	Condor w/Brad Turner	2	4	5
MA7002	Piranha w/Sly Rax	2	5	6
MA7003	Gator w/Dusty Hayes	3	6	7
MA7004	Thunderhawk w/Matt	3	6	7
MA7005	Jackhammer w/Cliff	3	6	7
MA7006	Switchblade w/Miles	3	6	7
MA7007	Rhino vehicle w/Bruce Sato & Matt Trakker	5	8	10
MA7008	Boulder Hill w/Alex Sector & Buddy Hawks	10	20	30
MA7009	Collector w/Alex Sector	2	4	5
MA7010	Afterburner w/Dusty	8	10	12
MA7011	Vampire w/Floyd	3	6	7
MA7012	Firefly w/Julio Lopez	3	6	7
MA7013	Raven w/Calhoun	3	6	7
MA7014	Firecracker w/Hondo	3	6	7
MA7015	Stinger w/Bruno	3	6	7
MA7016	Hurricane w/Hondo	3	6	7
MA7017	Slingshot w/Ace Riker	3	6	7
MA7018	Volcano w/Matt Trakker & Jaques La Fleur	3	6	7
MA7019	Outlaw w/Miles Mayhem/Nash Gorey	3	6	7
Action Figures MA7021-25				
MA7021	Matt Trakker/Miles Mayhem	2	4	5
MA7022	Alex Sector/Buddie Hawks	2	4	5
MA7023	Matt Trakker/ Hondo Mac Lean	2	4	5
MA7024	Bruce Sato/Brad Turner	2	4	5
MA7025	Cliff Dagger/Sly Rax	2	4	5
Adventure Packs MA7031-34				
MA7031	Jungle Challenge	3	5	6
MA7032	Rescue Mission	3	5	6
MA7033	Coast Patrol	3	5	6
MA7034	Venom's Revenge	3	5	6
MA7040	T-Bob w/Scott Trakker	4	6	8
MA7051	Skybolt	5	8	10

MASK, THE (Applause) 1995, (Hasbro/Kenner) 1995-96

Applause produced limited-articulation figures of *The Mask* and Milo for gift shops. A separate line was developed in the midst of Hasbro's acquisition of Kenner. The line was designed by Hasbro staff members, but sold by Kenner. First series figure packages are labeled "Hasbro Toy," while the vehicles and subsequent figures are labeled "Kenner." Belly Bustin' Mask was rumored to be cancelled because of concern over the squirting Milo packed with it, but limited quantities were sold in a few major markets. The rarest item from the line is the large talking figure, of which only 500 were produced.

Applause		CNP	MIP	MMP
MA7201	The Mask	20	-	-
MA7203	Milo	20	-	-
Hasbro/Kenner first series				
MA7211	Quick-Draw Mask	5	7	8
MA7213	Face-Blastin' Mask	6	8	12
MA7215	Killin' Time Mask	5	7	8
MA7217	Heads-up Mask	5	7	8
MA7219	Heads-up Dorian	4	6	7
MA7221	Mask Cycle	5	10	12
MA7223	Mask Mobile	7	12	20
Hasbro/Kenner second series				
MA7231	Wild Wolf Mask	10	18	30
MA7233	Belly Bustin' Mask	8	12	18
MA7235	Tornado Mask	6	10	16
MA7237	Chompin' Milo	6	10	16
MA7240	Talking Mask	75	450	600

MA7021

MA7031

MA7032

MA7034

MA7040

MA7201   MA7203   MA7221   MA7223

MA7211   MA7213   MA7215   MA7217   MA7219

MA7231   MA7233   MA7235   MA7237   MA7240

MA7351   MA7353   MA7355   MA7357   MA7359

MASK OF THE PHANTASM — See *Batman* — *Mask of the Phantasm*

MASKED RIDER, THE (Bandai) 1995

The success of *Mighty Morphin Power Rangers* encouraged Saban Entertainment to attempt other conversions of Japanese T.V.

shows. *Masked Rider*, was introduced in fall of 1995, with considerably less success.

		CNP	MIP	MMP
MA7351	Masked Rider	3	8	10
MA7353	Masked Rider Super Gold	3	8	10
MA7355	Cyclopter	3	8	10
MA7357	Count Dregon	3	8	10
MA7359	Double Face	3	8	10
MA7361	Robosect	3	8	10
MA7363	Skull Reaper	3	8	10
MA7371	Masked Rider/ Chopper set	7	14	20

MA7361   MA7363

MA7373   MA7375

		CNP	MIP	MMP
MA7373	Masked Rider Super Gold/Super Chopper set	7	14	20
MA7375	Magno	10	18	25

MASTER WARRIORS (Lido) 1986

A *Masters of the Universe* copy-cat, molded in die-cast metal. Identical figures have appeared under other names.

		CNP	MIP	MMP
MA7501	Thunder Prince	2	5	8
MA7502	Demon Man	2	5	8
MA7503	Power Lord	2	5	8
MA7504	Evil Karzu	2	5	8
MA7505	Zodiac	2	5	8
MA7506	Lava Monster	2	5	8

MASTERS OF THE UNIVERSE (Mattel) 1981-90

Masters of the Universe is significant for two reasons. It was the first major line which incorporated action features, making the figures more than just posable toys. As a result, many future lines would strive to include some sort of action feature…even if it was nothing more than an accessory which snapped onto the figure itself. Action features, however, were not the key factor in the success of the line.

Just prior to Christmas 1983, the Federal Communications Commission lifted a number of restrictions on children's television programming. Among the regulations which were overturned was a 1969 decision which prohibited television shows based on toy products. This precedent had been established when the Tonka corporation filed suit with the FCC to prevent Mattel from producing a *Hot Wheels* television program.

Filmation Associates, a subsidiary of Westinghouse, was quick to take advantage of the deregulation. With the cooperation of Mattel, they produced sixty-five half-hour episodes of *He Man and the Masters of the Universe*. Filmation was unable to sell the

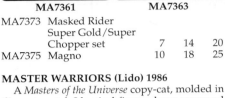

MA7501   MA7503   MA7504   MA7505

MA7502   MA7506

series to any of the major networks, so they tried a different approach. Instead of selling the show, they traded the animated sequences for a portion of the air time, allowing local stations to keep the advertising revenues.

The line ultimately ran for ten years, and inspired a spin-off for girls, called *Princess of Power*. The marketing approach was quickly copied. Product-based TV shows were created for *Transformers*, *Care Bears*, *G.I. Joe*, and many other toy lines which followed. Critics mourned the loss of educational programs, but there was no arguing with ratings.

Primary characters were often re-done with different features over the years. Figures were sold on bubble-packed cards which changed as new merchandise was released. In 1990, a new series of figures was marketed under the name He-Man (see listing at HE1001). Figures are listed here alphabetically.

		CNP	MIP	MMP
MA8303	Battle Armor He-Man	5	12	18
MA8305	Battle Armor Skeletor	5	12	18
MA8307	Beast Man	5	22	35
MA8309	Blade	5	15	22
MA8311	Blast-Attak	5	12	18
MA8313	Buzz-Off	5	12	18

MA8340

		CNP	MIP	MMP
MA8315	Buzz-Saw Hordak	5	12	18
MA8317	Clamp Champ	5	12	18
MA8319	Clawful	5	12	18
MA8325	Dragon Blaster Skeletor	5	12	18
MA8327	Dragstor	5	12	18
MA8329	Evil-Lyn	8	15	28
MA8331	Extendar	5	12	18
MA8333	Faker	5	20	40
MA8334	Faker (re-issue)	5	12	18
MA8337	Fisto	5	12	18
MA8339	Flying Fists He-Man	6	15	20
MA8340	Box: MA8339/MA8423	-	30	50
MA8341	Grizzlor	5	12	18
MA8343	Gwildor	5	12	20
MA8345	He-Man, original	5	15	25
MA8347	Hordak	5	12	18
MA8349	Horde Trooper	5	15	20

MA8303   MA8305   MA8307   MA8309   MA8311   MA8313

MA8315

MA8317

MA8319

MA8325

MA8327

MA8327

MA8329

MA8331

MA8334

MA8337

MA8341

MA8343

MA8345

MA8347

MA8349

MA8351

MA8353

MA8355

MA8357

MA8359

MA8361

MA8363

MA8365

MA8367

MA8369

MA8371

MA8373

MA8375

MA8377

MA8379

MA8381

MA8383

MA8385

MA8387

MA8389

MA8391

MA8393

MA8395

MA8397

MA8399

MA8401

MA8403

114

MA8405

MA8407

MA8409

MA8411 MA8413 MA8415 MA8419 MA8421 MA8427

MA8429 MA8423 MA8425 MA8435

MA8431 MA8437 MA8441 MA8443 MA8445 MA8571

MA8351	Hurricane Hordak	5	12	18	MA8389	Roboto	5	12	18	MA8427	Trap Jaw	8	18	25
MA8353	Jitsu	5	12	18	MA8391	Rokkon	5	12	18	MA8429	Tri-Klops	5	15	20
MA8355	King Hiss	5	12	18	MA8393	Rotar	5	12	18	MA8431	Tung Lashor	5	12	18
MA8357	King Radnor	10	18	30	MA8395	Saurod	6	15	20	MA8435	Twistoid	5	12	18
MA8359	Kobra Khan	5	12	18	MA8397	Scare Glow	10	15	25	MA8437	Two Bad	5	12	18
MA8361	Leech	5	12	18	MA8399	Skeletor, original	8	14	25	MA8441	Webstor	5	12	18
MA8363	Man-At-Arms	5	15	25	MA8401	Snake Face	5	12	18	MA8443	Whiplash	5	12	18
MA8365	Man-E-Faces	5	15	25	MA8403	Snout Spout	5	15	20	MA8445	Zodac	5	15	25
MA8367	Mantenna	5	12	18	MA8405	Sorceress	10	20	35	MA8571	Modulok	5	12	18
MA8369	Mekaneck	5	12	18	MA8407	Spikor	5	12	18	MA8572	Multi-Bot	5	12	18
MA8371	Mer-Man	10	20	35	MA8409	SSSqueeze	5	12	18	MA8573	Weapons Pak	2	4	5
MA8373	Mosquitor	8	14	20	MA8411	Stinkor	5	12	18	MA8574	Stilt Stalkers	3	8	12
MA8375	Moss Man	8	14	20	MA8413	Stonedar	5	12	18	MA8575	Point Dread Outpost			
MA8377	Ninjor	5	12	18	MA8415	Stratos (blue wings)	5	15	25		w/Talon Fighter	8	15	20
MA8379	Orko	5	15	20	MA8416	Stratos (red wings)	5	15	25	MA8576	Wind Raider	7	15	22
MA8381	Prince Adam	6	15	25	MA8419	Sy-Klone	5	12	18	MA8577	Battle Ram	7	15	22
MA8383	Ram Man	5	30	40	MA8421	Teela	15	25	35	MA8578	Attak Trak	10	20	25
MA8385	Rattlor	5	12	18	MA8423	Terror Claws Skeletor	5	15	20	MA8597	Zoar	5	12	15
MA8387	Rio Blast	5	12	18	MA8425	Thunder-Punch He-Man	5	15	20	MA8598	MA8597 w/MA8558	10	15	25

MA8572

MA8573

MA8574

MA8575

MA8576

MA8577

MA8578

MA8597

MA8599

MA8681

MA8683

MA8686

MA8688

MA8690

MA8693

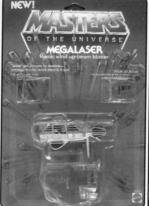

MA8694

MA8695

MA8599	Screeech			5	12	15		MA8691	Road Ripper		5	12	15
MA8600	MA8599 w/MA8547		10	15	25			MA8692	MA8691 w/MA8501		7	12	20
MA8681	Battle Cat			7	12	17		MA8693	Jet Sled		5	12	18
MA8682	MA8681 w/MA8520		14	20	25			MA8694	Megalaser		5	12	18
MA8683	Panthor			5	12	15		MA8695	Bashasaurus		5	12	18
MA8684	MA8683 w/MA8547		14	20	30			MA8696	Land Shark		5	12	18
MA8685	Dragon Walker			5	12	18		MA8697	Laser Bolt		5	12	18
MA8686	Stridor			5	12	18		MA8698	Monstroid		8	15	20
MA8687	MA8686 w/MA8516		6	15	20			MA8699	Fright Fighter				
MA8688	Night Stalker			6	13	19		MA8700	Mantisaur				
MA8689	MA8688 w/MA8524		7	16	21			MA8701	Spydor		5	10	14
MA8690	Roton			5	12	15		MA8702	Battle Bones Case		2	5	8

MA8703	Blasterhawk	8	15	20
MA8704	Beam-Blaster and Artilleray	8	15	20
Meteorbs MA8731-40				
MA8731	Cometroid	5	15	20
MA8732	Ty-Grrr	5	15	20
MA8733	Astro Lion	5	15	20
MA8734	Comet Cat	5	15	20
MA8735	Tuskor	5	15	20
MA8736	Dinosorb	5	15	20
MA8737	Crocobite	5	15	20
MA8738	Rhinorb	5	15	20

MA8696

MA8697

MA8698

MA8700

MA8699

MA8701

MA8739

MA8702

MA8703

MA8704

MA8850

MA8851

MA8855

MA8856

MA8857

117

MA8853

MA8985

MA8854

MA8739	Orbear	5	15	20
MA8740	Gore-illa	5	15	20
Playsets				
MA8850	Castle Grayskull	25	50	75
MA8851	Snake Mountain	25	50	75
MA8852	Fright Zone	25	50	85
MA8853	Slime Pit	15	25	35
MA8854	Eternia	50	150	275
GraySkull Dinosaur series				
MA8855	Bionatops	10	20	30
MA8856	Turbodaltyl	8	16	26
MA8857	Tyrantisaurus Rex	15	30	40

See also: *He-Man; Princess of Power*

MAXIMUM CARNAGE (Toy Biz) 1994

This was a one-shot tie-in with the release of the video game. The single-packed Carnage has two paint variations.

		CNP	MIP	MMP
MA9001	Carnage, black teeth	6	12	20
MA9002	Carnage, white teeth	5	10	15
MA9005	Carnage/Spider-Man	-	15	20
MA9007	Carnage/Venom	-	15	20
MA9009	Triple Threat set	-	20	30

MA9001		MA9002

MA9011	Die-cast set	4	8	12
MA9013	10" Carnage	8	17	20

See also: *Spider-Man*

MAXX FX (Matchbox) 1989

In the style of *Captain Action*, *Maxx FX* was intended to be a figure who wore costumes of horror-film monsters. The box shows unproduced outfits for Frankenstein, Dracula, and Geiger's Alien on the back.

MA9501

MA8853

MA9001

MA9005

118

MA9007

MA9009

MA9011

MA9013

MC1001

MC1002

MC1003

MC1004

MC1005

MC1006

MC1007

MC1010

	CNP	MIP	MMP
MA9501 Maxx FX/Freddy	15	25	35

McDONALDLAND CHARACTERS (Remco)
1976

Remco is largely known for producing generic figures copied after best-selling lines. One of the company's true contributions to action figure collecting was the 1976 line, *McDonaldland Characters*.

		CNP	MIP	MMP
MC1001	Ronald McDonald	15	28	45
MC1002	Big Mac	18	35	60
MC1003	Hamburglar	15	28	45
MC1004	Grimace	20	40	65
MC1005	Mayor McCheese	18	35	60
MC1006	Captain Crook	15	28	45

MC1007	Professor	15	28	45
MC1010	McDonaldland	40	75	125

MEGA MAN (Bandai) 1995-96

A series based on the Capcom video game. Bombman was pulled after the Oklahoma City bombing.

ME2001

ME2003

ME2005

ME2007

ME2009

ME2011

| | | ME2013 | ME2015 | ME2017 | ME2019 | | ME2021 |

			CNP	MIP	MMP
ME2001	Mega Man		2	5	7
ME2003	Rush		2	5	7
ME2005	Cutman		2	5	7
ME2007	Bombman		5	10	20
ME2009	Proto Man		2	5	7
ME2011	Gutsman		2	5	7
ME2013	Drillman		2	5	7
ME2015	Brightman		2	5	7
ME2017	Eleckman		2	5	7
ME2019	Snakeman		2	5	7
ME2021	Air Raider		8	14	20

ME5002   ME5021   ME5021

MEN OF MEDAL (Mattel) 1989

These were tiny action figures which fit into clip-on badges.

		CNP	MIP	MMP
ME5001	"Machine Gun" Traub	2	3	5
ME5002	Kyle "The Kid" Wise	2	3	5
ME5003	"Hair Trigger" Hamilton	2	3	5
ME5004	Jim "Bam-Bam" Briggs	2	3	5
ME5005	"The Shark" Schaar	2	3	5
ME5006	"Beachbum" Aldrete	2	3	5
ME5007	John "Flyboy" Moody	2	3	5
ME5008	"Thunderclap" West	2	3	5
ME5009	Don "The Man" Larkin	2	3	5
ME5010	"Hawkeye" Hollister	2	3	5
ME5011	"Cross-Hairs" Peterman	2	3	5
ME5012	"Cool Hand" Russo	2	3	5
ME5013	Penn "Piranha" Jones	2	3	5
ME5014	"Boom-Boom" Hailey	2	3	5
ME5021	"The Mole" Spy	3	4	6
ME5022	"Nitro" Bomber	3	4	6
ME5023	"Quick Chop" Judo Man	3	4	6
ME5024	"Snake" Sniper	3	4	6
ME5031	Armored Transport	5	10	15

MEN OF STEEL (Nylint Toys) 1989

The four Men of Steel were designed for use with Nylint trucks.

		CNP	MIP	MMP
ME6001	Fire Fighter	2	4	5
ME6002	Construction Worker	2	4	5
ME6003	Farmer	2	4	5
ME6004	Truck Driver	2	4	5

MERA, QUEEN OF ATLANTIS — See *Comic Heroines*

ME6001   ME6002   ME6003   ME6004

METAL-MAN (Zee Toys) 1978

Each die-cast *Metal-Man* came on a card with an action play accessory. Some larger sets came with more than one figure.

		CNP	MIP	MMP
ME8001	Rocket Repair Unit set	4	7	9
ME8002	Levitation Platform set	4	7	9
ME8003	Rocket Backpack set	4	7	9
ME8004	Sky Sled set	4	7	9
ME8005	Armor/Ray Gun set	4	7	9
ME8006	Stretcher/Medical Backpack and Bag	5	8	10
ME8007	Commando Raft, Paddle & Dynamite	5	8	10
ME8008	Flamethrower/Grenade Belt/Machine Gun	5	8	10
ME8009	Recharge Capsule	8	16	20
ME8010	Roadblock and Radio Backpack	8	16	20
ME8011	Searchlight & Bullhorn	10	18	25
ME8012	Jet Pack	10	18	25

MICKEY & FRIENDS (Sears Exclusive) 1988

These Sears figures were part of a store-wide Disney tie-in.

		CNP	MIP	MMP
MI1501	Mickey Mouse	4	8	12
MI1502	Minnie Mouse	4	8	12
MI1503	Donald Duck	4	8	12
MI1504	Daisy Duck	4	8	12
MI1505	Goofy	4	8	12
MI1506	Pluto	4	8	12

MICKEY & FRIENDS, EPCOT '94 ADVENTURE (McDonald's) 1994

Eight Disney characters were used as premiums in a Happy Meal promotion which ran from July 8 - August 4, 1994. Each is dressed in an international costume representing a different World Showcase pavilion at EPCOT center. Canadian restaurants received two versions of Chip, one in a Chinese costume (the same one used in the U.S.) and one dressed as a Canadian

ME8001   MI1501   MI1503   MI1506

MI1701   MI1702   MI1703   MI1704   MI1705   MI1706   MI1707   MI1708   MI1709

MI2011   MI2013   MI2014   MI2015   MI2016

MI3007   MI3010   MI3011   MI3021

Mounty. The Mickey Mouse figure was available in regular or "under 3" packaging.

	CNP	MIP	MMP
MI1701 Donald in Mexico	1	2	3
MI1702 Daisy in Germany	1	2	3
MI1703 Mickey in U.S.A.	1	2	3
MI1704 Minnie in Japan	1	2	3
MI1705 Pluto in France	1	2	3
MI1706 Chip in China	1	2	3
MI1707 Goofy in Norway	1	2	3
MI1708 Dale in Morocco	1	2	3
MI1709 Chip in Canada (Canadian exclusive)	1	3	4
MI1710 Mickey USA (under 3)	-	3	4

MICKEY MOUSE (Durham) c.1975

Durham figures featured Mickey dressed in different costumes. They were sold in boxes with full view plastic fronts.

	CNP	MIP	MMP
MI2011 Chef	10	15	20
MI2012 Cowboy	10	15	20
MI2013 Drum Major	10	15	20
MI2014 Ring Master	10	15	20
MI2015 Sailor	10	15	20
MI2016 Super Mickey	10	15	20

See also: *Disney; Disney Clubhouse Collection; Hollywood Mickey; Mickey & Friends; Mickey & Friends, EPCOT '94 Adventure; Santa Mickey; Walt Disney Characters on Safari; Walt Disney Golden Fantasy*

MICRONAUTS (Mego) 1977-79

This popular line was an American version of the Japanese *Micro Man* series by Takara. Every item in the *Micronauts* line incorporated 5 millimeter holes and matching 5 millimeter posts. The result was a fully interchangeable line of toys: everything from the smallest figure to the largest building set could be assembled in various ways by itself or in combination with other items. Items were made from die-cast metal and/or plastic, and some incorporated small spring-loaded missiles which were later banned by legislation. Figures were molded in assorted colors.

Following the demise of the Mego corporation, *Micro Man* toys continued to be imported

MI3012

MI3013

MI3015

MI3022

MI3023

MI3030

MI3020

MI3031

MI3032

MI3034   MI3033

MI3035

to the U.S. in similar packages under the title of *The Inter-Changeables*. See IN8001-IN8032 for more details.

		CNP	MIP	MMP
MI3001	Time Traveler, clear	2	5	10
MI3002	Time Traveler, opaque	5	8	15
MI3003	Space Glider, ea	4	7	10
MI3004	Galactic Warriors, ea	4	7	10
MI3005	Acroyear, ea	6	15	25
MI3006	Acroyear II, ea	7	10	15
MI3007	Pharoid w/Time Chamber, ea	5	8	10
MI3008	Galactic Defender, ea	7	10	18
MI3010	Galactic Cruiser	8	10	18

MI3045   MI3046

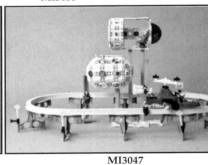

MI3047

MI3011	Hydro Copter	10	15	23
MI3012	Ultronic Scooter	5	10	15
MI3013	Crater Cruncher	5	10	15

MI3014	Photon Sled	5	10	15
MI3015	Warp Racer	5	10	15
MI3020	Biotron	8	12	20

MI3081

MI3082

MI3101

MI3041

MI3061

MI3062

MI3063

MI3071

MI3072

MI3091

MI3092

MI3110

MI3111

MI3121

MI3093

MI4001

MI4002

MI4004

MI4005

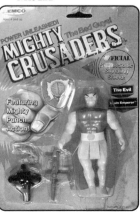

MI4006

MI3021	Microtron	5	10	18		MI3036	Rhodium Orbiter	7	12	19		MI3046	Galactic Command
MI3022	Stratastation playset	10	15	23		MI3037	Thorium Orbiter	7	12	19			Center	10	20	30
MI3023	Astro Station playset	8	10	18		MI3038	Neon Orbiter	7	12	19		MI3047	Microrail City	15	20	30
MI3030	Battle Cruiser	20	40	75		MI3039	Phobos	8	12	18		**Alien Invaders MI3061-66**				
MI3031	Force Commander	10	15	30		MI3040	Nemesis	5	8	12		MI3061	Repto	15	25	45
MI3032	Oberon	10	15	25		MI3041	Giant Acroyear	10	15	23		MI3062	Membros	15	25	45
MI3033	Baron Karza	10	15	30		**Micropolis playsets MI3045-47**						MI3063	Antron	15	25	45
MI3034	Andromeda	10	15	25		MI3045	Interplanetary					MI3064	Kronos	35	75	150
MI3035	Megas	15	20	30			Headquarters	10	20	30		MI3065	Sentaurus	35	75	150

123

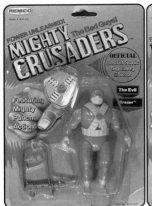

MI4007   MI4008

MI4505   MI4503

MI4507   MI4501   MI4509

MI5001   MI5002   MI5003   MI5004   MI5005

MI3066	Lobros	35	75	150
MI3071	Solarion	10	15	25
MI3072	Taurion	10	15	25
MI3073	Aquatron	8	12	20
MI3074	Hydra	8	10	18
MI3081	Hornetroid	15	20	30
MI3082	Terraphant	15	20	30
MI3091	Alphatron	5	8	11
MI3092	Betatron	5	8	11
MI3093	Gammatron	5	8	11
MI3101	Star Searcher	15	25	40
MI3110	Karrio	5	10	15
MI3111	Mobile Exploration Lab	15	20	28
MI3121	Mega City	20	30	40
MI3130	Rocket Tubes playset	20	30	40
MI3131	Deluxe Rocket Tubes	20	40	50

See also: *Inter-Changeables, The*

MIGHTY CRUSADERS (Remco) 1974

Based on the comic series of the same name. Each figure came with a shield-shaped whistle.

		CNP	MIP	MMP
MI4001	Shield	5	10	15
MI4002	Web	5	10	15
MI4003	Comet	5	10	15
MI4004	Fox	5	10	15
MI4005	Sting	5	10	15
MI4006	Brain Emperor	5	10	15
MI4007	Eraser	5	10	15
MI4008	Buzzard	5	10	15

MIGHTY DUCKS (Mattel) 1996

Battling the forces of evil to save Earth, the *Mighty Ducks* were announced at the 1996 Toy Fair for fall release. Mattel action figures were displayed, scheduled to debut in conjunction with the show.

		CNP	MIP	MMP
MI4501	Wildwing		undetermined	
MI4503	Ducques		undetermined	
MI4505	Grin		undetermined	
MI4507	Mallory		undetermined	
MI4509	Nosedive		undetermined	
MI4511	Draconis		undetermined	
MI4521	Duck Cycle		undetermined	

MIGHTY MORPHIN POWER RANGERS (Bandai) 1993-96

The *Mighty Morphin Power Rangers* had been on TV for several years in Japan before Saban Entertainment decided to try the program in the U.S. Bandai produced the toys for both countries. U.S. toy buyers considered the line was too geared for the Japanese market and purchased comparatively little product. Then kids went wild for the American cast, and *Power Rangers* became the hottest selling action figure line buyers had seen in years. Product for 1993 was starved. Supplies surpassed demand by fall 1994. The film helped demand in 1995, but availability suggested U.S. kids couldn't be content with the sleek sameness of the line. Rita Repulsa and first year space aliens were replaced by Lord Zedd and new monsters the third year, and yet another cast of villains were used in the film. However, while same old/same old is revered in Japan, it still doesn't play in Peoria. The line was always a mix of rangers in various sizes, space aliens,

and transformer-type dinosaur alter-egos which combined with higher-priced accessories to make super robots and monsters.

Tyrannosaurus, Sabertooth Tiger, Mammoth, Triceratops, and Pterodactyl Dinozords only came packaged in the Megazord gift set. These smaller transforming figures were different for the Ninja Megazord (movie edition). They were the Ape, Bear, Crane, Wolf, and Frog. The transforming Alter Ego animals for 1994 were the Firebird, Unicorn, Lion, and Griffin found packaged only as part of the Thunderzord Assault Team. Ninjazords came only in the Ninja Megazord gift set. The deluxe Shogun Megazord was comprised of Red, Blue, Pink, Yellow, and Black Ranger Shogunzords, and came only in the deluxe Shogun Megazord set.

8" Power Rangers, 1993		CNP	MIP	MMP
MI5001	Red Ranger	7	10	15
MI5002	Black Ranger	7	10	15
MI5003	Blue Ranger	7	10	15
MI5004	Pink Ranger	10	18	25
MI5005	Yellow Ranger	10	18	25
MI5010	Deluxe Megazord	25	45	60
MI5011	Tyrannosaurus Dinozord	5	-	-
MI5012	Sabertooth Tiger Dinozord	5	-	-
MI5013	Mammoth Dinozord	5	-	-
MI5014	Triceratops Dinozord	5	-	-
MI5015	Pterodactyl Dinozord	5	-	-
MI5021	Squatt	12	20	35
MI5022	Goldar	12	20	35
MI5023	Baboo	12	20	35

MI5021	MI5022	MI5023	MI5024	MI5025	MI5026

MI5027	MI5041	MI5042	MI5043	MI5051

MI5010	MI5053	MI5055	MI5061

MI5071	MI5072	MI5073	MI5074	MI5075	MI5076

MI5024	King Sphinx	12	20	35
MI5025	Bones	12	20	35
MI5026	Finster	12	20	35
MI5027	Putty Patrol	12	20	35
MI5041	T-Rex Battle Bike	10	15	20
MI5042	Mammoth Battle Bike	10	15	20
MI5043	Triceratops Battle Bike	10	15	20
MI5051	Megazord, 8"	15	25	35
MI5053	Dragonzord			
	w/Green Ranger	30	50	65
MI5054	Green Ranger, 8"	15	-	-
MI5055	Titanus	30	50	80
MI5061	Special Edition			
	Black Megazord, 1994	50	60	75

5½" Auto Morphin Power Rangers, 1994

MI5071	Green Ranger	3	7	9
MI5072	Red Ranger	2	4	6
MI5073	Black Ranger	2	4	6
MI5074	Blue Ranger	2	4	6
MI5075	Pink Ranger	2	4	6
MI5076	Yellow Ranger	2	4	6

8" Karate Action Power Rangers, 1994

MI5081	Red Ranger	3	5	7
MI5082	Black Ranger	3	5	7
MI5083	Blue Ranger	3	5	7
MI5084	Pink Ranger	3	5	7
MI5085	Yellow Ranger	3	5	7

5½" Evil Space Aliens, 1994

MI5091	Food Gobbling			
	Pudgy Pig	3	5	7
MI5092	Killer Bite			
	Slippery Shark	3	5	7
MI5093	Slash & Block Minotaur	3	5	7
MI5094	Missile Launching			
	Pete & Repeat	3	5	7
MI5095	Devouring Snizard			
	Lips	3	5	7
MI5096	Eye Popping Eye Guy	3	5	7
MI5097	Sword Slashing			
	Knasty Knight	3	5	7

CNP: Complete, no package, with all weapons and accessories; MIP: Mint in package; MMP: Mint item in Mint package. Values in U.S. dollars. See page 3 for details.

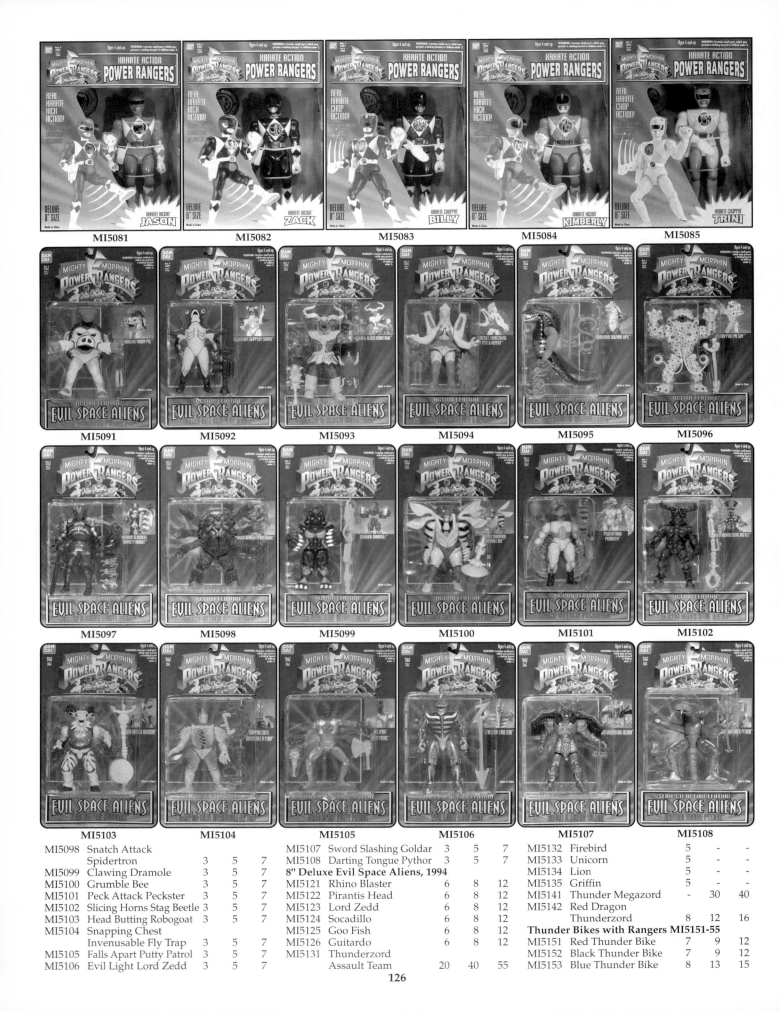

MI5081	MI5082	MI5083	MI5084	MI5085

MI5091	MI5092	MI5093	MI5094	MI5095	MI5096

MI5097	MI5098	MI5099	MI5100	MI5101	MI5102

MI5103	MI5104	MI5105	MI5106	MI5107	MI5108

MI5098	Snatch Attack Spidertron	3	5	7
MI5099	Clawing Dramole	3	5	7
MI5100	Grumble Bee	3	5	7
MI5101	Peck Attack Peckster	3	5	7
MI5102	Slicing Horns Stag Beetle	3	5	7
MI5103	Head Butting Robogoat	3	5	7
MI5104	Snapping Chest Invenusable Fly Trap	3	5	7
MI5105	Falls Apart Putty Patrol	3	5	7
MI5106	Evil Light Lord Zedd	3	5	7

MI5107	Sword Slashing Goldar	3	5	7
MI5108	Darting Tongue Pythor	3	5	7
8" Deluxe Evil Space Aliens, 1994				
MI5121	Rhino Blaster	6	8	12
MI5122	Pirantis Head	6	8	12
MI5123	Lord Zedd	6	8	12
MI5124	Socadillo	6	8	12
MI5125	Goo Fish	6	8	12
MI5126	Guitardo	6	8	12
MI5131	Thunderzord Assault Team	20	40	55

MI5132	Firebird	5	-	-
MI5133	Unicorn	5	-	-
MI5134	Lion	5	-	-
MI5135	Griffin	5	-	-
MI5141	Thunder Megazord	-	30	40
MI5142	Red Dragon Thunderzord	8	12	16
Thunder Bikes with Rangers MI5151-55				
MI5151	Red Thunder Bike	7	9	12
MI5152	Black Thunder Bike	7	9	12
MI5153	Blue Thunder Bike	8	13	15

MI5121

MI5123

MI5124

MI5125

MI5126

MI5131

MI5141

MI5181

MI5151

MI5161

MI5162

MI5171

MI5172

MI5175

MI5176

MI5142

MI5154	Pink Thunder Bike	9	14	18
MI5155	Yellow Thunder Bike	9	14	18
MI5161	White Tigerzord	25	38	50
MI5162	Tor the Shuttle Zord	18	30	40
MI5171	White Tigerzord Special Size (Target Exclusive)	20	30	40
MI5172	Tor The Shuttlezord (Target Exclusive)	20	30	40
MI5175	Red Dragon Thunderzord Special Size (Toys "Я" Us Exclusive)	15	25	35
MI5176	Mega Tigerzord (Toys "Я" Us Exclusive)	15	25	35
MI5181	Power Dome	15	40	65

Power Rangers for Girls, 1994

MI5191	Trini	6	8	14
MI5192	Kimberly	6	8	14
MI5193	Trini/Kimberly 2-pack	-	16	22

Movie Edition Products, 1995
8" Power Rangers

MI5201	White Ranger	8	12	16
MI5202	Red Ranger	6	10	14
MI5203	Black Ranger	6	10	14
MI5204	Blue Ranger	6	10	14
MI5205	Pink Ranger	6	10	14
MI5206	Yellow Ranger	6	10	14

5½" Power Rangers, 1995

MI5211	White Ranger	5	7	9
MI5212	Red Ranger	4	6	8
MI5213	Black Ranger	4	6	8
MI5214	Blue Ranger	4	6	8
MI5215	Pink Ranger	4	6	8
MI5216	Yellow Ranger	4	6	8

8" Evil Space Aliens, 1995

MI5221	Hornitor	5	8	10
MI5222	Ivan Ooze	5	8	10

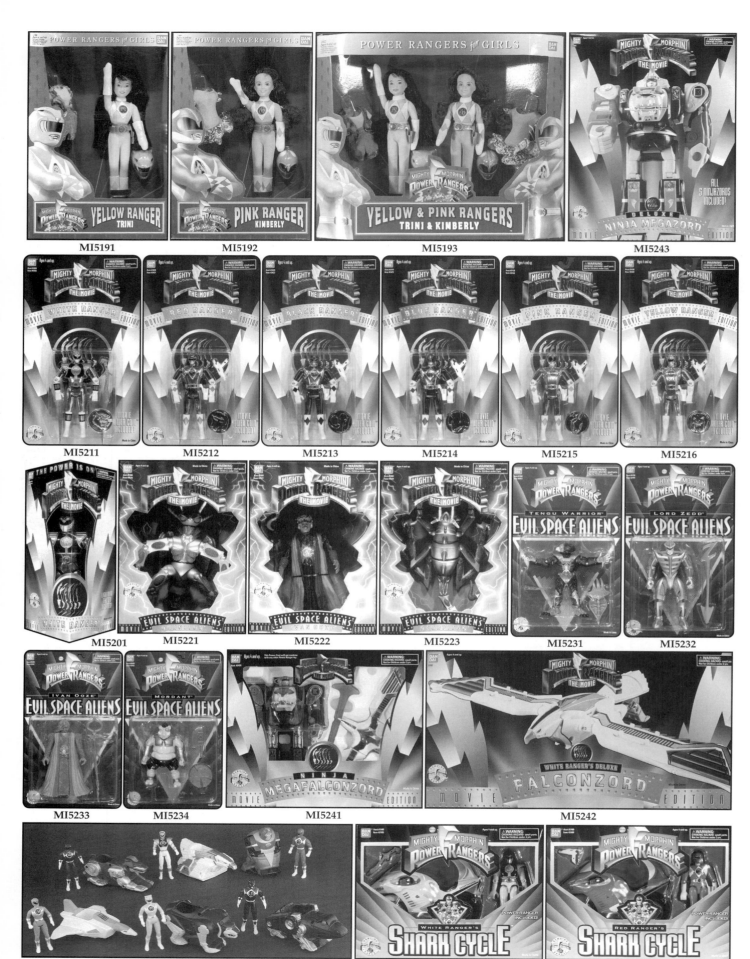

MI5191

MI5192

MI5193

MI5243

MI5211

MI5212

MI5213

MI5214

MI5215

MI5216

MI5201

MI5221

MI5222

MI5223

MI5231

MI5232

MI5233

MI5234

MI5241

MI5242

MI5251-56

MI5261

MI5262

| MI5271 | MI5272 | MI5273 | MI5281 | MI5282 | MI5283 |

| MI5287 | MI5291 | MI5292 | MI5293 | MI5294 | MI5312 |

| MI5301 | MI5302 | MI5303 | MI5304 | MI5305 | MI5306 |

| MI5316 | MI5321 | MI5322 | MI5332 | MI5333 |

MI5223	Scorpitan	5	8	10

5½" Evil Space Aliens, 1995

MI5231	Tengu Warrior	2	4	6
MI5232	Lord Zedd	2	4	6
MI5233	Ivan Ooze	2	4	6
MI5234	Mordnt	2	4	6
MI5241	Megafalconzord	15	30	40
MI5242	Falconzord	10	18	25
MI5243	Ninja Megazord	20	30	45
MI5244	Ape	4	-	-
MI5245	Bear	4	-	-
MI5246	Crane	4	-	-
MI5247	Wolf	4	-	-
MI5248	Frog	4	-	-

McDonald's Happy Meal Premiums, 1995

MI5251	Blue	2	4	6
MI5252	White	2	4	6
MI5253	Red	2	4	6
MI5254	Pink	2	4	6
MI5255	Yellow	2	4	6
MI5256	Black	2	4	6

1995 Standard *Power Rangers* Line, 1995
Shark Cycles w/Rangers

MI5261	White	4	8	12
MI5262	Red	4	8	12
MI5263	Black	4	8	12
MI5264	Blue	4	8	12
MI5265	Pink	4	8	12
MI5266	Yellow	4	8	12

5½" Ninja Rangers, 1995

MI5271	White Ninja	3	5	7
MI5272	Red Ninja	3	5	7
MI5273	Black Ninja	3	5	7
MI5274	Blue Ninja	3	5	7
MI5275	Pink Ninja	3	5	7
MI5276	Yellow Ninja	3	5	7

5½" Auto Morphin Rangers, 1995

MI5281	White Ranger	2	6	7
MI5282	Red Ranger	2	6	7
MI5283	Black Ranger	2	6	7
MI5284	Blue Ranger	2	6	7
MI5285	Pink Ranger	2	6	7
MI5286	Yellow Ranger	2	6	7

MI5323	MI5328	MI5341	MI5342

MI5353	MI5354	MI5355	MI5361	MI5363	MI5365

MI5367	MI5368	MI5369	MI5370	MI5391

MI5287	Ninjor Deluxe Auto Morphin	6	9	14
8" Evil Space Aliens, 1995				
MI5291	Merrick the Barbaric	5	8	10
MI5292	Calcifire	5	8	10
MI5293	Master Vile	5	8	10
MI5294	Silent Knight	5	8	10
5½" Evil Space Aliens, 1995				
MI5301	Flap Attack Vampirus	2	4	6
MI5302	Air-Pump Cannon Rito Revolto	2	4	6
MI5303	Spinning Head Attack Master Vile	2	4	6
MI5304	Dual-Attack Slotsky	2	4	6
MI5305	Slicing Action Erik the Barbaric	2	4	6
MI5306	Rapid-Fire Steamy Meany	2	4	6
8" Talking Power Rangers, 1995				
MI5311	White Talking Ranger	5	8	12
MI5312	Red Talking Ranger	5	8	12
MI5313	Black Talking Ranger	5	8	12
MI5314	Blue Talking Ranger	5	8	12
MI5315	Pink Talking Ranger	5	8	12
MI5316	Talking Lord Zedd	6	10	15
Deluxe Ninja Warriors, 1995				
MI5321	Deluxe Ninja Megazord	10	20	30
MI5322	Deluxe Shogun Megazord	15	30	45

MI5323	Deluxe Falconzord	10	18	28
MI5328	Serpentera	15	35	45
Power Rangers for Girls, 1995				
MI5331	Kimberly	6	8	14
MI5332	Aisha	6	8	14
MI5333	Kimberly/Aisha Set	-	16	22
MI5334	Carrying Case Playset	10	15	22
Alien Rangers, 1996				
MI5341	White	3	5	7
MI5342	Red	3	5	7
MI5343	Black	3	5	7
MI5344	Blue	3	5	7
MI5345	Yellow	3	5	7
Ninja Borgs, 1996				
MI5351	White	3	6	8
MI5352	Red	3	6	8
MI5353	Black	3	6	8
MI5354	Blue	3	6	8
MI5355	Yellow	3	6	8
Power Rangers Zeo, 1996				
MI5361	Zeo Ranger I	3	5	7
MI5362	Zeo Ranger II	3	5	7
MI5363	Zeo Ranger III	3	5	7
MI5364	Zeo Ranger IV	3	5	7
MI5365	Zeo Ranger V	3	5	7
Evil Space Aliens				
MI5367	Cogs	4	6	8
MI5368	Drill Master	4	6	8
MI5369	Mechanizer	4	6	8

MI5370	Quadra Fighter	4	6	8
Zeo Jet Cycles, 1996				
MI5371	Zeo Jet Cycle I	6	10	12
MI5372	Zeo Jet Cycle II	6	10	12
MI5373	Zeo Jet Cycle III	6	10	12
MI5374	Zeo Jet Cycle IV	6	10	12
MI5375	Zeo Jet Cycle V	6	10	12
Deluxe Zords, 1996				
MI5381	Deluxe Zeo Megazord	18	30	40
MI5383	Deluxe Red Battlezord	20	35	45
MI5385	Deluxe Pyramidas	undetermined		
MI5387	Super Zeo Megazord	undetermined		
Zeo Zords, 1996				
MI5391	Zeo Megazord	7	10	14
MI5393	Pyramidas	undetermined		
MI5395	Super Zeo Megazord	undetermined		
MI5397	Red Battlezord	undetermined		
MI5399	Warrior Wheel	undetermined		
MI5401	Auric	undetermined		
Evil Space Aliens, 1996				
MI5411	Clawing Alien	undetermined		
MI5413	Drilling Digster	undetermined		
MI5415	Missile-Firing Staroid	undetermined		
MI5417	1-2-3 Punch-A-Bunch	undetermined		
MI5419	Missile-Aiming Silo	undetermined		
8" Zeo Rangers, 1996				
MI5421	Zeo Ranger I	undetermined		
MI5422	Zeo Ranger II	undetermined		
MI5423	Zeo Ranger III	undetermined		

| MI5371 | MI5372 | MI7001 | MI7023 | MI8001 |

| MI5381 | MI5383 | MI6001 | MI6011 |

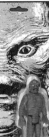

| MI9001 | MI9002 | MI9003 | MI9020 | MI9031 |

| MI9011 | MI9012 | MI9013 | MI9014 | MI9015 | MI9016 |

MI5424	Zeo Ranger IV	undetermined
MI5425	Zeo Ranger V	undetermined
MI5426	Gold Ranger	undetermined

Zord Morphin Zeo Rangers, 1996

MI5433	Zeo Ranger III	undetermined
MI5434	Zeo Ranger IV	undetermined
MI5435	Zeo Ranger V	undetermined

See also: *Projectors*

MIKE HAZARD (Marx) 1967

Marx secret agent with spy equipment.

| MI6001 | Mike Hazard | 100 | 280 | 320 |
| MI6011 | Display stand | 375 | - | - |

MILITARY ONE (Porto Play, Inc.) 1982-85

		CNP	MIP	MMP
MI7001	Army	2	4	5
MI7002	Navy	2	4	5
MI7003	Marine	2	4	5

MI7004	Pilot	2	4	5
MI7005	Terrorist	2	4	5
MI7006	Paratrooper	2	4	5
MI7007	Frogman	2	4	5
MI7008	Paratrooper w/parachute	2	4	5
MI7009	Terrorist w/parachute	2	4	5
MI7010	Beret w/parachute	2	4	5
MI7011	Frogman set	3	5	7
MI7021	Female Marine	1	2	3
MI7022	Female Navy	1	2	3
MI7023	Female Army	1	2	3
MI7024	Female Air Force	1	2	3

MINI GODAIKIN (Bandai) c. 1986

A series of poseable robot figures from Japan. The bodies were die-cast metal with plastic limbs.

		CNP	MIP	MMP
MI8001-06	Mini Godaikin Robots, ea	2	4	5

MINI MONSTERS (Remco) 1983

These were originally released as plain figures, but later had glow-in-the dark hands and faces. Each was 3¾" tall. Wolfman and Mummy are the least common.

		CNP	MIP	MMP
MI9001	Creature from the Black Lagoon	10	25	45
MI9002	Dracula	10	20	25
MI9003	Frankenstein	10	20	25
MI9004	Mummy	20	50	75
MI9005	The Phantom of the Opera	10	20	25
MI9006	Wolfman	20	40	60

Glow-in-the-Dark figures MI9010-16

MI9011	Creature from the Black Lagoon	5	15	25
MI9012	Dracula	5	15	20
MI9013	Frankenstein	5	15	20
MI9014	Mummy	15	30	45

131

| MO1001 | MO1003 | MO1005 | MO1007 | MO1009 |

| MO1011 | MO1013 | MO2001 | MO2002 | MO2003 | MO3011 |

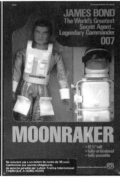

| MO3001-12 | MO3012 | MO4000 | MO4001 | MO4002 | MO4003 |

| MO5001 | MO5002 | MO5005 | MO5010 | MO6002 | MO6003 |

		CNP	MIP	MMP
MI9015	The Phantom of the Opera	5	15	20
MI9016	Wolfman	15	30	40
MI9020	Monsterizer	25	60	125
MI9031	Play Case	5	15	25

MISS LIBERTY BELL — See *Dakin*

MISTER BUMPY — See *Bump in the Night*

MONSTER FORCE (Playmates) 1994

A new twist on classic Universal monsters, inspired by the animated series. Each figure was packaged with a display stand designed to hold a cut-out from the back of the package. Frankenstein was the low-packed figure.

		CNP	MIP	MMP
MO1001	Doc Reed Crawley	4	6	8
MO1003	Lance McGruder	4	6	8
MO1005	Tripp Hansen	4	6	8
MO1007	Luke Talbot	4	6	8
MO1009	Frankenstein	8	15	20
MO1011	Dracula	4	6	8
MO1013	Creature From the Black Lagoon	5	8	10

MONSTER MAN (Woolworth) c. 1986

A series of generic glow-in-the-dark monsters.

		CNP	MIP	MMP
MO2001	Muck Man	6	10	12
MO2002	Lizard Man	6	10	12
MO2003	Rock Man	6	10	12
MO2004	Tree Man	6	10	12
MO2005	Fire Man	6	10	12
MO2006	Bird Man	6	10	12

MOON MCDARE (Gilbert) 1966

Gilbert's action space man.

		CNP	MIP	MMP
MO3001	Moon McDare figure	40	85	135
MO3011	Space Suit	10	25	55
MO3012	Space Mutt	10	25	55
MO3013	Moon Explorer Set	10	25	55
MO3014	Action Communication Set	8	18	35
MO3015	Space Gun Set	8	18	35
MO3016	Space Accessory Set	8	18	35

| MO6007 | MO6010 | MO6012 | MO6014 | MO6016 | MO6017 |

| MO6019 | MO6021 | MO6023 | MO6025 | MO6027 | MO6029 |

| MO6030 | MO6031 | MO6041 | MO6043 |

| MO6045 | MO6051 | MO6052 | MO6053 |

MOONRAKER (Mego) 1979

A series of 12" figures inspired by the James Bond film. Jaws is the hardest to find.

		CNP	MIP	MMP
MO4000	James Bond	25	45	85
MO4001	James Bond w/suit accessories	150	250	300
MO4002	Holly	50	100	150
MO4003	Jaws	175	350	600
MO4004	Drax	50	100	150

MORK AND MINDY (Mattel) 1980

The 9" Mork figure came with a talking spacepack. To emphasize the strangeness of the character, the Mork figure was shipped in the box upside-down. (A drawing of Mindy at the bottom of the box asks "Mork, why are you standing on your head?") Mindy figures are less common. The 4" Mork figure and egg were sold on blister cards.

		CNP	MIP	MMP
MO5001	Mork	10	18	25
MO5002	Mindy	15	25	35
MO5005	4-Wheel Drive	10	20	25
MO5010	4" Mork w/Egg	10	15	22

MORLOCK — See *Famous Monsters of Legend*

MORTAL KOMBAT (Hasbro) 1994

In spite of collector anticipation, *Mortal Kombat* was a disappointing line which made extensive use of repainted *G.I. Joe* molds. Reptile, Scorpion, Smoke, and Sub-Zero were the same figure painted different colors. Hasbro added pop-up cards with game tips in later shipments, but this did little to boost the line.

		CNP	MIP	MMP
MO6001	Liu Kang	2	4	5
MO6002	MO6001 w/pop-up	2	4	5
MO6003	Johnny Cage	2	4	5
MO6004	MO6003 w/pop-up	2	4	5
MO6005	Goro	2	4	5
MO6006	MO6005 w/pop-up	2	4	5
MO6007	Sonya Blade	2	4	5
MO6008	MO6007 w/pop-up	2	4	5
MO6009	Rayden	2	4	5
MO6010	MO6009 w/pop-up	2	4	5
MO6011	Scorpion	2	4	5
MO6012	MO6011 w/pop-up	2	4	5
MO6013	Smoke	2	4	5
MO6014	MO6013 w/pop-up	2	4	5
MO6015	Sub-Zero	2	4	5

CNP: Complete, no package, with all weapons and accessories; MIP: Mint in package; MMP: Mint item in Mint package. Values in U.S. dollars. See page 3 for details.

| MO7001 | MU7005 | MU7007 | MU7009 | MU7011 | MU7017 |

| MU7501 | MU7502 | MU7503 | MU7504 | MU7521 |

| MY7007 | NI1002 | NI1003 | NI1004 | NI1006 | NI5013 |

MO6016	MO6015 w/pop-up	2	4	5
MO6017	Shang Tsung	2	4	5
MO6018	MO6017 w/pop-up	2	4	5
MO6019	Goro vs. Johnny Cage			
	2-pack	4	7	9

Movie Edition Figures MO6021-31

MO6021	Liu Kang	4	8	12
MO6023	Sonya Blade	5	10	15
MO6025	Rayden	4	8	12
MO6027	Shang Tsung	4	8	12
MO6029	Scorpion	4	8	12
MO6030	Sub-Zero	4	8	12
MO6031	Goro vs. Johnny Cage			
	2-pack	5	10	15
MO6041	Kombat Cycle	6	8	12
MO6043	Dragon MK-1	8	14	18
MO6045	Dragon Wing	12	20	28

12" figures

MO6051	Johnny Cage	10	18	25
MO6052	Rayden	10	18	25
MO6053	Scorpion	10	18	25

MOTO-BOT (Intex Recreation) 1984

Moto-Bot was a series of die-cast metal and plastic vehicles which transformed into (not very convincing) robots. Each included a motorized wheel section, which could be used to power either form.

		CNP	MIP	MMP
MO7001	Dump Truck	1	3	4
MO7002	Pick-Up	1	3	4
MO7003	Locomotive	1	3	4
MO7004	4WD Vehicle	1	3	4

MO7005	F-15 Jet Fighter	1	3	4
MO7006	Military Jeep	1	3	4

MUSICAL PRINCESS (Mattel) 1994

A collection of Disney "Princess" heroines and their associated Princes. Each figure included a musical base.

		CNP	MIP	MMP
MU7001	Cinderella	5	8	12
MU7003	Prince Charming	5	8	12
MU7005	Belle	5	8	12
MU7007	The Beast	5	8	12
MU7009	Jasmine	5	8	12
MU7011	Aladdin	5	8	12
MU7013	Snow White	5	8	12
MU7017	Sleeping Beauty	5	8	12
MU7021	Gift Set	-	24	34

See also: *Bubble Princess; Perfume Princess*

MUTANT LEAGUE (Galoob) 1995

Monsters with detachable parts, sold in football and hockey configurations.

		CNP	MIP	MMP
MU7501	Bones Justice (football)	2	4	6
MU7502	Razor Kidd	2	4	6
MU7503	Spewter	2	4	6
MU7504	K.T. Slayor	2	4	6
MU7511	Bones Justice (hockey)	undetermined		
MU7512	Grim McSlam	undetermined		
MU7521	BoneSykle	3	5	8
MU7522	Mutalator	undetermined		

MUMMY, THE — See *Classic Movie Monsters; Mad Monster Series, The; Mini Monsters; Monster Force; Official World Famous Super Monsters; Real Ghostbusters, The; Universal Monsters*

MYSTERIANS (Marchon, Inc.) 1984

An early *Transformers* copy-cat, *Mysterians* were robot-like boxes which unfolded into box-like robots. Each had a Freudian "secret" compartment containing a smaller robot, an accessory, or other hunk of plastic.

		CNP	MIP	MMP
MY7001	Tank Commander	1	3	4
MY7003	Bomber	1	3	4
MY7005	Major Repair	1	3	4
MY7007	Air Commander	1	3	4
MY7009	Explorer Scout	1	3	4
MY7011	Enforcer	1	3	4

NATIONAL DEFENSE (Agglo) 1985-86

This is a spin-off line of the first series of *American Defense* figures by Agglo. Unlike the previous series, they were sold on individual packages. The figures are identical to *American Defense* if unpackaged.

		CNP	MIP	MMP
NA7001	Bazooka Marine	2	5	8
NA7002	UDT	2	5	8
NA7003	Machine Gunner	2	5	8
NA7004	Army Infantry	2	5	8
NA7005	Marine	2	5	8
NA7006	Ranger	2	5	8

NA7007	NA7020	NI6011	NO1001	

  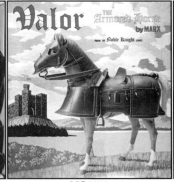 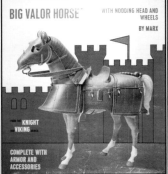 

NO1002	NO1011	NO1011 (packaging variation)	NO1015

OF2001	OF2012	OF2024	OF2050

NA7007	Pilot	2	5	8
NA7008	Special Forces	2	5	8
NA7009	Commando	2	5	8
NA7010	Green Beret	2	5	8
NA7011	Weapons Officer	3	6	10
NA7012	Assault Officer	3	6	10
NA7013	Enemy Leader	3	6	10
NA7014	U.D.T.	3	6	10
NA7015	Spy Leader	3	6	10
NA7016	Flight Leader	3	6	10
NA7019	City Attack	2	5	8
NA7020	Accessory Pack 1	2	5	8

NIGHTMARE BEFORE CHRISTMAS — See
Tim Burton's Nightmare Before Christmas

NIGHTMARE WARRIORS (MTC) 1983

Nightmare Warriors were 5½" skeletal warriors with bones that glow in the dark. They were loosely based on popular culture, historical, or legendary characters.

		CNP	MIP	MMP
NI1001	Spartacus	4	8	12
NI1002	Major Bones	4	8	12
NI1003	Geronimo	4	8	12
NI1004	Sir Lancelot	4	8	12

NI1005	Captain Kidd	4	8	12
NI1006	Pancho Villa	4	8	12

NINJA ASSASSINS/NINJA DEFENDERS (Select Merchandise) 1985

Plastic figures with cloth costumes.

Ninja Assassins NI5001-05		CNP	MIP	MMP
NI5001	Werewolf	4	6	10
NI5002	Reaper	4	6	10
NI5003	Terminator	4	6	10
NI5004	Pincer	4	6	10
NI5005	Strykor	4	6	10
Ninja Defenders NI5011-15				
NI5011	Rotund San	4	6	10
NI5012	Wipeout	4	6	10
NI5013	Mentor	4	6	10
NI5014	Ringo	4	6	10
NI5015	Tyro	4	6	10

NINJA WARRIORS (Child's Play) 1985

		CNP	MIP	MMP
NI6001	Jonin	2	4	6
NI6002	Whirl-Wind	2	4	6
NI6003	Swift-Strike	2	4	6
NI6004	Night-Wing	2	4	6

NI6005	Dragon Mark	2	4	6
NI6006	Star Caster	2	4	6
NI6007	Scorpia	2	4	6
NI6008	Castle Keep	2	4	6
NI6009	Shadow San	2	4	6
NI6011	Lord Taka	2	4	6
NI6020	Topi-Ken (Horse)	6	10	12

NOBLE KNIGHTS, THE (Marx) 1968-72

More complex than most later action figures, the *Noble Knights* each came with a fully detailed suit of 15th Century-style armor. The armor came in approximately 18 pieces which had to be "buckled" onto the figure. Three helmets were also included, along with assorted weapons, a shield, and a banner. An instruction sheet identified all of the armor pieces by name. Horses were sold separately. Multiple packaging variations exist, but do not have a significant effect on values.

		CNP	MIP	MMP
NO1001	The Silver Knight	60	100	140
NO1002	The Gold Knight	60	100	140
NO1003	The Black Knight	60	170	200
NO1011	Valour (black w/ silver armor)	80	100	125
NO1012	Victor (bay w/gold armor	80	100	125
NO1013	Valiant (grey w/ black armor)	80	100	125
NO1015	Bravo (brown with bronze armor)	80	100	125

See also: *World's Greatest Super Knights*

OFFICIAL SCOUT HIGH ADVENTURE (Kenner) 1974-75

Boy Scout figures appeared in 1974. Cub Scouts were introduced the following year, and packages for the original two figures were redesigned.

		CNP	MIP	MMP
OF2001	Steve Scout, original	8	15	20
OF2002	Bob Scout, original	12	20	25

OF2011	Steve Scout, 2nd	8	15	20
OF2012	Bob Scout, 2nd	12	20	25
OF2013	Craig Cub	8	15	20
OF2014	Dave Cub	8	15	20
OF2021	The Pathfinder	15	24	32
OF2022	Escape Glide from Eagle Mountain	10	18	24
OF2023	Porta-Power Rescue Cycle	10	16	20
OF2024	Balloon Race to Devil's Canyon	10	20	35
OF2031	Warning from Thunderhead Weather Station	10	18	24
OF2032	Lost in the High Country	10	18	24
OF2033	Danger at Snake River	10	18	24
OF2034	Search for the Spanish Galleon	10	18	24
OF2035	Avalanche on Blizzard Ridge	10	18	24

High Adventure Gear OF2041-44

OF2041	Metal Detector	5	10	18
OF2042	Fire Fighter	5	10	18
OF2043	Mountain Medic	5	10	18
OF2044	Signal Launcher	5	10	18
OF2050	Scout Base	10	20	30

OFFICIAL WORLD FAMOUS SUPER MONSTERS (AHI/Remco) 1973-76

These figures were based on the classic Aurora model kits. The back of each Kresge-style card displays artwork based on the 1972 Aurora Glow-Kit boxes. AHI made a number of running changes, resulting in 2-5 significantly different variations for each character. The most sought-after is the wide-waist Creature from the Black Lagoon.

		CNP	MIP	MMP
Creature from the Black Lagoon				
OF2511	Thin waist, "female" rubber limbs	100	200	400
OF2512	Wide waist, "male" plastic limbs	150	300	600
Mummy				
OF2515	Right arm across chest	45	125	175
OF2516	Yellow body	35	100	150
OF2517	Tan body	30	100	150
Wolfman				
OF2521	Fierce face, hairy chest, hands, and feet	45	125	175
OF2522	Placid face, br. body	38	100	150
OF2523	Tan body	35	100	150
Dracula				
OF2525	Wrinkled Face	42	100	150
OF2526	Aurora face, red body	45	125	175
OF2527	Aurora-style face, jointed wrists	50	125	175
OF2528	Aurora face, tan body	35	125	175
OF2529	OF2528, European box	35	150	200
Frankenstein				
OF2535	Karloff head	50	125	175
OF2536	Fat head, green body	35	100	150
OF2537	Ears sticking out, jointed wrists	38	115	145
OF2538	Crude, stern face	35	100	150
OF2539	Fat head, tan body	32	90	145

OFFICIAL WORLD'S GREATEST SUPER HEROES (Mego) 1972-78

These cloth-costumed 8" figures were produced from 1972 to 1982, and were sold until Mego ceased action figure sales in 1983. The last new figures or accessories were introduced in 1978. A total of 37 different super heroes, alter-ego identities and villains were included in the line. A total of 33 characters were available boxed. All but the alter-ego costumes were available carded. There are numerous box, card, and figure variations, plus hundreds of costume differences.

The first four figures were Batman, Robin, Superman, and Aquaman. These were introduced early in 1972 in solid boxes (the picture on the back of the window box also appeared on the front of solid boxes). The Batman with removable cowl came in both solid and early window boxes. Robin with removable mask has been found only in a solid box. Both versions also appear on Kresge-style cards. Tarzan (then appearing in DC Comics) and Captain America are advertised on solid boxes, but only window box versions have been found.

The other key to recognizing the earliest boxes is the appearance of Captain America as the middle figure in the upper row of the box logo. He was replaced by Shazam on boxes for the first six DC characters in late 1972. The two Marvel figures were packaged in boxes with pictures of Spider-Man and Captain America. Figures introduced in 1973 and later have no character drawings on the front of the box, just the logo and wording. The logo was changed in 1974. Copyright dates can cause confusion, because the date on the box is not necessarily the year it was sold.

Contrary to popular belief, carded figures did not replace the boxed versions. From the first year, the S.S. Kresge Company (the forerunner of K mart) demanded peg-board packaging. These "Kresge Cards" are of special interest to the definitive Mego collector. They are worth 20% to 50% more than regular carded figures, depending on condition and character demand. Only Kresge-style cards were available in 1972, 1973, and early 1974, but a version without the Kresge name was used by Grants, Two Guys, and other retailers. Regular-style cards were introduced in 1974. Only the *Teen Titans* were not available boxed...though boxed Isis figures are extremely rare.

In the '70s, Superman, Batman, Spider-Man, Captain America and The Incredible Hulk were available in a 12½" size, both as stand-alone toys and with "fly-away action" (a piece of string and a skyhook to mount on furniture so the figure could be elevated from a remote location). A more muscular 12½" Spider-Man came carded with a web of netting. A 9½" Robin and a Web-Shooting Spider-Man were also produced. These items are listed elsewhere in the appropriate sections. The rarest figure outfits are the four "alter-ego" figures offered exclusively by Montgomery Ward in their 1974 Christmas catalog. These outfits came in individual plain corrugated cardboard boxes. You didn't even get complete figures...just the clothes, shoes, and a replacement head. The heads for Bruce Wayne and Dick Grayson were identical to those of Batman with removable cowl and Robin with removable mask. The Superman head only required glasses to become Clark Kent. The Peter Parker head was made from the Shazam mold with a few paint modifications. The eyes were changed to blue, the hair to brown, and the hair paint mask was altered to modify the hairline. Even this was not enough to disguise Spider-Man, however, since the actual figure had red hands. None of the Ward "alter-ego" heads had DC or Marvel identification incised on the back.

The *Teen Titans* are very rare, but were available through most toy retailers in 1976. Aquaman vs. the Great White Shark was the lone "adventure" packaging of figure and adversary. This was offered in 1978 for $12.98. It is the rarest Mego package to find. There were also four special "Fist Fighting" figures. A switch caused the figure's arms to "punch" up and down.

Mego made vehicles for prominent characters, three playsets, a Supervator doorknob elevator, and a carrying case. Smaller vehicles were sold both carded and boxed. Vehicles and playsets for use with Mego figures were also made by third parties. Leading pieces produced by outside companies included the Spider-Man and Batman Vans and Helicopters by Empire (scaled for assorted figure sizes), and a Hulk Hideaway Playset by Tara.

See color photos on pages 145-151.

1972-76, boxed figures		CNP	MIP	MMP
OF4000	Superman (solid box)	40	250	400
OF4001	Superman (window box)	40	125	150
OF4002	Batman (removable cowl, solid box)	125	450	600
OF4003	Batman (removable cowl, window box)	125	350	450
OF4004	Batman (painted mask)	55	125	200
OF4005	Robin (removable mask, solid box)	600	1000	1400
OF4006	Robin (painted mask, window box)	45	115	165
OF4007	Aquaman (solid box)	45	350	500
OF4008	Aquaman (window box)	45	125	180
OF4009	Captain America	75	145	195
OF4011	Spider-Man	12	75	125
OF4018	Tarzan	45	125	175
OF4020	Shazam	60	125	220
OF4031	Green Arrow	100	200	320
OF4032	Mr. Mxyzptlk (open mouth)	25	50	75
OF4033	Mr. Mxyzptlk (smirking mouth)	50	100	150
OF4034	Riddler	75	225	300
OF4035	Penguin	40	75	125
OF4036	Joker	55	175	225
OF4037	Supergirl	150	275	450
OF4038	Batgirl	100	275	450
OF4039	Wonder Woman	85	175	350
OF4040	Catwoman	95	150	225
OF4071	Green Goblin	100	175	295
OF4072	The Hulk	20	75	125
OF4073	The Falcon	85	125	185
OF4074	The Lizard	85	150	250
OF4075	Iron Man	85	125	200
OF4101	Fist Fighting Batman	75	250	475
OF4102	Fist Fighting Robin	75	250	475
OF4103	Fist Fighting Joker	75	300	500
OF4104	Fist Fighting Riddler	100	350	525
OF4111	Mr. Fantastic	45	95	175
OF4112	Invisible Girl	45	95	175
OF4113	Human Torch	25	50	95
OF4114	The Thing	45	95	175
OF4115	Thor	150	250	400
OF4116	Conan	100	250	400
OF4139	Isis	65	250	400
1972-73, Kresge carded figures				
OF4200	Superman	40	250	350
OF4202	Batman (removable cowl)	150	500	800
OF4204	Batman (painted mask)	55	250	350
OF4205	Robin (removable mask)	750	1200	1700
OF4206	Robin (painted mask)	50	250	350
OF4207	Aquaman	45	300	450
OF4209	Captain America	75	300	450
OF4211	Spider-Man	12	275	375
OF4218	Tarzan	45	250	350
OF4220	Shazam	60	300	450
OF4231	Green Arrow	100	400	750
OF4232	Mr. Mxyzptlk (open mouth)	25	175	300
OF4233	Mr. Mxyzptlk (smirking mouth)	50	300	450

OF2511

OF2512

OF2515

OF2516

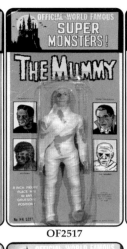

OF2517

OF2521

OF2522

OF2523

OF2525

OF2526

OF2528

OF2529

OF2535

OF2536

OF2537

OF2538

OF2539

OF2521   OF2522

OF2525   OF2528

OF4234	Riddler	75	350	500
OF4235	Penguin	40	250	350
OF4236	Joker	55	250	350
OF4237	Supergirl	150	350	500
OF4238	Batgirl	100	350	500
OF4239	Wonder Woman	85	350	500
OF4240	Catwoman	95	350	450

Ward's Exclusive Costumes (Christmas, 1974)

OF4301	Clark Kent	600	800	1500
OF4302	Peter Parker	600	800	1500
OF4303	Bruce Wayne	600	800	1500
OF4304	Dick Grayson	600	800	1500

1974-83, Regular carded figures

OF4400	Superman	40	85	125
OF4404	Batman (painted mask)	55	95	150
OF4406	Robin (painted mask)	50	75	125
OF4407	Aquaman	45	350	500
OF4409	Captain America	75	95	175

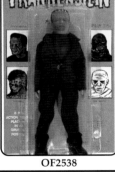

OF4005   OF4006   OF4002   OF4004

OF4000   OF4001   OF4002   OF4003   OF4004   OF4005

OF4006   OF4007   OF4008   OF4009   OF4011   OF4018

OF4020   OF4031   OF4032   OF4033   OF4033   OF4034

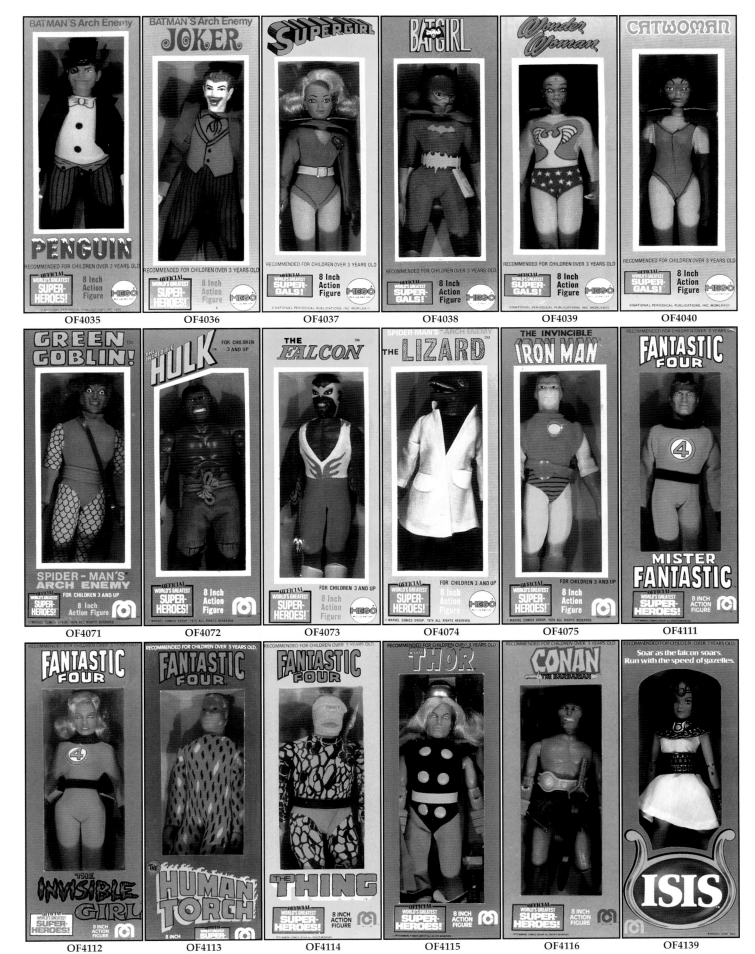

BATMAN'S Arch Enemy
PENGUIN
OFFICIAL WORLD'S GREATEST SUPER-HEROES!
8 Inch Action Figure
MEGO
RECOMMENDED FOR CHILDREN OVER 3 YEARS OLD
OF4035

BATMAN'S Arch Enemy
JOKER
OFFICIAL WORLD'S GREATEST SUPER-HEROES!
8 Inch Action Figure
MEGO
RECOMMENDED FOR CHILDREN OVER 3 YEARS OLD
OF4036

SUPERGIRL
OFFICIAL WORLD'S GREATEST SUPER-GALS!
8 Inch Action Figure
MEGO
RECOMMENDED FOR CHILDREN OVER 3 YEARS OLD
OF4037

BATGIRL
OFFICIAL WORLD'S GREATEST SUPER-GALS!
8 Inch Action Figure
MEGO
RECOMMENDED FOR CHILDREN OVER 3 YEARS OLD
OF4038

Wonder Woman
OFFICIAL WORLD'S GREATEST SUPER-GALS!
8 Inch Action Figure
MEGO
RECOMMENDED FOR CHILDREN OVER 3 YEARS OLD
OF4039

CATWOMAN
OFFICIAL WORLD'S GREATEST SUPER-GALS!
8 Inch Action Figure
MEGO
RECOMMENDED FOR CHILDREN OVER 3 YEARS OLD
OF4040

GREEN GOBLIN!
SPIDER-MAN'S ARCH ENEMY
OFFICIAL WORLD'S GREATEST SUPER-HEROES!
FOR CHILDREN 3 AND UP
8 Inch Action Figure
OF4071

THE INCREDIBLE **HULK**
FOR CHILDREN 3 AND UP
OFFICIAL WORLD'S GREATEST SUPER-HEROES!
8 Inch Action Figure
MEGO
OF4072

THE **FALCON**
OFFICIAL WORLD'S GREATEST SUPER-HEROES!
FOR CHILDREN 3 AND UP
8 Inch Action Figure
MEGO
OF4073

SPIDER-MAN'S ARCH ENEMY
THE **LIZARD**
OFFICIAL WORLD'S GREATEST SUPER-HEROES!
FOR CHILDREN 3 AND UP
8 Inch Action Figure
MEGO
OF4074

THE INVINCIBLE IRON MAN
IRON MAN
OFFICIAL WORLD'S GREATEST SUPER-HEROES!
FOR CHILDREN 3 AND UP
8 Inch Action Figure
OF4075

FANTASTIC FOUR
MISTER FANTASTIC
OFFICIAL WORLD'S GREATEST SUPER-HEROES!
8 INCH ACTION FIGURE
OF4111

FANTASTIC FOUR
THE **INVISIBLE GIRL**
OFFICIAL WORLD'S GREATEST SUPER-HEROES!
8 INCH ACTION FIGURE
RECOMMENDED FOR CHILDREN OVER 3 YEARS OLD
OF4112

FANTASTIC FOUR
THE **HUMAN TORCH**
OFFICIAL WORLD'S GREATEST SUPER-HEROES!
8 INCH
RECOMMENDED FOR CHILDREN OVER 3 YEARS OLD
OF4113

FANTASTIC FOUR
THE **THING**
OFFICIAL WORLD'S GREATEST SUPER-HEROES!
8 INCH ACTION FIGURE
RECOMMENDED FOR CHILDREN OVER 3 YEARS OLD
OF4114

THOR
OFFICIAL WORLD'S GREATEST SUPER-HEROES!
8 INCH ACTION FIGURE
RECOMMENDED FOR CHILDREN OVER 3 YEARS OLD
OF4115

CONAN THE BARBARIAN
OFFICIAL WORLD'S GREATEST SUPER-HEROES!
8 INCH ACTION FIGURE
RECOMMENDED FOR CHILDREN OVER 3 YEARS OLD
OF4116

Soar as the falcon soars. Run with the speed of gazelles.
ISIS
RECOMMENDED FOR CHILDREN OVER 3 YEARS OLD
OF4139

OF4101

OF4102

OF4103

OF4104

OF4209

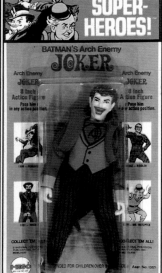

OF4236

OF4238

OF4400

OF4301   OF4302   OF4303   OF4304

OF4404

OF4406

OF4411

OF4436

OF4437

OF4438

OF4472

OF4481

OF4482

OF4483

OF4484

OF4487

OF4600

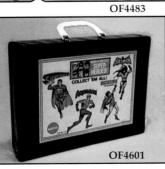
OF4601

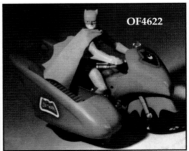
OF4622

OF4621

OF4501

OF4502

OF4503

OF4504

OF4540

OF4611

OF4617

OF4630

OF4640

OF4650

OF4655

OF4660

OF4663

OF4667

OF4705

OF4670

OF4703

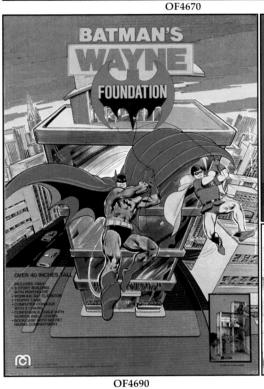

OF4690

ON0501   ON0503   ON0505   ON0507

ON1012

ON1013

ON1001

ON1002   ON1003   ON1004

OU7001   OU7002   OU7003   OU7004   OU7005   OU7006

OU7010

OU7011

OU8001

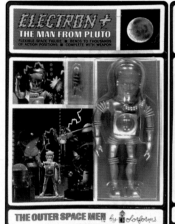

OU8002

OU8003

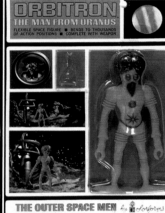

OU8004

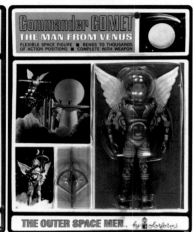

OU8005

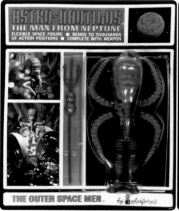

OU8006

OU8007

OU8011

OU8012

OU8013

OU8014

OU8015

OU8016

OL4001					OL4003		OL4005		OL4007			

OF4411	Spider-Man	12	20	60
OF4420	Shazam	60	125	210
OF4431	Green Arrow	100	300	400
OF4432	Mr. Mxyzptlk			
	(open mouth)	25	85	150
OF4434	Riddler	75	225	400
OF4435	Penguin	40	75	160
OF4436	Joker	55	150	220
OF4437	Supergirl	150	300	460
OF4438	Batgirl	100	150	260
OF4440	Catwoman	95	250	450
OF4471	Green Goblin	100	250	400
OF4472	The Hulk	20	35	50
OF4473	The Falcon	85	150	300
OF4474	The Lizard	95	195	420
OF4475	Iron Man	85	300	500
OF4481	Mr. Fantastic (US card)	45	60	150
OF4482	Invisible Girl (US card)	45	85	175
OF4483	Human Torch (US card)	25	35	150
OF4484	The Thing (US card)	45	75	150
OF4485	Thor	150	250	450
OF4486	Conan	100	225	400
OF4487	Isis	65	95	160
OF4501	Kid Flash	150	300	475
OF4502	Aqualad	150	300	500
OF4503	Wonder Girl	175	300	450
OF4504	Speedy	250	425	650

1978-79

OF4540	Aquaman vs. Great			
	White Shark	200	350	650

Accessories and playsets

OF4600	Retailer Display Box			
	(1973)	-	300	550
OF4601	Super Hero Carry			
	Case (1973)	45	-	-
OF4611	Batmobile, boxed			
	(1974)	45	95	155
OF4612	Batmobile, carded			
	(1974)	45	125	225
OF4616	Batcopter, boxed (1974)	45	85	165
OF4617	Batcopter, carded (1974)	45	85	150
OF4621	Batcycle, black (1974)	85	150	250
OF4622	Batcycle, blue (1974-78)	50	130	175
OF4630	Batcave playset (1974)	85	175	350
OF4640	Supervator (1974)	50	80	150
OF4650	Mobile Bat Lab (1975)	95	225	425
OF4655	Jokermobile (1975)	95	225	425
OF4660	Spider-Car (1976)	45	85	135
OF4663	Captain Americar			
	(1976)	75	125	275
OF4667	Green Arrowcar (1976)	100	250	400
OF4670	Hall of Justice (1976)	75	200	375
OF4690	Batman's Wayne			
	Foundation			
	Penthouse (1977)	300	625	1200

Empire accessories and playsets OF4701-04

OF4701	Spider-Man Van	25	60	80
OF4702	Batman Van	25	60	80
OF4703	Spider-Man Helicopter	35	80	100
OF4704	Batman Helicopter	35	80	100
OF4705	Hulk Hideaway (Tara,			
	Sears Exclusive)	35	60	70

See also: *Amazing Spider-Man, The; Batman; Captain America; Incredible Hulk, The; Superman; Wonder Woman*

OLIVER & COMPANY (Sears Exclusive) 1988

Flocked PVC figures for *Oliver and Co.* were part of a failed Disney tie-in. Most figures were sold on closed-out.

		CNP	MIP	MMP
OL4001	Oliver	2	6	8
OL4003	Dodger	2	6	8
OL4005	Tito	2	6	8
OL4007	Francis	2	6	8
OL4009	Georgette	2	6	8
OL4011	Einstein	2	6	8
OL4013	Rita	2	6	8

See also: *Mickey & Friends*

101 DALMATIONS (McDonald's) 1991

Four action figures inspired by the re-release of the Disney film were given away as Happy Meal premiums.

See color photo on page 151.

		CNP	MIP	MMP
ON0501	Pongo	1	2	3
ON0503	Cruella De Vil	1	2	3
ON0505	The Colonel and			
	Sergeant Tibs	1	2	3
ON0507	Lucky	1	2	3

ONE MILLION B.C. (Mego) 1976

Each figure from *One Million B.C.* except Mada had a throwing-arm feature, and came with a foam rubber club. A small magnet inside the club would stick to metal or magnetic spots on the dinosaur figures. Spinning a knob on the dinosaurs made a "roaring" sound.

See color photos on page 151.

		CNP	MIP	MMP
ON1001	Trag	15	35	50
ON1002	Mada	15	40	65
ON1003	Zon	15	40	65
ON1004	Orm	15	35	50
ON1005	Grok	15	38	50
ON1011	Tyrannosaur	100	150	350
ON1012	Dimetrodon	90	140	325
ON1013	Hairy Rhino	90	140	325
ON1020	Tribal Lair playset	75	125	250
ON1021	Tribal Lair Gift Set			
	w/ON1001-05	-	175	300

OUR GANG (Mego) 1975

Another popular television series interpreted by Mego.

		CNP	MIP	MMP
OU7001	Buckwheat	35	45	65
OU7002	Spanky	35	45	65
OU7003	Porky	35	45	65
OU7004	Mickey	35	50	75
OU7005	Alfalfa	35	45	65
OU7006	Darla	40	55	85

OU7010	Paddle Boat	25	40	60
OU7011	Car	25	40	60
OU7021	Clubhouse	50	100	175

OUTER SPACE MEN, THE (Colorforms) 1968-70

One of the few 3-dimensional toys produced by Colorforms, the *Outer Space Men* were soft plastic "flexie" figures with accordion joints similar to *Major MATT MASON.*

A second series of six figures was planned, titled *The World of the Future.* Mockups of five sets of carded figures were made to be shown at the 1969 Toy Fair. Unfortunately, a New York dock strike tied up the figures in transit, and they were never shown. By the time the next Toy Fair came around, men had actually walked on the Moon, and interest in space travel had declined. Prototypes of one of two sets known to survive are shown here. Special thanks to Mel Birnkrant for photographing his set of the second series.

Outer Space Men		CNP	MIP	MMP
OU8001	Alpha 7	125	350	500
OU8002	Electron +	150	375	500
OU8003	Xodiac	150	375	500
OU8004	Orbitron	150	375	500
OU8005	Commander Comet	175	400	525
OU8006	Astro-Nautilus	200	425	550
OU8007	Colossus Rex	150	375	500

World of the Future				
OU8011	Cyclops		not produced	
OU8012	Gamma-X		not produced	
OU8013	Gemini		not produced	
OU8014	Inferno		not produced	
OU8015	Metamorpho		not produced	
OU8016	Mystron		not produced	

OVER THE TOP (LewCo) 1986

Arm wrestling was the major theme of these figures. By turning a knob on the back of a figure, a kid could control a specially-jointed right forearm for wrestling with other figures. A figure-sized wrestling table was also sold.

		CNP	MIP	MMP
OV1001	Lincoln Hawks	4	10	16
OV1002	John "Golden Boy"			
	Brzenk	5	12	16
OV1003	Cleve "Armbender"			
	Dean	5	12	16
OV1004	John Grizzly	5	12	16
OV1005	Johnny "Ice Man"			
	Walker	5	12	18
OV1006	Bob "Bull" Hurley	5	12	18
OV1011	Wrestling table	5	10	12
OV1021	Lincoln Hawks, 20"	15	20	40

PEE-WEE'S PLAYHOUSE (Matchbox) 1988

The first-run *Pee-Wee* figures were sold on cards with blue graphics which were later

CNP: Complete, no package, with all weapons and accessories; MIP: Mint in package; MMP: Mint item in Mint package. Values in U.S. dollars. See page 3 for details.

145

OV1001	OV1011	OV1021	PE1000	PE1001
PE1002	PE1003	PE1004	PE1005	PE1006	PE1007

PE1070

PE6011

changed to pink. The figure of Pee-Wee Herman was sold by itself and on a special card which included his helmet and scooter. The Reba and Ricardo figures are less common, and did not appear on the package backs.

		CNP	MIP	MMP
PE1000	Pee-Wee Herman	5	10	15
PE1001	Pee-Wee w/helmet and scooter	8	15	24
PE1002	Chairry	5	8	15
PE1003	Miss Yvonne	8	14	22
PE1004	Cowboy Curtis	8	14	22
PE1005	King of Cartoons	5	10	12
PE1006	Reba	5	12	18
PE1007	Ricardo	5	8	15
PE1070	Pee-Wee's Playhouse	15	30	40

PERFUME PRINCESS (Mattel) 1995-96

A collection of Disney princess characters, following the success of *Musical Princess*. Each doll was hollow to store perfume, and came with an applicator. The refill bottle could be stored in a "secret" compartment inside the enclosed doll stand.

		CNP	MIP	MMP
PE6001	Belle	4	8	12
PE6003	Cinderella	4	8	12
PE6005	Jasmine	4	8	12
PE6007	Sleeping Beauty	4	8	12

PE6009	Snow White	4	8	12
PE6011	Box set w/PE6001-09	-	25	40

See also: *Bubble Princess; Musical Princess*

PETER PAN (Sears Exclusive) 1988-89

These figures were produced in conjunction with the 1988 re-release of Peter Pan. Sears does not permit identification of the manufacturer on exclusive merchandise, so the origin of the figures is unknown.

		CNP	MIP	MMP
PE8001	Peter Pan	7	18	25
PE8002	Wendy	7	18	25
PE8003	Tinkerbell	7	18	25
PE8004	Captain Hook	7	18	25

See also: *Fox's Peter Pan and the Pirates; Hook; Walt Disney Golden Fantasy*

PETER PAN AND THE PIRATES — See *Fox's Peter Pan and the Pirates*

PHANTOM OF THE OPERA, THE — See *Lincoln International Monsters; Mini Monsters; Universal Monsters*

PHOTON (LJN) 1986

A boxed set of two figures, each of which could fire light beams to hit targets.

		CNP	MIP	MMP
PH6000	Bhodi Li vs. Warriarr	12	25	45

PINK PANTHER — See *Dakin*

PIRATES OF DARK WATER, THE (Hasbro) 1991

Based on the Hanna-Barbera TV series.

		CNP	MIP	MMP
PI4501	Ren	3	5	8
PI4502	Ioz	3	5	8
PI4503	Niddler	3	5	8
PI4504	Zoolie	3	5	8
PI4505	Bloth	3	5	8
PI4506	Joat	3	5	8
PI4507	Mantus	3	5	8
PI4508	Konk	3	5	8
PI4520	Wraith ship	8	15	25

PIRATES OF THE CARRIBEAN (Mattel) 1993

A pirate captain figure from the Disney attraction was produced as part of an ongoing series of 12" Disney characters.

PI4700	Captain	6	10	16

PIRATES OF THE EVIL SEAS (Remco) 1991

Two different three-packs of generic pirates.

PI4951	Three-packs, each	3	6	9

PIRATES OF THE GALAXSEAS (Remco) 1984

Another generic pirate series. Two playsets were listed in the manufacturer's catalog, but no production evidence could be found.

PE8001	PE8002	PE8003	PE8004	PH6000	PI4700

PI4501	PI4502	PI4503	PI4504	PI4505

PI4506	PI4507	PI4508	PI4520

PI4951	PI5004	PI6001

PIRATES OF THE HIGH SEAS (Imperial) 1991

Six public domain pirates of legend were thrown together for this series, each with one or two accessories which were duplicated among the figures. It was probably no accident that the line was released around the same time as *The Pirates of Dark Water*, *Fox's Peter Pan and the Pirates*, and *Hook*.

		CNP	MIP	MMP
PI6001	Captain Kidd	1	2	3
PI6002	Bad Bart	1	2	3
PI6003	Blackbeard	1	2	3
PI6004	One Eyed John	1	2	3
PI6005	Long John Silver	1	2	3
PI6006	Captain Hook	1	2	3

PLANET OF THE APES (Mego) 1973-75

Planet of the Apes figures were 8" tall, packaged on bubble cards or in window boxes. The first five appeared in 1973, the rest were produced in 1975. Apes figures were all produced in the '70s, even though most items carry a 1967 copyright date.

The Action Stallion is similar to the remote-controlled horse from the *American West Series*, molded in a different color plastic. The tree-

PI5001	Tattoo	2	6	8
PI5002	Patch	2	6	8
PI5003	Pegleg	2	6	8

PI5004	Cutlass	2	6	8
PI5005	Ribs	2	6	8
PI5006	Crossbones	2	6	8

CNP: Complete, no package, with all weapons and accessories; MIP: Mint in package; MMP: Mint item in Mint package. Values in U.S. dollars. See page 3 for details.

| PL6040 | PL6041 | PL6042 | PL6044 | PL6045 |

| PL6046 | PL6047 | PL6048 | PL6049 | PL6050 |

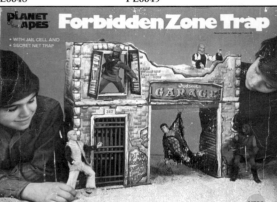

PL6201

| PL6056 | PL6060 | PL6203 |

| PL6205 | PL6207 | PL6209 | PL6211 | PL6213 | PL6215 |

house playset is similar to other toys made by Mego, including *Dinah-Mite's* Beach House and *Action Jackson's* Jungle House. The Village Playset is similar to the Mego Batcave and *Action Jackson* Lost Continent playsets.

Boxed figures PL5990-99		CNP	MIP	MMP
PL5990	Cornelius	30	110	150
PL5991	Dr. Zaius	30	150	175
PL5992	Zira	30	150	175
PL5993	Soldier Ape	45	110	150
PL5994	Astronaut	50	110	150
PL5995	Galen	40	110	150
PL5996	General Ursus	50	110	150
PL5997	General Urko	50	110	150
PL5998	Astronaut Burke	40	110	150
PL5999	Astronaut Verdon	40	110	150
Carded figures PL6040-49				
PL6040	Cornelius	30	55	75
PL6041	Dr. Zaius	30	55	75
PL6042	Zira	30	55	75

PL6043	Soldier Ape	45	75	125
PL6044	Astronaut	50	75	125
PL6045	Galen	40	95	125
PL6046	General Ursus	50	100	130
PL6047	General Urko	50	100	130
PL6048	Astronaut Burke	40	60	85
PL6049	Astronaut Verdon	40	60	85
PL6050	Action Stallion	40	75	125
PL6053	Catapult and wagon	15	25	45
PL6054	Fortress	45	75	150
PL6055	Treehouse	50	75	125
PL6056	Village playset	45	75	150
PL6057	Battering Ram	10	25	30
PL6058	Jail	10	25	30
PL6059	Dr. Zaius' Throne	10	25	30
PL6060	Forbidden Zone Trap	25	45	75

PLAY ASTERIX (Goscinny & Uderzo) 1980

This series was based on the *Asterix* comics and cartoons. Produced in England, it was sold in the U.S. through comic book shops, but not

in traditional toy stores. Many sets were combinations of figures and accessories found elsewhere in the line.

		CNP	MIP	MMP
PL6201	Asterix	5	15	20
PL6203	Obelix	5	15	20
PL6205	Getafix	6	20	25
PL6207	Vitalstatistix	6	20	25
PL6209	Impedimenta	6	20	25
PL6211	Cacophonix	8	19	26
PL6213	Geriatrix	8	19	26
PL6215	Panacea	6	20	25
PL6217	Unhygienix	15	30	35
PL6219	Bacteria	15	30	35
PL6221	Fullyautomatix	8	18	26
PL6223	Voluptua	6	20	25
PL6225	Operatix & Acoustix	20	30	35
PL6227	Farmer w/wagon	6	20	25
PL6229	Farmer w/woodcrib	6	20	25
PL6231	Carrier w/platter	6	20	25
PL6233	Carrier w/cooked boar	6	20	25

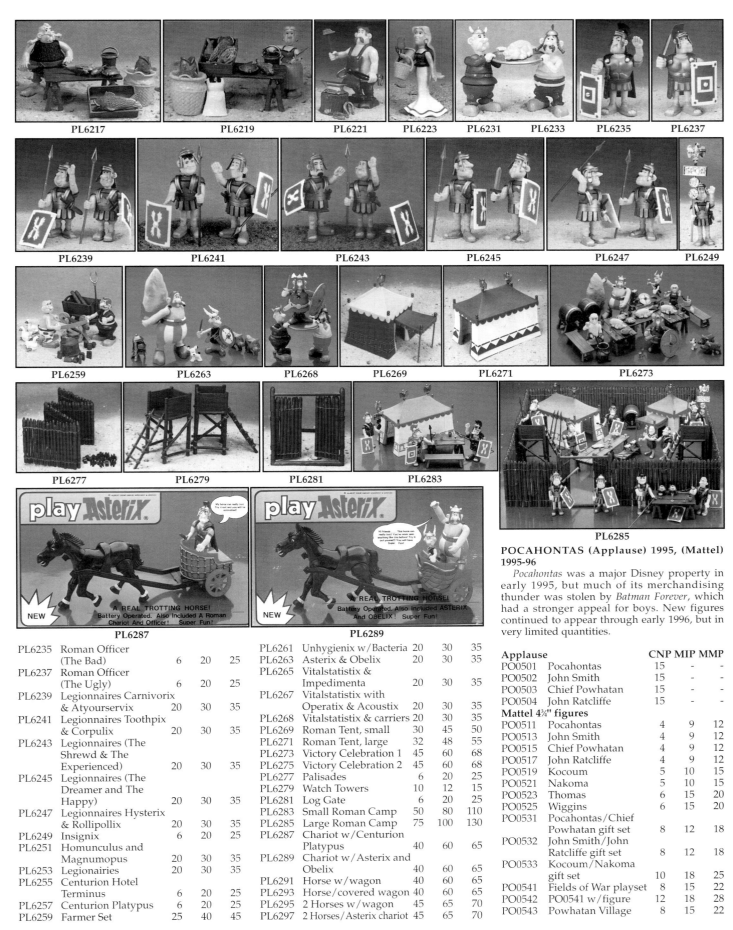

PL6217 PL6219 PL6221 PL6223 PL6231 PL6233 PL6235 PL6237

PL6239 PL6241 PL6243 PL6245 PL6247 PL6249

PL6259 PL6263 PL6268 PL6269 PL6271 PL6273

PL6277 PL6279 PL6281 PL6283

PL6285

PL6287 PL6289

POCAHONTAS (Applause) 1995, (Mattel) 1995-96

Pocahontas was a major Disney property in early 1995, but much of its merchandising thunder was stolen by *Batman Forever*, which had a stronger appeal for boys. New figures continued to appear through early 1996, but in very limited quantities.

Applause		CNP	MIP	MMP
PO0501	Pocahontas	15	-	-
PO0502	John Smith	15	-	-
PO0503	Chief Powhatan	15	-	-
PO0504	John Ratcliffe	15	-	-
Mattel 4¾" figures				
PO0511	Pocahontas	4	9	12
PO0513	John Smith	4	9	12
PO0515	Chief Powhatan	4	9	12
PO0517	John Ratcliffe	4	9	12
PO0519	Kocoum	5	10	15
PO0521	Nakoma	5	10	15
PO0523	Thomas	6	15	20
PO0525	Wiggins	6	15	20
PO0531	Pocahontas/Chief Powhatan gift set	8	12	18
PO0532	John Smith/John Ratcliffe gift set	8	12	18
PO0533	Kocoum/Nakoma gift set	10	18	25
PO0541	Fields of War playset	8	15	22
PO0542	PO0541 w/figure	12	18	28
PO0543	Powhatan Village	8	15	22

PL6235	Roman Officer (The Bad)	6	20	25
PL6237	Roman Officer (The Ugly)	6	20	25
PL6239	Legionnaires Carnivorix & Atyourservix	20	30	35
PL6241	Legionnaires Toothpix & Corpulix	20	30	35
PL6243	Legionnaires (The Shrewd & The Experienced)	20	30	35
PL6245	Legionnaires (The Dreamer and The Happy)	20	30	35
PL6247	Legionnaires Hysterix & Rollipollix	20	30	35
PL6249	Insignix	6	20	25
PL6251	Homunculus and Magnumopus	20	30	35
PL6253	Legionairies	20	30	35
PL6255	Centurion Hotel Terminus	6	20	25
PL6257	Centurion Platypus	6	20	25
PL6259	Farmer Set	25	40	45

PL6261	Unhygienix w/Bacteria	20	30	35
PL6263	Asterix & Obelix	20	30	35
PL6265	Vitalstatistix & Impedimenta	20	30	35
PL6267	Vitalstatistix with Operatix & Acoustix	20	30	35
PL6268	Vitalstatistix & carriers	20	30	35
PL6269	Roman Tent, small	30	45	50
PL6271	Roman Tent, large	32	48	55
PL6273	Victory Celebration 1	45	60	68
PL6275	Victory Celebration 2	45	60	68
PL6277	Palisades	6	20	25
PL6279	Watch Towers	10	12	15
PL6281	Log Gate	6	20	25
PL6283	Small Roman Camp	50	80	110
PL6285	Large Roman Camp	75	100	130
PL6287	Chariot w/Centurion Platypus	40	60	65
PL6289	Chariot w/Asterix and Obelix	40	60	65
PL6291	Horse w/wagon	40	60	65
PL6293	Horse/covered wagon	40	60	65
PL6295	2 Horses w/wagon	45	65	70
PL6297	2 Horses/Asterix chariot	45	65	70

CNP: Complete, no package, with all weapons and accessories; MIP: Mint in package; MMP: Mint item in Mint package. Values in U.S. dollars. See page 3 for details.

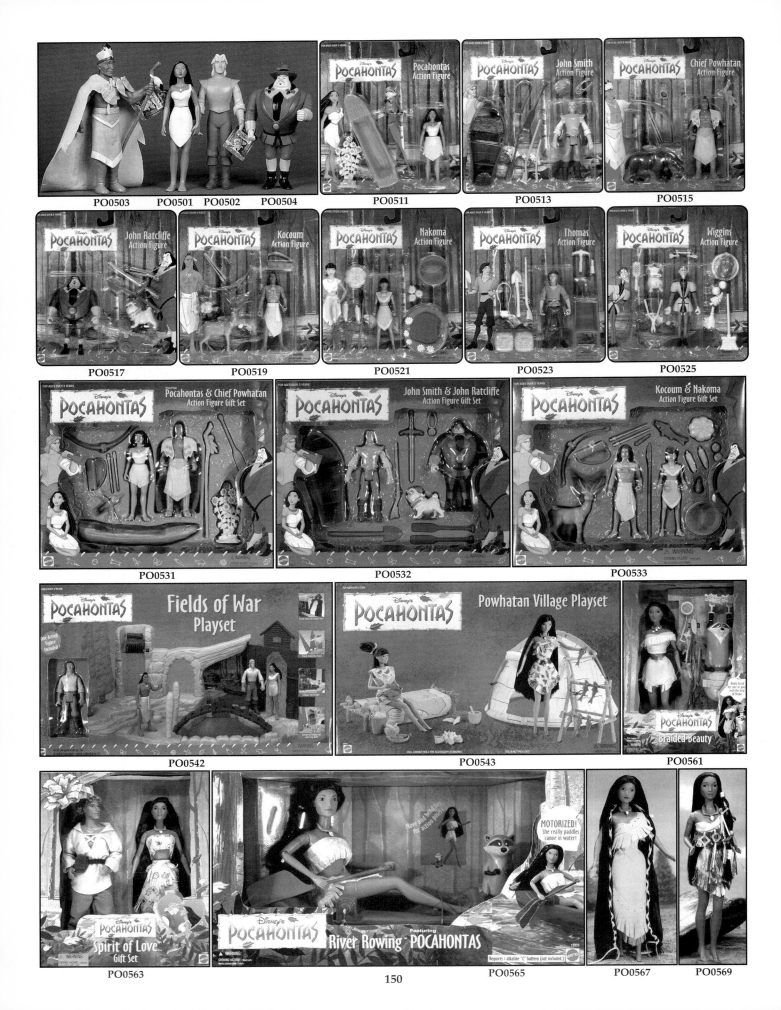

PO0503   PO0501   PO0502   PO0504

PO0511

PO0513

PO0515

PO0517   PO0519   PO0521   PO0523   PO0525

PO0531

PO0532

PO0533

PO0542

PO0543

PO0561

PO0563

PO0565

PO0567

PO0569

150

PO0571	PO0581	PO0583	PO0585	PO0587	PO0593 PO0591	PO0592

PO1001	PO1002	PO1003	PO1004	PO1005	PO1006

PO1007	PO1008	PO1010	PO1031	PO1034	PO1035

PO1050 Batcave   75   150   200

Mattel large figures

PO0561	Braided Beauty	12	20	30
PO0563	Spirit of Love set	15	25	35
PO0565	River Rowing Pocahontas	15	35	40
PO0567	Shining Braids Pocahontas	6	12	18
PO0569	Bead-so-Pretty Pocahontas	6	12	18

Dress 'n Play outfits

PO0571	Dance	4	10	14
PO0573	Swimming	4	10	14
PO0575	Wilderness	4	10	14
PO0577	Winter	4	10	14

Sun Colors Figures

PO0581	Pocahontas	6	12	18
PO0583	John Smith	6	12	18
PO0585	Kocoum	6	12	18
PO0587	Nakoma	6	12	18

Color Splash Figures

PO0591	Pocahontas	6	12	18
PO0592	John Smith	6	12	18
PO0593	Nakoma	6	12	18

POCKET SUPER HEROES (Mego) 1979

Marvel and DC comic characters were sold in this series. DC and Marvel characters had different packaging styles, and DC characters came on white or red cards. The names of the characters were not printed on red cards.

White Cards PO1001-10

		CNP	MIP	MMP
PO1001	Spider-Man	10	35	75

PO1050

PO1002	Hulk	10	20	40
PO1003	Captain America	20	95	150
PO1004	Green Goblin	20	95	150
PO1005	Superman	10	35	75
PO1006	Batman	10	35	80
PO1007	Robin	10	35	75
PO1008	Wonder Woman	10	55	100
PO1010	Aquaman	20	100	150

Red cards PO1021-35

PO1021	Spider-Man	10	20	35
PO1022	Hulk	10	20	35
PO1025	Superman	10	35	55
PO1026	Batman	10	45	65
PO1027	Robin	10	45	65
PO1031	Lex Luthor	5	10	20
PO1034	Jor-El	5	10	20
PO1035	General Zod	5	10	20

POGO (Proctor and Gamble) 1969

A series based on the popular comic strip by Walt Kelly. The figures came with Proctor and Gamble soap products, but never had their own packages.

		CNP
PO2001	Pogo Possum	8
PO2002	Uncle Albert Alligator	8
PO2003	Porky Pine	8
PO2004	Beaureguard Hound	8
PO2005	Churchy La Femme	8
PO2006	Howland Owl	8

The lack of any packaging for the Pogo series eliminates the need for Mint in Packaga and Mint in Package prices.

POLICE ACADEMY (Kenner) 1989-90, 1991

Mr. Sleaze was extremely difficult to find, but other first series figures were widely availible. Captain Harris was a mail-in offer. Lack of interest from retailers killed the second series figures, which were closed out in 1991. Several characters in the second series were still very difficult to find. Only one Snack Attack House was available for every ten of other figures in the assortment. Less than twelve Stakeout Sweetchuck figures are known.

PO2001　PO2002　PO2003　PO2004　PO2005　PO2006　PO3001　PO3002

PO3003

PO3004

PO3005

PO3006

PO3007

PO3008

PO3010

PO3011

PO3012

PO3013

PO3014

PO3015

PO3016　　PO3017

PO3020

PO3021

PO3031

	CNP	MIP	MMP
PO3001 Carey Mahoney	5	8	10
PO3002 Zed	5	8	10
PO3003 Larvelle Jones	5	8	10
PO3004 Moses Hightower	5	8	10
PO3005 Eugene Tackleberry	5	8	10
PO3006 Mr. Sleaze	8	15	18
PO3007 Numskull	5	8	10
PO3008 Claw	5	8	10
PO3009 Captain Harris (mail-in premium)	25	30	45
PO3010 Stakeout Sweetchuck	60	125	175
PO3011 Flung Hi (yellow or orange gear)	8	15	18
PO3012 Karate Larvell Jones	8	15	18
PO3013 S.W.A.T. Eugene Tackleberry	8	15	18
PO3014 Sky Glidin' Zed	10	18	20
PO3015 Kingpin	8	15	18
PO3016 Undercover Carey Mahoney	8	15	18
PO3017 Snack Attack House	15	25	45
PO3020 Crazy Cruiser	8	14	16
PO3021 Crash Cycle	2	6	8
PO3031 Precinct Police Station	12	35	45

POLICE WOMAN (Horsman)

The 9" *Police Woman* figure is classified here as an action figure, even though it was sold as

PO5301   PO5303   PO5305   PO5307   PO5308

PO5001   PO6001   PO6002   PO6003   PO6004   PO6005

   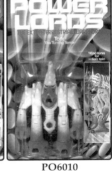      

PO6006   PO6010   PO6021   PO6030

PO6020

a doll. Several assignment-packs for the figure were sold separately, each including a change of clothes and plastic accessories.

		CNP	MIP	MMP
PO5001	Police Woman figure	15	20	30
Assignment packs PO5011-15				
PO5011	Sabotage Under the Sea	5	12	15
PO5012	Race Against Time	5	12	15
PO5013	Undercover Mission	5	12	15
PO5014	Surprise from the Skies	5	12	15
PO5015	Hostess to Danger	5	12	15

POOH AND FRIENDS (Sears Exclusive) 1988

These Sears figures were part of a store-wide Disney tie-in.

		CNP	MIP	MMP
PO5301	Pooh	2	6	8
PO5302	Tigger	2	6	8
PO5303	Owl	2	6	8
PO5304	Kanga	2	6	8
PO5305	Roo	2	6	8
PO5306	Rabbit	2	6	8
PO5307	Eyore	2	6	8
PO5308	Piglet	2	6	8

See also: *Disney; Mickey and Friends*

POPEYE — See *Dakin and Dakin-Style Figures*

POWER LORDS (Revell) 1982

The basic *Power Lords* figures were double-sided, either with a revolving torso or two sets of feet. Their joints were designed to be moved 180 or 360 degrees, so the figures could be convincingly moved from either side. Most included an action feature, plastic accessories, and a sticker. A cut-out description of each character was printed on the back of the blister packages. A *Power Lords* fan club was also advertised.

		CNP	MIP	MMP
PO6001	Adam Power/			
	Lord Power	3	6	8
PO6002	Shaya	3	6	8
PO6003	Sydot	3	6	8
PO6004	Arkus	3	6	8
PO6005	Raygoth	3	6	8
PO6006	Ggripptogg	3	6	8
PO6007	Disguyzor	3	8	10
PO6008	Drrench	3	8	10
PO6009	Bakatak	3	8	10
PO6010	Tork	3	8	10
PO6020	Power Ship	5	12	15
PO6021	Trigore	5	12	15
PO6030	Volcan Rock	10	25	35

POWER OF THE FORCE, THE — See *Star Wars*

POWER RANGERS, POWER RANGERS ZEO
— See *Mighty Morphin Power Rangers*

PREDATOR (Kenner) 1993-95

Alien warriors based on the *Predator* films were launched in conjunction with the second year of Kenner's *Aliens* line. The concept was sold to the trade as *Aliens vs. Predator*, but this name only appeared on one special two-pack (see AL5601).

Molds were re-used on several occasions. Electronic Lasershot Predator figures were produced in very limited quantities in early 1995.

First series		CNP	MIP	MMP
PR1501	Cracked Tusk Predator	5	8	10
PR1503	Scavage Predator	5	8	10
PR1505	Ambush Predator	10	20	30
	mail-in (clear re-mold			
	of figure from AL5601)			
Second series				
PR1511	Stalker Predator	5	8	10
PR1513	Spiked Tail Predator	5	8	10

CNP: Complete, no package, with all weapons and accessories; MIP: Mint in package; MMP: Mint item in Mint package. Values in U.S. dollars. See page 3 for details.

| | PR1501 | | PR1503 | | | PR1505 | | PR1511 | | PR1513 |

| | PR1515 | | PR1521 | | PR1523 | | PR1525 | | PR1535 |

| | PR1531 | | PR2001 | | PR2003 | | PR2005 | | PR2007 |

| | PR2009 | | PR2011 | | PR2013 | | PR3041 | | PR3043 |

PR1515	Predator Clan Leader	6	10	14
Third series				
PR1521	Lava Planet Predator (re-mold of PR1501)	5	8	12
PR1523	Nightstorm Predator (re-mold of PR1503)	5	8	12
PR1525	Lasershot Predator	10	18	25
PR1531	Blade Fighter	8	15	22
PR1535	Ultimate Predator	9	20	30

PRIMAL RAGE (Playmates) 1996

Part articulated figure, part bend-em, fantasy dinosaurs based on the video game.

		CNP	MIP	MMP
PR2001	Diablo	6	10	14
PR2003	Sauron	6	10	14
PR2005	Chaos	6	10	14
PR2007	Blizzard	6	10	14
PR2009	Armadon	6	10	14
PR2011	Vertigo	6	10	14
PR2013	Talon	6	10	14

PRINCESS OF POWER (Mattel) 1985-87

She-Ra, He-Man's sister, was Mattel's female counterpart to the popular Masters of the Universe line. The series was probably pro-

duced in response to Galoob's "Golden Girl" line. Each figure included a mini-comic.

		CNP	MIP	MMP
PR3001	She-Ra	4	8	12
PR3002	Catra	4	8	12
PR3003	Bow	4	8	12
PR3004	Frosta	4	8	12
PR3005	Castaspella	4	8	12
PR3006	Double Trouble	4	8	12
PR3007	Angella	4	8	12
PR3008	Glimmer	4	8	12
PR3009	Kowl	4	10	14

154

PR3001

PR3002

PR3003

PR3004

PR3005

PR3006

PR3007

PR3008

PR3009

PR3021

PR3033

PR3022

PR3023

PR3024

PR3025

PR3026

PR3027

PR3028

PR3032

PR3035

PR3045

PR3046

PR3021	Star Burst She-Ra	5	15	25
PR3022	Entrapta	8	15	30
PR3023	Sweet Bee	8	15	30
PR3024	Peekablue	8	15	30
PR3025	Perfuma	8	15	30
PR3026	Mermista	8	15	30
PR3027	Scratchin' Sound Catra	8	15	30
PR3028	Flutterina	8	15	30
PR3031	Bubble Power She-Ra	8	15	30

PR3049	PR3050	PR3062	
PR3063	PR3064	PR3066	

PR6001	PR6003	PR6005	PR6007	PR6009	PR6011	PR6013

PR6015	PR6021	PR6023	PR6025	PR6027	PR6029	PR6031

PR6033	PR6035	PR6039	PR6041	PR6043	PR6045	PR6047

PR3032	Netossa	8	15	35
PR3033	Shower Power Catra	8	15	30
PR3034	Spinnerella	8	15	30
PR3035	Loo-Kee	10	25	45
PR3041	Swift Wind	8	14	16
PR3042	Storm	8	14	16
PR3043	Arrow	8	14	16
PR3044	Crystal Swift Wind	15	22	25
PR3045	Crystal Moon Beam	15	22	25
PR3046	Crystal Sundancer	15	22	25
PR3047	Royal Swift Wind	15	22	25
PR3048	Silver Storm	8	14	16
PR3049	Clawdeen	8	14	16

PR3050	Peekablue w/Crystal Moon Beam			
PR3055	Enchanta	12	18	20
PR3061	Bubble Carriage	6	22	28
PR3062	Crystal Falls playset	8	18	24
PR3063	Crystal Castle playset	12	25	40
PR3064	Butterflyer	6	15	18
PR3066	Sea Harp			
PR3071	Fantastic Fashions, ea			

PROJECTORS (Toy Biz) 1994-95

These figures incorporated miniature lamps and lenses, enabling kids to project scenes from Marvel TV shows onto any flat surface. Each figure came with three "adventure wheel" film disks.

Figures were packaged in window boxes. Individual boxes were designed to match the sub-series the character was from (*X-Men*, *Spider-Man*, etc.).

		CNP	MIP	MMP
PR6001	Apocalypse	8	12	16
PR6003	Wolverine	8	12	16
PR6005	Magneto	8	12	16
PR6007	Sabretooth	8	12	16

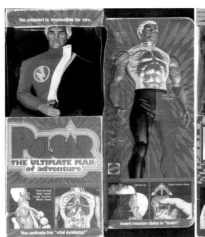

| PU1001 | PU1002 | PU1010 |

| RA2004 | RA2005 | RA2006 | RA2011 | RA2012 | RA2013 |

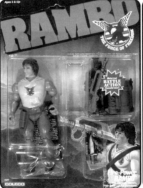

| RA4001 | RA4002 | RA4003 | RA4004 | RA4005 |

PR6009	Cyclops	8	12	16
PR6011	Spider-Man	8	12	16
PR6013	Hobgoblin	8	12	16
PR6015	Venom	8	12	16
PR6021	Civilian Wolverine	8	12	16
PR6023	Beast	8	12	16
PR6025	Lizard	8	12	16
PR6027	Iron Man	8	12	16
PR6029	The Thing	8	12	16
PR6031	Bishop	8	12	16
PR6033	Cable	8	12	16
PR6035	Mr. Sinister	8	12	16
PR6037	Dr. Octopus	8	12	16
PR6039	Spider-Sense Spider-Man	8	12	16
PR6041	White Ranger	8	12	16
PR6043	Red Ranger	8	12	16
PR6045	Black Ranger	8	12	16
PR6047	Blue Ranger	8	12	16

PULSAR (Mattel) 1977-78

Pulsar, "The Ultimate Man of Adventure" had a see-through chest containing visible internal organs. Pressing his back made his heart beat, lungs breath, and bloodstream to flow. Lifting his face exposed a computer brain which could be fitted with one of two mission disks. Hypnos was his ultimate enemy, who came with a removeable face mask and sparkling color wheels in his chest. The Life Systems Center included an X-Ray effect, circuitry connections, and a lever which activated Pulsar's "vital systems."

		CNP	MIP	MMP
PU1001	Pulsar	15	35	65
PU1002	Hypnos	15	45	75
PU1010	Life Systems Center	15	38	45

RACING SUPERSTARS (Racing Champions Inc.) 1991-93

A series of race car drivers, released with two different packaging variations. The first run included only the figure and helmet. The second series included a die-cast version of the driver's car and a collector's card.

Figures only		CNP	MIP	MMP
RA2001	Bill Elliott	1	3	4
RA2002	Ken Schrader	1	3	4
RA2003	Sterling Marlin	1	3	4
RA2004	Bobby Hamilton	1	3	4
RA2005	Richard Petty	1	4	5
RA2006	Derrike Cope	1	3	4
Figures with die-cast cars and collector cards				
RA2011	Bill Elliott	1	3	4
RA2012	Ken Schrader	1	3	4
RA2013	Sterling Marlin	1	3	4
RA2014	Bobby Hamilton	1	3	4
RA2015	Richard Petty	1	4	5
RA2016	Derrike Cope	1	3	4

RAMBO (Coleco) 1985-86

Each Rambo figure came packaged with a statistics card and a small catalog, in addition to the usual plastic accessories. The Nomad figure was taken off the market because of complaints from Arab communities.

The Force of Freedom		CNP	MIP	MMP
RA4001	Rambo	8	15	18
RA4002	Fire-Power Rambo	8	15	18
RA4003	Colonel Trautman	8	15	18
RA4004	Turbo	8	15	18
RA4005	K.A.T.	8	16	20
RA4006	White Dragon	8	16	20
S.A.V.A.G.E. RA4011-16				
RA4011	General Warhawk	8	15	18
RA4012	Sergeant Havoc	8	15	18
RA4013	Black Dragon	8	15	18
RA4014	Nomad	8	15	18
RA4015	Gripper	8	15	18
RA4016	Mad Dog	8	15	18

CNP: Complete, no package, with all weapons and accessories; MIP: Mint in package; MMP: Mint item in Mint package. Values in U.S. dollars. See page 3 for details.

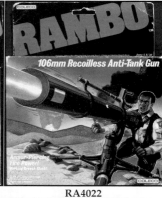

| RA4012 | RA4014 | RA4019 | RA4021 | RA4022 |

| RA4023 | RA4024 | RA4032 | RA4034 |

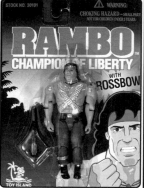

| RA4041 | RA4201 | RA7505 | RE1001 | RE1002 |

RA4019	Weapons Pack	2	6	8
RA4021	.50 Caliber Anti-Aircraft Gun	2	6	8
RA4022	106mm Recoilless Anti-Tank Gun	2	6	8
RA4023	81mm Mortar	2	6	8
RA4024	.50 Caliber Machine Gun	2	6	8
RA4031	Defender 6 x 6	6	15	20
RA4032	Skyfire Assault Copter	6	15	30
RA4033	Skywolf One-Man Assault Jet	4	12	16
RA4034	S.A.V.A.G.E. Strike Cycle	4	12	16
RA4041	S.A.V.A.G.E. Strike Headquarters	12	25	35

RAMBO — CHAMPION OF LIBERTY (Toy Island) 1995

Toy Island picked up the Rambo license and produced a few toys some time after the character's heyday had died down. The same figures were sold on larger cards at Kay-Bee stores.

		CNP	MIP	MMP
RA4201	Rambo w/crossbow	2	5	8
RA4202	RA4201 on large card	2	5	8

RAPID DEPLOYMENT FORCE (In Time Products Co., Ltd.) 1992-93, 1995

This line began as a knock-off of *G.I. Joe* Hall of Fame figures. Low-quality figures and

accessory packs "suitable for *G.I. Joe…*" were produced. Figures were packaged in generic boxes, which were updated when new figures were introduced. The "Skull" figure generated some collector interest because of its similarity to The Punisher. The line was carried exclusively by Wal-Mart during 1993. Stickers reading "Marketed by Wal-Mart Stores Inc." were added to older packages. New figures manufactured for 1993 had no names, fewer accessories, and sold for about $3 less.

A carded 6" series was made exclusively for K mart in 1995. Each figure included a temporary tattoo matching the design on the character's chest.

		CNP	MIP	MMP
RA7501	Airborne Ranger	6	10	14
RA7502	Sky Raider	6	10	14
RA7503	Para Ninja	6	10	14
RA7504	Night Fighter	6	10	14
RA7505	"Skull"	6	10	14
RA7506	"Scuba"	6	10	14
RA7507	Marine	6	10	14
RA7508	Snoweagle	6	10	14
RA7509	Night Paratrooper	6	10	14
RA7510	Sirocco (Desert Fighter)	6	10	14
RA7511	Top Gun	6	10	14
RA7512	Havco	6	10	14
RA7513	Sniper	6	10	14
RA7514	Techno	6	10	14

RA7515	Delta One	6	10	14
RA7531	Carded Commando Accessory Packs, ea	4	8	12
RA7551	Gift Sets, ea	20	30	35
RA7571	Air Borne (sic) Accessory Set	20	30	35
RA7581	Foot Locker	undetermined		
RA7585	1993 12" figures (no names), ea	6	10	14
6" figures (K mart)				
RA7600	Red Dragon	5	8	12
RA7601	Navy Seal	5	8	12
RA7602	"Claw"	5	8	12
RA7603	Green Beret	5	8	12
RA7604	"Tiger"	5	8	12
RA7605	Para Ninja	5	8	12

REAL GHOSTBUSTERS, THE (Kenner) 1986-90

The Real Ghostbusters animated series inspired this line of action figures. The show would have been called *Ghostbusters* after the film it was based on, but the rights to the name were owned by Filmation. The "companion" ghosts could prove to be collectible in the future. They get lost or are separated from the figures so easily that there are bound to be more figures than ghosts. The Ecto-Glow Ghostbusters featured glow in the dark outfits, and came with glowing head covers to complete the effect.

RE1003   RE1004   RE1005   RE1006   RE1011

RE1012   RE1013   RE1021   RE1014

RE1022   RE1023   RE1024   RE1016

RE1025   RE1026   RE1031   RE1032   RE1033

RE1001	Peter Venkman				RE1004	Winston			
	w/Grabber Ghost	5	12	20		w/Chomper Ghost	5	12	20
RE1002	Ray Stantz				RE1005	Stay-Puft			
	w/Wrapper Ghost	5	12	20		Marshmallow Man	10	18	25
RE1003	Egon Spengler				RE1006	Green Ghost (Slimer)			
	w/Gulper Ghost	5	12	20		w/Pizza	12	20	35

RE1011	Bug-Eyed Ghost	10	18	25
RE1012	H2Ghost	10	18	25
RE1013	Bad to the Bone Ghost	10	18	25
RE1014	Squisher w/Ecto Plazm	10	18	25
RE1015	Banshee Bomber			
	w/Ecto Plazm	6	12	18

CNP: Complete, no package, with all weapons and accessories; MIP: Mint in package; MMP: Mint item in Mint package. Values in U.S. dollars. See page 3 for details.

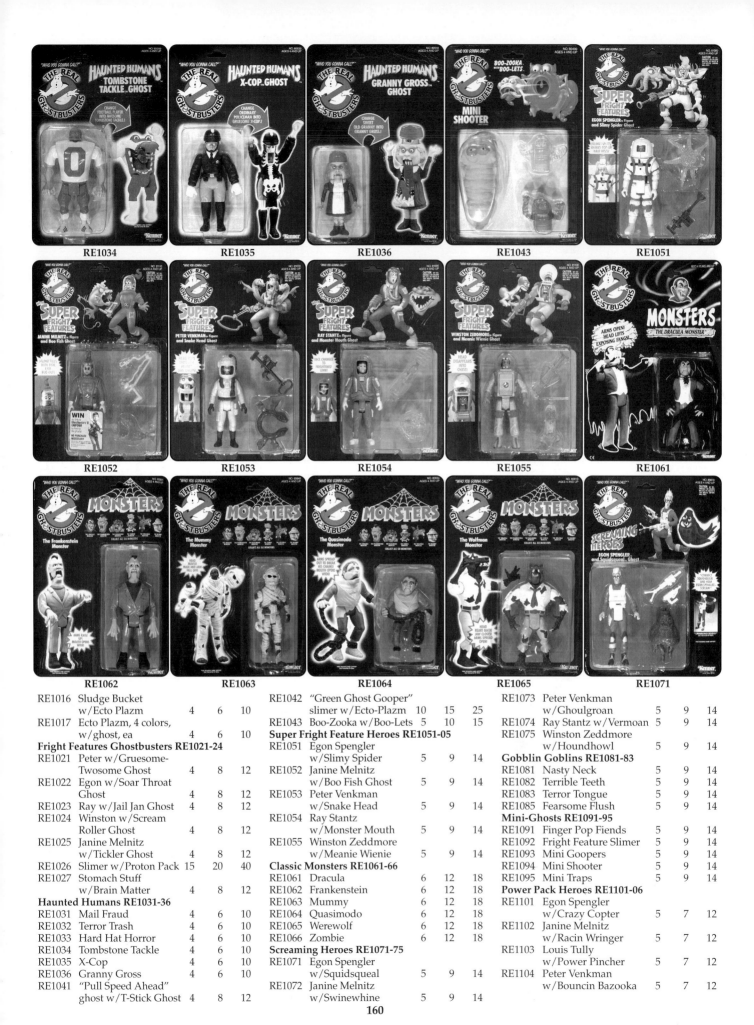

RE1034	RE1035	RE1036	RE1043	RE1051
RE1052	RE1053	RE1054	RE1055	RE1061
RE1062	RE1063	RE1064	RE1065	RE1071

RE1016	Sludge Bucket w/Ecto Plazm	4	6	10
RE1017	Ecto Plazm, 4 colors, w/ghost, ea	4	6	10
Fright Features Ghostbusters RE1021-24				
RE1021	Peter w/Gruesome-Twosome Ghost	4	8	12
RE1022	Egon w/Soar Throat Ghost	4	8	12
RE1023	Ray w/Jail Jan Ghost	4	8	12
RE1024	Winston w/Scream Roller Ghost	4	8	12
RE1025	Janine Melnitz w/Tickler Ghost	4	8	12
RE1026	Slimer w/Proton Pack	15	20	40
RE1027	Stomach Stuff w/Brain Matter	4	8	12
Haunted Humans RE1031-36				
RE1031	Mail Fraud	4	6	10
RE1032	Terror Trash	4	6	10
RE1033	Hard Hat Horror	4	6	10
RE1034	Tombstone Tackle	4	6	10
RE1035	X-Cop	4	6	10
RE1036	Granny Gross	4	6	10
RE1041	"Pull Speed Ahead" ghost w/T-Stick Ghost	4	8	12

RE1042	"Green Ghost Gooper" slimer w/Ecto-Plazm	10	15	25
RE1043	Boo-Zooka w/Boo-Lets	5	10	15
Super Fright Feature Heroes RE1051-05				
RE1051	Egon Spengler w/Slimy Spider	5	9	14
RE1052	Janine Melnitz w/Boo Fish Ghost	5	9	14
RE1053	Peter Venkman w/Snake Head	5	9	14
RE1054	Ray Stantz w/Monster Mouth	5	9	14
RE1055	Winston Zeddmore w/Meanie Wienie	5	9	14
Classic Monsters RE1061-66				
RE1061	Dracula	6	12	18
RE1062	Frankenstein	6	12	18
RE1063	Mummy	6	12	18
RE1064	Quasimodo	6	12	18
RE1065	Werewolf	6	12	18
RE1066	Zombie	6	12	18
Screaming Heroes RE1071-75				
RE1071	Egon Spengler w/Squidsqueal	5	9	14
RE1072	Janine Melnitz w/Swinewhine	5	9	14

RE1073	Peter Venkman w/Ghoulgroan	5	9	14
RE1074	Ray Stantz w/Vermoan	5	9	14
RE1075	Winston Zeddmore w/Houndhowl	5	9	14
Gobblin Goblins RE1081-83				
RE1081	Nasty Neck	5	9	14
RE1082	Terrible Teeth	5	9	14
RE1083	Terror Tongue	5	9	14
RE1085	Fearsome Flush	5	9	14
Mini-Ghosts RE1091-95				
RE1091	Finger Pop Fiends	5	9	14
RE1092	Fright Feature Slimer	5	9	14
RE1093	Mini Goopers	5	9	14
RE1094	Mini Shooter	5	9	14
RE1095	Mini Traps	5	9	14
Power Pack Heroes RE1101-06				
RE1101	Egon Spengler w/Crazy Copter	5	7	12
RE1102	Janine Melnitz w/Racin Wringer	5	7	12
RE1103	Louis Tully w/Power Pincher	5	7	12
RE1104	Peter Venkman w/Bouncin Bazooka	5	7	12

RE1072

RE1073

RE1074

RE1085

RE1093

RE1081

RE1082

RE1083

RE1095

RE1101

RE1102

RE1103

RE1105

RE1106

RE1111

RE1112

RE1113

RE1114

RE1105	Ray Stanz w/Grabbin Grappler	5	7	12
RE1106	Winston Zeddmore w/Cyclin Slicer	5	7	12
Slimed Heroes RE1111-15				
RE1111	Egon Spengler w/Brain Ghost	5	7	12
RE1112	Louis Tully w/Four-Eyed Ghost	5	7	12
RE1113	Peter Venkman w/Tooth Ghost	5	7	12

RE1114	Ray Stantz w/Vapor Ghost	5	7	12
RE1115	Winston Zeddmore w/Sucker Ghost	5	7	12
Backpack figures RE1121-26				
RE1121	Peter Venkman w/Bouncin' Bazooka	5	7	12
RE1122	Egon Spengler w/Crazy Copter	5	7	12
RE1123	Ray Stantz w/Grabbin' Grappler	5	7	12

RE1124	Louis Tully w/Power Pincher	5	7	12
RE1125	Winston Zeddmore w/Cyclin' Slicer	5	7	12
RE1126	Janine Melnitz w/Racin' Wringer	5	7	12
Ecto-Glow Heroes RE1131-35				
RE1131	Peter Venkman w/Spider Ghost	8	14	20
RE1132	Egon Spengler w/Jail Jaw Ghost	8	14	20

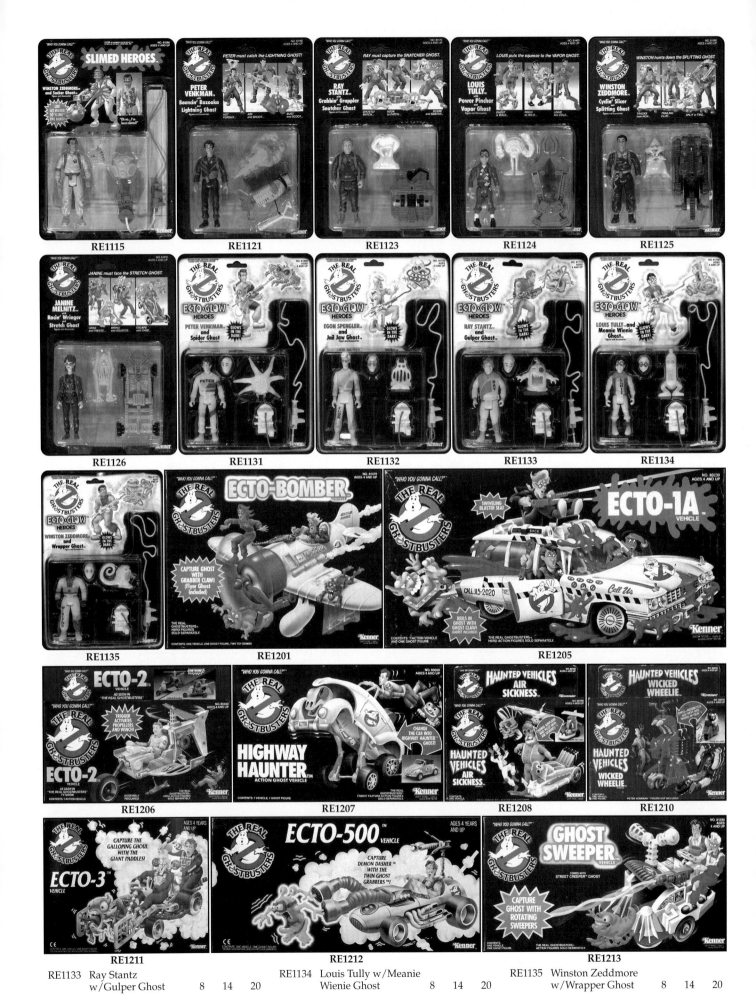

RE1115   RE1121   RE1123   RE1124   RE1125

RE1126   RE1131   RE1132   RE1133   RE1134

RE1135   RE1201   RE1205

RE1206   RE1207   RE1208   RE1210

RE1211   RE1212   RE1213

| RE1133 | Ray Stantz w/Gulper Ghost | 8 | 14 | 20 | | RE1134 | Louis Tully w/Meanie Wienie Ghost | 8 | 14 | 20 | | RE1135 | Winston Zeddmore w/Wrapper Ghost | 8 | 14 | 20 |

RE1300

RE2001

RE2002

RE2003

RE2535

RE1201	Ecto-Bomber			
	w/Bomber Ghost	10	20	25
RE1204	Ecto-1 Ambulance			
	w/Orange Ghost	6	15	20
RE1205	Ecto-1A w/Ambulance			
	Ghost	6	12	18
RE1206	Ecto-2 Helicopter	6	12	18
RE1207	Highway Haunter	6	12	18
RE1208	Air Sickness w/pilot	6	12	18
RE1210	Wicked Wheelie			
	w/driver	4	8	12
RE1211	Ecto-3 w/Companion			
	Ghost	4	8	12
RE1212	Ecto-500 Racecar			
	w/Companion Ghost	4	8	12
RE1213	Ghost Sweeper			
	w/Street Creeper	4	8	12
RE1300	Firehouse Headquarters	15	45	60

See also: *Filmation's Ghostbusters*

REAL MEN (Mattel) 1986

Action figures combined with puppets. A child's fingers provided the arms or legs of the figure, adding plastic gloves or shoes.

RE2001	Boxer/Wrestler	2	4	6
RE2002	Cheerleader	2	4	6
RE2003	Skateboarder	2	4	6
RE2004	Deluxe Soccer Set	3	5	7
RE2005	Deluxe Football Set	3	5	7

REBOOT (Irwin) 1995-96

The computer-generated TV show *ReBoot* was one of the surprise successes of 1995. Hexadecimal was the short-packed figure.

Second series figures were repaints of the first series, with color-changing paint for heroes and splashy new deco jobs for villians. These were primarily available in Canada.

First Series, 1995		CNP	MIP	MMP
RE2501	Bob	5	8	10
RE2503	Enzo	5	8	10
RE2505	Dot	5	8	10
RE2507	Megabyte	5	8	10
RE2509	Hexadecimal	5	10	15
RE2511	Hack	5	8	10
RE2513	Slash	5	8	10
Second Series, 1996 (Canada)				
RE2521	Bob	8	12	20

RE2501   RE2503   RE2505   RE2507   RE2509   RE2511   RE2513

RE2521   RE2523   RE2525   RE2527   RE2529   RE2531   RE2533

RE6001   RE6002   RE6003   RE6004   RE6005   RE6006

| RE6007 | RE6008 | RO1001 | RO1002 | RO1003 | RO1004 |

| RO2001 | RO2002 | RO2003 | RO2004 | RO2005 | RO2006 |

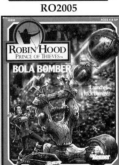

| RO2007 | RO2008 | RO2009 | RO2010 | RO2021 | RO2024 |

RO2022   RO2031

RE2523	Enzo	8	12	20
RE2525	Dot	8	12	20
RE2527	Megabyte	8	12	20
RE2529	Hexadecimal	8	12	20
RE2531	Hack	8	12	20
RE2533	Slash	8	12	20
RE2535	Drophead Car	10	20	30

REN AND STIMPY SHOW, THE (Mattel) 1993

The Nickelodeon cartoon was the inspiration for this short-lived series. Late-run figures saw limited distribution at Suncoast Video stores and possibly a few other franchises.

		CNP	MIP	MMP
RE6001	Slap-Happy Ren	10	15	20
RE6002	Bump-A-Riffic Stimpy	10	15	20
RE6003	Commander Ren	10	15	20
RE6004	Space Cadet Stimpy	10	15	20
RE6005	Army Ren	10	15	20
RE6006	Boot Camp Stimpy	10	15	20
RE6007	Bathtub Ren	15	20	25
RE6008	Gritty Kitty Stimpy	15	20	25

RETURN OF THE JEDI — See *Star Wars*

R.I.O.T. VS. EAGLE FORCE — See *Eagle Force*

ROBIN HOOD AND HIS MERRY MEN (Mego) 1974

A less common series of Mego figures. Friar Tuck is the easiest to find, Will Scarlet is the most difficult.

		CNP	MIP	MMP
RO1001	Robin Hood	75	125	225
RO1002	Little John	45	65	115
RO1003	Friar Tuck	20	40	55
RO1004	Will Scarlet	75	125	200

ROBIN HOOD — PRINCE OF THIEVES (Kenner) 1991

Inspired by the 1991 Warner Brothers film, this series was a constant challenge to collectors. Shortly after the first shipment of figures hit the stands, both Robin Hood figures were given new heads which looked a lot more like actor Kevin Costner (the original designs are rarer). Friar Tuck was a low-production figure, and was not available until the second shipment. Much of the series was made from left-over *Star Wars* and *Super Powers Collection* molds.

		CNP	MIP	MMP
RO2001	Long Bow Robin Hood (original head)	4	8	12
RO2002	RO2001 (Costner head)	4	6	8
RO2003	Crossbow Robin Hood (original head)	4	8	12
RO2004	RO2003 (Costner head)	4	6	8

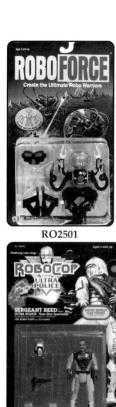

| RO2501 | RO3001 | RO3002 | RO3003 | RO3004 | RO3005 |

| RO3006 | RO3007 | RO3008 | RO3009 | RO3010 | RO3011 |

| RO3012 | RO3013 | RO3014 | RO3015 | RO3018 | RO3040 |

RO2005	Azeem	5	7	10
RO2006	Little John	4	6	9
RO2007	Will Scarlett	5	8	12
RO2008	Friar Tuck	8	14	18
RO2009	Sheriff of Nottingham	4	6	8
RO2010	The Dark Warrior	5	8	12
RO2021	Bola Bomber	4	6	10
RO2022	Battle Wagon	8	15	25
RO2023	Net Launcher	4	6	10
RO2031	Sherwood Forest	10	25	45

ROBO FORCE (Galoob) 1992-93

A series of robotic aliens with interchangeable parts.

		CNP	MIP	MMP
RO2501	Robo Force figures, ea	2	5	7

ROBO-LEADERS — See *Robotron*

ROBOCOP AND THE ULTRA POLICE (Kenner) 1989-90, Toy Island (1994)

The Kenner *RoboCop* figures were cap-firing. Each was originally sold with two rolls of "RoboCaps." A large talking action figure was proposed, but never produced.

Toy Island acquired the rights to RoboCop in 1994, producing a number of look-alike figures with digital sound chips and accessories. A 12" "Audiotronic" figure was also produced.

| RO3021 | RO3022 |

Kenner		CNP	MIP	MMP
RO3001	RoboCop	4	8	12
RO3002	"Wheels" Wilson	2	4	6
RO3003	"Birdman" Barnes	2	4	6
RO3004	"Ace" Jackson	2	4	6
RO3005	Anne Lewis	2	4	6
RO3006	Sgt. Reed	2	4	6
RO3007	Chainsaw	2	4	6
RO3008	Dr. McNamara	2	4	6
RO3009	Nitro	2	4	6
RO3010	Headhunter	2	4	6
RO3011	Torpedo Thompson	2	4	6
RO3012	"Claw" Callahan	2	4	6
RO3013	Gatlin' Blaster RoboCop	5	12	18
RO3014	Scorcher	2	4	6
RO3015	Toxic Waster	2	4	6
RO3017	Nightfighter (mail-in)	5	8	12

RO3018	RO3017 on card	5	6	8
RO3021	Robo-Coptor	5	12	15
RO3022	Robo-1 police car	4	10	12
RO3023	Robo-Cycle	2	5	8
RO3024	Skull Hog	2	5	8
RO3025	ED-260	5	12	15
RO3026	Robo-Jailer	12	20	25
RO3027	Robo-Command	6	15	20
RO3028	Robo-Hawk	6	15	18
RO3029	Vandal-1	4	13	15
RO3030	Robo-Tank	6	15	18
RO3040	RoboCaps	-	1	2
Toy Island				
Electronic RoboCop figures				
RO3151	w/Flight Pack	3	5	7
RO3152	w/Weapon Arm	3	5	7
RO3153	w/Recharging Station	3	5	7

| RO3023 | RO3024 | RO3025 | RO3026 |

| RO3151 | RO3152 | RO3153 | RO3161 | RO3501 |

| RO3503 | RO3504 | RO3507 | RO3509 | RO3511 | RO3550 |

| RO3523 | RO3525 | RO3527 |

RO3521

Talking RoboCop figures

		CNP	MIP	MMP
RO3155	w/Flight Pack	3	5	7
RO3156	w/Weapon Arm	3	5	7
RO3157	w/Bazooka	3	5	7

12" Audiotronic RoboCop figures

| RO3161 | Wide box | 8 | 14 | 20 |
| RO3162 | Narrow box | 8 | 14 | 20 |

ROBOCOP THE SERIES (Toy Island) 1994-95

Toy Island initially produced five 4½" figures for *RoboCop the Series*. Madigan was the toughest figure, and had two package variations.

A smaller *RoboCop the Series* figure was made in 1995 as part of a multi-character assortment.

		CNP	MIP	MMP
RO3501	RoboCop	2	5	7
RO3503	Madigan (hat)	3	7	10
RO3504	Madigan (helmet)	3	7	10
RO3507	Stan Parks	2	5	7

RO3509	Pudface	2	5	7
RO3511	Commander Cash	3	7	10
RO3521	OCP Interceptor	7	15	22
RO3523	Tactical Field Vehicle	7	15	22
RO3525	Tactical Field Ambulance	7	15	22
RO3527	Mobile Armored Detention Vehicle	7	15	22
RO3531	Cryochamber		not produced	
RO3550	3⅞" RoboCop	2	5	8

ROBOT DEFENDERS/ROBOT RENEGADES (Remco) 1984

		CNP	MIP	MMP
RO4001	Mazrak	2	4	5
RO4002	Epaxion	2	4	5
RO4003	Zoton	2	4	5
RO4004	Wargor	2	4	5
RO4005	Zebok	2	4	5
RO4006	Diotrax	2	4	5

RO4007	Strike Cruiser	2	4	5
RO4008	Marauder	2	4	5

ROBOTECH (Matchbox) 1986, (Harmony Gold) 1992-94

The *Robotech* story was the U.S. Translation of three popular Japanese animated features: *Super-Dimension Fortress Macross, Super-Dimension Cavalry Southern Cross,* and *Genesis Climber Mospeada*. The Robotech Master and Zor Prime are the easiest to find, Lunk is the hardest. Zentraedi figures are taller, and were

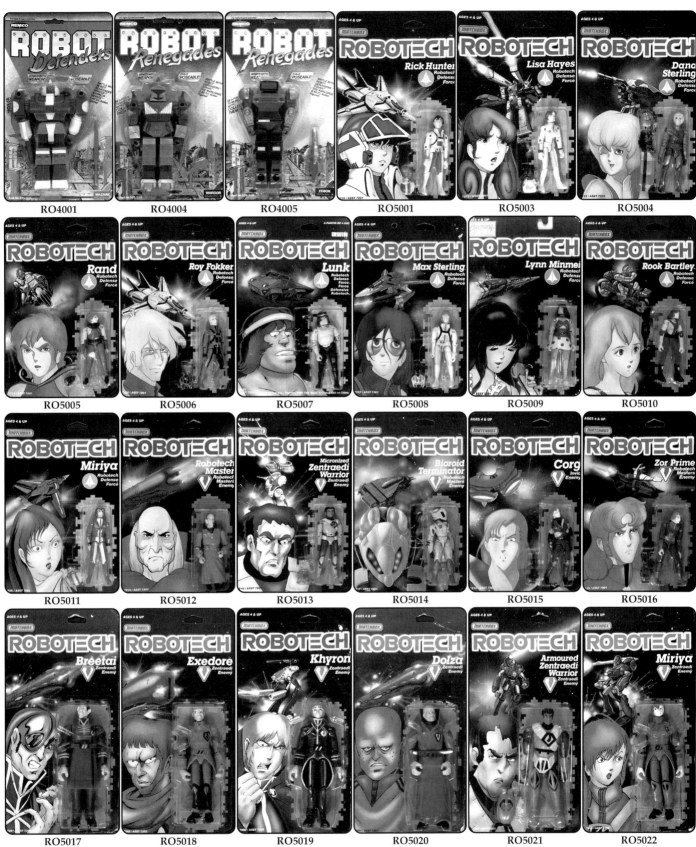

RO4001	RO4004	RO4005
RO5001	RO5003	RO5004
RO5005	RO5006	RO5007 RO5008 RO5009 RO5010
RO5011	RO5012	RO5013 RO5014 RO5015 RO5016
RO5017	RO5018	RO5019 RO5020 RO5021 RO5022

shipped on longer cards than the 3¾" figures. Miriya is "micronized" and switches sides in the story, so two different figures of her were made. Twelve-inch figures with cloth clothing and accessories were made, and a fan club promotion was offered.

Harmony Gold acquired the rights to the Robotech line in 1992, and began selling leftover product in the United Kingdom. Lynn Minmei was not produced until this acquisition. Most other products sold by Harmony Gold are the Matchbox versions with stickers added to the packaging. Harmony Gold attempted to revive the line in the U.S. at the 1994 Toy Fair There was little retail buyer interest, but some product was imported by U.S. collectors and dealers.

Vehicle molds from this line were later licensed to Playmates as part of an *Exosquad* expansion.

3¾", 6" figures		CNP	MIP	MMP
RO5001	Rick Hunter	4	8	12
RO5002	Scott Bernard	5	18	20
RO5003	Lisa Hayes	4	8	10
RO5004	Dana Sterling	4	8	10
RO5005	Rand	3	5	7
RO5006	Roy Fokker	4	10	15
RO5007	Lunk	10	18	25
RO5008	Max Sterling	4	8	10
RO5009	Lynn Minmei (HG)	5	12	18

| RO5050 | RO5051 | RO5055 | RO5056 |

| RO5057 | RO5061 | RO5062 | RO5063 | RO5073 |

RO5066

RO5080

ROBOTRON (Buddy L) 1984, (Diversified Specialists Inc.) 1992

A low-quality *Transformers* copy-cat. The Buddy L line featured four different figures, each design molded in two color combinations to produce eight in all. One packaging design was used for all eight. In vehicle form they could be dragged along the floor and released for a spring-loaded mechanized action. Figures in the later Diversified Specialists line converted to spaceships and dinosaurs.

| RO5503 | RO5525 | RO5527 | RO5528 |

		CNP	MIP	MMP
Buddy L, 1984				
RO5501	Turbotron	1	2	4
RO5502	Gastron	1	2	4
RO5503	Loadtron	1	2	4
RO5504	Trashtron	1	2	4
RO5505	Traktron	1	2	4
RO5506	Locotron	1	2	4
RO5507	Autotron	1	2	4
RO5508	Dragtron	1	2	4
Diversified Specialists Inc., 1992				
Robo Leaders				
RO5525	Commander Red	1	2	3
RO5526	Commander Blue	1	2	3
RoboTron Dinotron				
RO5527	Rextron	1	2	3
RO5528	Stegatron	1	2	3
RO5529	Brontotron	1	2	3
See also: *Chargertron*				

RO5010	Rook Bartley	15	20	30
RO5011	Miriya (short version)	6	9	10
RO5012	Robotech Master	4	8	10
RO5013	Micronized Zentraedi	4	6	8
RO5014	Bioroid Terminator	4	8	10
RO5015	Corg	3	5	7
RO5016	Zor Prime	3	5	7
RO5017	Breetai	5	9	11
RO5018	Exedore	5	9	11
RO5019	Khyron	5	8	10
RO5020	Dolza	5	8	10
RO5021	Armoured Zentraedi Warrior	6	10	13
RO5022	Miriya (tall version)	6	10	12
RO5050	Armoured Cyclone	6	10	14
RO5051	Bioroid Hover Craft	6	10	14

RO5055	Invid Scout Ship	8	16	20
RO5056	Raidar X	8	16	20
RO5057	Spartan	8	16	20
RO5061	Invid Shock Trooper	10	22	30
RO5062	Tactical Battle Pod	10	22	30
RO5063	Zentraedi Officer's Battle Pod	10	22	30
RO5065	Veritech Fighter	15	28	40
RO5066	Veritech Hover Tank	15	28	40
12" figures				
RO5071	Rick Hunter	15	25	35
RO5072	Lisa Hayes	15	25	35
RO5073	Lynn Minmei	15	25	35
RO5074	Dana Sterling	15	25	35
RO5080	Dana's Hover Cycle	10	22	35
See also: *Exosquad*				

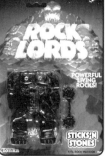

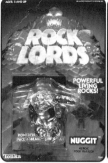

| RO6001 | RO6002 | RO6003 | RO6004 | RO6005 | RO6022 |

| RO6021 | RO60231 | RO60233 |

| RO6502 | RO6851 | RO6901 | RO7004 | SA1501 |

ROCK LORDS (Tonka) 1986

Rock Lords are a variant of the transforming robot figures. Instead of robots, they fold up into rocks.

		CNP	MIP	MMP
RO6001	Boulder	5	8	10
RO6002	Sticks 'n Stones	5	8	10
RO6003	Granite	5	8	10
RO6004	Nuggit	5	8	10
RO6005	Magmar	5	8	10
RO6006	Tombstone	5	8	10
RO6007	Crackpot	5	8	10
RO6008	Pulver-Eyes	5	8	10
RO6009	Slimestone	5	8	10
RO6010	Marbles	5	8	10
RO6011	Brimstone	5	8	10
RO6012	Stoneheart	5	8	10
Narlies RO6013-20				
RO6013	Narliphant	5	8	10
RO6014	Narlihog	5	8	10
RO6015	Narlizard	5	8	10
RO6016	Narligator	5	8	10
RO6017	Narlibat	5	8	10
RO6018	Narlirhino	5	8	10
RO6019	Narlilion	5	8	10
RO6020	Narlibaboon	5	8	10
RO6021	Rock Pot Vehicle	6	14	18
RO6022	Stone Wing Vehicle	6	14	18
RO6031	Terra-Roc	8	20	24
RO6033	Spikestone	6	14	18

ROCKY (Phoenix Toys) 1983

These figures were based on characters in the *Rocky* films. Each figure came with cloth

RO6700

trunks, removeable boxing gloves, and heavy-weight championship belts.

		CNP	MIP	MMP
RO6501	Sylvester Stallone as Rocky	10	20	25
RO6502	Mr. T as Clubber Lang	10	20	25
RO6503	Carl Weathers as Apollo Creed	15	25	30
RO6504	Hulk Hogan as Thunderlips	15	25	35
RO6505	Drago	15	25	30
RO6511	Rocky Sock 'Em Set	20	40	50

RODAN (Mattel) 1977

Much sought-after by monster collectors, this large figure of Rodan has a 38" wingspan.

		CNP	MIP	MMP
RO6700	Rodan	95	150	225

See also: *Godzilla; Shogun Warriors*

ROGER RABBIT — See *Who Framed Roger Rabbit?*

ROLLER WARRIORS (Lanard Toys) 1991

Action figures on roller skates. Each figure came with two sets of skates; one which

matched their costume and one re-used from another figure.

		CNP	MIP	MMP
RO6851	Iron Mike	2	5	6
RO6852	Scorpion	2	5	6
RO6853	Metallica Rex	2	5	6
RO6854	Hornet	2	5	6

RONIN WARRIORS (Playmates) 1995

This line combined snap-on armor pieces — a Japanese favorite — with "power coil" spring articulation. Each figure had a special post sticking out of the heels of its feet, enabling it to become tangled with the feet of other figures or grabbed by their "power hands." Doubtless this feature was designed to enhance play value.

		CNP	MIP	MMP
RO6901	Ryo	5	8	10
RO6903	Rowen	5	8	10
RO6905	Kento	5	8	10
RO6907	Sage	5	8	10
RO6909	Hariel	5	8	10
RO6911	Cye	5	8	10
RO6915	Anubis	5	8	10
RO6917	Cale	5	8	10
RO6919	Dais	5	8	10
RO6921	Talpa	5	8	10
RO6923	Sekhmet	5	8	10

ROOKIES, THE (LJN) 1973

		CNP	MIP	MMP
RO7001	Mike	10	20	28
RO7002	Willie	10	20	28

CNP: Complete, no package, with all weapons and accessories; MIP: Mint in package; MMP: Mint item in Mint package. Values in U.S. dollars. See page 3 for details.

| SA2001 | SA2002 | SA2004 | SA2003 | SA2005 | SA2006 | SA2011 | SA2013 | SA2014 | SA2015 |

SA3001	SA4001

		CNP	MIP	MMP
RO7003	Terry	10	20	28
RO7004	Chris	10	20	28

SAFARI ADVENTURE (Marx) 1976-77

This series of cloth-dressed human figures was issued with plastic jungle animals, vehicles and accessories. All but the heads and clothing were made in the United States. The scale was 7½".

		CNP	MIP	MMP
SA1501	Buck Hunter	10	25	35
SA1502	Sgt. Kogo	10	25	35
SA1503	Kim	10	25	35
SA1507	Elephant	12	30	40
SA1508	Gorilla	9	25	35
SA1509	Tiger	9	25	35
SA1512	Lion	9	25	35
SA1513	Crocodile	9	25	35
SA1514	Rhino	9	25	35
SA1520	Jeep	10	20	30
SA1521	Pursuit Truck	12	25	35
SA1522	Capture Cage	4	10	18
SA1523	Lookout Tower	12	20	30
SA1524	Camp	15	35	45

SAMBO'S RESTAURANTS — See Dakin

SAILOR MOON (Bandai) 1995

Boxed dolls based on the series. Figures were made in 6" and 11½" sizes.

6" Adventure Dolls		CNP	MIP	MMP
SA2001	Sailor Moon	2	4	6
SA2002	Sailor Mercury	2	4	6
SA2003	Sailor Venus	2	4	6
SA2004	Sailor Mars	2	4	6
SA2005	Sailor Jupiter	2	4	6
SA2006	Queen Beryl	2	4	6
11½" Deluxe Adventure Dolls				
SA2011	Sailor Moon	4	7	12
SA2012	Sailor Mercury	4	7	12
SA2013	Sailor Venus	4	7	12
SA2014	Sailor Mars	4	7	12
SA2015	Sailor Jupiter	4	7	12
SA2016	Queen Beryl	undetermined		

SANTA MICKEY (ARCO) 1981

A Christmas-oriented Mickey Mouse figure.

		CNP	MIP	MMP
SA3001	Santa Mickey	5	10	12

See also: *Disney; Mickey Mouse*

SARGE TEAM (Remco) 1984

These were probably leftovers from the Sgt. Rock series which were repackaged.

Sarge Team SA4001-04		CNP	MIP	MMP
SA4001	Sarge	2	4	5
SA4002	Bull	2	4	5
SA4003	Chutes	2	4	5
SA4004	Ranger	2	4	5

See also: *Bad Guys, The; Sgt. Rock*

SAVAGE DRAGON, THE (Playmates) 1996

Erik Larsen's The Savage Dragon comic book inspired this line which was distributed with Jim Lee's *Teenage Mutant Ninja Turtles*. There wee two versions of the She-Dragon which were found interchangeably the entire time the line was on sale.

		CNP	MIP	MMP
SA9001	The Savage Dragon	4	7	9
SA9003	Battle Damage Savage Dragon	4	7	9
SA9005	Barbaric	4	7	9
SA9007	She-Dragon (big hair)	6	12	18
SA9009	She-Dragon (mohawk)	6	12	18

SCHWARZENEGGER COMMANDO (Diamond Toymakers) 1985

A series inspired by the film *Commando*. Figures came in 2 sizes.

3¾" figures SC8001-08		CNP	MIP	MMP
SC8001	Matrix	5	10	15
SC8002	Spex	5	10	12
SC8003	Blaster	5	10	12
SC8004	Chopper	5	10	12
SC8005	Sawbones	5	10	12
SC8006	Stalker	5	10	12
SC8007	Lead Head	5	10	12
SC8008	Psycho	5	10	12
8" figures SC8011-18				
SC8011	Matrix	15	50	85
SC8012	Spex	6	12	16
SC8013	Blaster	6	12	16
SC8014	Chopper	6	12	16
SC8015	Sawbones	6	12	16
SC8016	Stalker	6	12	16
SC8017	Lead Head	6	12	16
SC8018	Psycho	6	12	16
SC8021	18" Matrix	45	75	135

SCOOBY DOO — See Dakin

SCOUT HIGH ADVENTURE — See *Official Scout High Adventure*

SEA DEVILS (Mattel) 1970-71

Mattel was riding the crest of *Major MATT MASON* when they developed this underwater counterpart. The air pumps used on many *Matt Mason* toys were adapted for underwater play, enabling figures to dive and surface. Battery-operated "sea jet" vehicles enabled them to swim. The Aqualander featured a motor for water use, and "hand powered" wheels to roll like a car on land. Two figures and playsets were offered the first year, with Zark and Kretor following in 1971.

		CNP	MIP	MMP
SE0401	Commander Chuck Carter	25	75	100

| SA9001 | SA9003 | SA9005 | SA9007 | SA9009 |

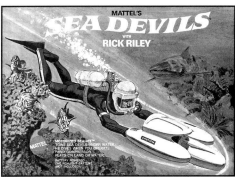

SC8011	SC8012	SE0401	SE0403

SE0405	SE0407	SE0409	SE0411

SE0501	SE0502	SE0503	SE0504	SE0505

SE0506	SE0507	SE0508	SE0509	SE1005

SE0403	Rick Riley	25	75	100		SE0504	Hitchcock	5	7	12		SE1004	Tae Kwon Do Warrior	2	4	5
SE0405	Zark	40	100	150		SE0505	Chief Crocker	5	7	12		SE1005	Golden Shaolin Monk	2	4	5
SE0407	Kretor	50	135	175		SE0506	O'Neill	5	7	12		SE1006	Thai Kick Boxer	2	4	5
SE0409	Aqualander	25	75	95		SE0507	Dr. Z	5	7	12						
SE0411	Search & Rescue set					SE0508	The Regulator	5	10	15		**SECRET WARS** — See *Marvel Super Heroes*				
	w/SE0401 & SE0409	-	250	350		SE0509	Darwin	5	12	20		*Secret Wars*				

SEAQUEST (Playmates) 1993-94

Inspired by the Amblin Entertainment television series. The Darwin figure was a late arrival, and was in short supply for some time.

	CNP	MIP	MMP
SE0501 Captain Bridger	5	7	12
SE0502 Commander Ford	5	7	12
SE0503 Lucas Wolenczak	5	7	12

SECRET OF THE NINJA (Remco) 1984

Each figure had action features which were triggered by turning a dial on the back.

	CNP	MIP	MMP
SE1001 Ninja	2	4	5
SE1002 Karate Black Belt			
Champion	2	4	5
SE1003 Kung Fu Master	2	4	5

SECTAURS (Coleco) 1984

Each of the *Sectaurs* came with a giant insect companion, and were packaged as a pair in a window box. Larger, hand-puppet insect steeds were also sold, complete with figures. In addition to plastic accessories, the boxes included instructions, a mini-comic (by Marvel) and an application to become a "Royal Guard Warrior" (i.e. fan club member).

CNP: Complete, no package, with all weapons and accessories; MIP: Mint in package; MMP: Mint item in Mint package. Values in U.S. dollars. See page 3 for details.

| SE2002 | SE2003 | SE2004 | SE2005 | SE2011 |

| SE2012 | SE2031 | SE7010 |

| SE7001 | SE7002 | SG5005 | SG5021 | SH1501 |

SE2001	Dargon w/Parafly	6	15	18
SE2002	Zak w/Bitaur	4	12	15
SE2003	Mantor w/Raplor	4	12	15
SE2004	Skito w/Toxcid	4	12	15
SE2005	Commander Waspax			
	w/Wingid	4	12	15
SE2011	Dargon w/Dragonflyer	10	25	30
SE2012	Pinsor w/Battle Beetle	10	20	25
SE2013	General Spidrax			
	w/Spiderflyer	10	15	30
SE2014	Skulk w/Trancula	10	20	25
SE2031	HYVE action playset	15	35	50

SESAME STREET (Tara Toy Corp.) 1986

The figures were sold on blister cards which came in two styles. Grover is actually a bendie, but is considered part of the series.

		CNP	MIP	MMP
SE7001	Cookie Monster	1	3	4
SE7002	Bert	1	3	4
SE7003	Ernie	1	3	4
SE7004	Big Bird	1	3	4
SE7005	Oscar the Grouch	1	3	4
SE7007	Grover	1	3	4
SE7010	Gift Set w/SE7001-07	-	20	26

SGT. ROCK (Remco) 1982-83

Based on a DC comic series. Dog tags with unique serial numbers were included.

		CNP	MIP	MMP
SG5001	Sgt. Rock	3	6	8
SG5002	Leatherneck	3	6	8
SG5003	Gunner	3	6	8
SG5004	Raider	3	6	8
SG5005	Marksman	3	6	8
SG5006	Mack	3	6	8
SG5007	Tanker	3	6	8
SG5008	Chutes	3	6	8
SG5009	Special Forces	3	6	8
SG5010	Cowboy	3	6	8
SG5011	The Instructor	3	6	8
SG5012	Airman	3	6	8
SG5013	Snow Force	3	6	8
SG5014	Dock	3	6	8
SG5015	MP	3	6	8
SG5016	Gyrene	3	6	8
SG5021	Action Playcase	2	4	5
SG5022	L.E.M. Attack			
	Command Vehicle	4	6	10
SG5023	Forward Recon Post	4	6	10
SG5024	River Commando			
	Patrol	4	6	10
SG5025	Action Machine			
	Gun Nest	4	6	10
SG5026	Climbing Assault Unit	4	6	10
SG5027	Track Attack Cat	4	6	10
SG5028	Airborne Parachute			
	Invader	4	6	10
SG5031	ATC Troop Carrier	6	8	12
SG5032	ATA Weapon	6	8	12
SG5033	LEM Attack Vehicle	6	8	12

See also: *Bad Guys, The; Sarge Team*

SHADOW, THE (Kenner) 1994

The weed of re-makes bore bitter fruit for the 1994 film revival of *The Shadow*. Kenner offered a mail-in hologram ring with the purchase of two figures.

		CNP	MIP	MMP
SH1501	Transforming			
	Lamont Cranston	5	8	12
SH1503	Lightning			
	Draw Shadow	5	8	12
SH1505	Ambush Shadow	5	8	12
SH1507	Ninja Shadow	5	8	12
SH1509	Dr. Mocquino	5	8	12
SH1511	Shiwan Khan	5	8	12
SH1513	Battle Shiwan Khan	5	8	12
SH1515	Mongol Warrior	5	8	12
SH1517	Bullet-Proof Shadow	6	12	20
SH1521	Nightmist Cycle	8	12	15
SH1523	Serpent Bike	8	12	15
SH1525	Mirage SX-100	10	18	28
SH1527	Thunder Cab	10	18	28

SHOGUN CYBER WARRIORS (Trendmasters) 1994-95

"Shape-changing liquid metal" (snap-on armor) was the central concept of this line.

| SH1503 | SH1505 | SH1507 | SH1509 | SH1511 | SH1513 |

| SH1515 | SH1517 | SH1521 | SH1523 |

		CNP	MIP	MMP
SH4501	Jason (Stealth)	3	5	7
SH4503	Mitch (Talon)	3	5	7
SH4505	Sean (Raptor)	3	5	7
SH4507	Michael (Titan)	3	5	7
SH4509	Lord Tyrantus	3	5	7
SH4511	Skragg	3	5	7
SH4521	Stealth's Power Cycle	4	6	8
SH4523	Talon's Power Cycle	4	6	8
SH4525	Raptor's Power Cycle	4	6	8
SH4527	Titan's Power Cycle	4	6	8

| SH1525 | SH1527 |

SHOGUN WARRIORS (Mattel) 1979-80

The original *Shogun Warriors* were 23½ inches tall. Each included spring-loaded weapons which delighted small children and caused concern among parents. The 3" figures were die-cast metal, and were sold individually or with vehicles. Three of the vehicles could be linked like a train. Four 5" die-cast metal figures were also made.

23½" figures		CNP	MIP	MMP
SH5001	Daimos	35	75	110
SH5002	Great Mazinga	35	75	110
SH5003	Raydeen	35	75	110
SH5004	Gaiking	35	75	110
SH5005	Dragun	35	85	125

3" figures and accessories SH5011-33				
SH5011	Dragun	2	6	8
SH5012	Grandizer	2	6	8
SH5013	Gaiking	2	6	8
SH5014	Poseidon	2	6	8
SH5015	Great Mazinga	2	6	8
SH5016	Combatra	2	6	8
SH5017	"17"	2	6	8
SH5018	Voltus V	2	6	8
SH5019	Dangard	2	6	8
SH5020	Leopaldon	2	6	8
SH5031	Dangard/Armor Crab	10	15	22
SH5032	Voltus V/Space Shark	10	15	22
SH5033	Leopaldon/ Mecadragon	10	15	22
SH5034	Varitank	8	10	15
SH5035	Vertilift	8	10	15
SH5036	Solar Saucer	8	10	15
5" figures SH5051-54				
SH5051	Raider	18	35	55
SH5052	Dragun	18	35	55
SH5053	Great Mazinga	18	35	55
SH5054	Poseidon	18	35	55

See also: *Godzilla; Rodan*

SILVERHAWKS (Kenner) 1986-88

This line was one of the first to widely use vac-metalizing, a process which later became almost routine. Third series figures were extremely rare until Kenner shut down a major Cincinnati warehouse. A large supply of last-series figures was closed out about 5 years after the fact through Kay-Bee. Now the first series is hardest to find carded.

| SH4501 | SH4523 | SH5003 | SH5002 | SH5005 | SH5004 | SI5001 |

Under the photos (package codes):

SI5002 · SI5003 · SI5005 · SI5006 · SI5007 · SI5008

SI5009 · SI5010 · SI5011 · SI5012 · SI5031 · SI5032

SI5033 · SI5034 · SI5035 · SI5036 · SI5037 · SI5038 · SI5039

SI5021 · SI5023 · SI5024 · SI5025

SI5050 · SI6515

SI5001	Flashback w/Backlash	5	12	16
SI5002	Stargazer w/Sly-Bird	4	8	12
SI5003	Bluegrass w/Side Man	2	7	9
SI5004	Hotwing w/Gyro	4	8	12
SI5005	Steelheart w/Rayzor	8	15	20
SI5006	Quicksilver w/Tally-Hawk	5	12	16
SI5007	Copper Kidd/May-Day	4	8	10
SI5008	Steelwill w/Stronghold	4	8	10
SI5009	Mumbo-Jumbo/Airshock	4	8	10
SI5010	Buzz-Saw w/Shredator	4	8	10
SI5011	Mon*Star w/Sky-Shadow	4	8	10
SI5012	Mo-Lec-U-Lar w/Volt-Ture	4	8	10
SI5021	Stronghold	10	12	20
SI5022	Sky-Shadow	8	14	16
SI5023	Tally-Hawk	10	18	22
SI5024	Sky-Runner	6	14	18
SI5025	Sprinthawk	6	14	16
SI5031	Quicksilver in Ultra Suit	6	15	20
SI5032	Moon Stryker/Tail-Spin	6	15	20
SI5033	Condor w/Jet Stream	6	15	20
SI5034	Hardware w/Prowler Launcher	6	15	20
SI5035	Bluegrass w/Amp	6	15	20
SI5036	Steelwill w/Laser Spark	7	15	20
SI5037	Windhammer w/Pitch Fork	7	15	20
SI5038	Mon*Star w/Laser Lance	8	20	25
SI5039	Copper Kid w/Laser Discs	8	20	25
SI5050	Maraj space ship	15	30	50

SIMPSONS, THE (Mattel) 1990

The FOX TV network animated series added a new and different dimension to action figures by having plastic word balloons attached to each character's head.

		CNP	MIP	MMP
SI6501	Bart		5	8	12
SI6502	Homer		5	8	12
SI6503	Marge		5	8	12
SI6504	Lisa		10	17	24
SI6505	Maggie		10	17	24
SI6506	Nelson		5	10	15
SI6507	Bartman		5	8	12
SI6515	Sofa & Boob Tube		8	14	22

SIX MILLION DOLLAR MAN, THE (Kenner) 1975-78

The Bionic Man figure is frequently found damaged or incomplete. The complete item included rubber skin on its right arm, which could be rolled up to reveal two plastic arm modules. The same arm could be removed and

174

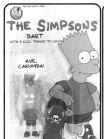      

| SI6501 | SI6502 | SI6503 | SI6504 | SI6505 | SI6506 | SI6507 |

SI7001   SI7005   SI7007

SI7020   SI7025   SI7031   SI7033

SI7035   SI7041   SI7044   SI7080

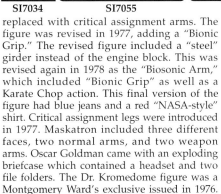      

SI7010

SI7034   SI7055   SI7056   SI7057   SI7070

replaced with critical assignment arms. The figure was revised in 1977, adding a "Bionic Grip." The revised figure included a "steel" girder instead of the engine block. This was revised again in 1978 as the "Biosonic Arm," which included "Bionic Grip" as well as a Karate Chop action. This final version of the figure had blue jeans and a red "NASA-style" shirt. Critical assignment legs were introduced in 1977. Maskatron included three different faces, two normal arms, and two weapon arms. Oscar Goldman came with an exploding briefcase which contained a headset and two file folders. The Dr. Kromedome figure was a Montgomery Ward's exclusive issued in 1976. Smaller figures of Steve Austin and Bigfoot were included with cycle sets in 1977.

Special thanks to Mike Vanplew for his assistance with this section.

		CNP	MIP	MMP
Colonel Steve Austin figures SI7001-03				
SI7001	with engine block	15	45	65
SI7002	with "Bionic Grip"	15	65	100
SI7003	with "Biosonic Arm"	20	100	175
SI7005	Critical Assignment Arms	10	20	30
SI7007	Critical Assignment Legs	10	20	30
SI7010	Bionic Transport/ Repair Station	8	20	35
SI7020	Back Pack Radio	5	20	25
SI7025	Porta-Communicator	8	15	25
SI7031	Maskatron	30	75	165
SI7033	Oscar Goldman w/ Exploding Briefcase	20	50	75
SI7034	Dr. Kromedome	150	250	400
SI7035	Bionic Bigfoot	45	95	155
SI7041	Mission Control Center	10	20	35
SI7044	Venus Space Probe	40	125	200
Bionic Adventure Suits SI7055-57				
SI7055	Mission to Mars	10	25	45
SI7056	Test Flight at 75,000 Ft.	10	25	45
SI7057	O.S.I. Undercover Assignment	10	25	45
SI7070	Bionic Mission Vehicle	20	40	80
SI7080	O.S.I. Headquarters	25	50	85
SI7090	Dual Launch Drag set	30	75	135
SI7091	Bionic Cycle	10	30	60
SI7092	Tower and Cycle set	20	45	85

See also: *Bionic Woman, The*

| SK9002 | SK9003 | SK9004 | SK9005 | SK9006 |

| SM1011 | SM5002 | SM7001 | SM7020 | SM7030 |

| SM7040 | SM7101 | SO8501 |

SKELETON WARRIORS (Playmates) 1994-95

Playmates pulled out the stops for this line, creating some of the most detailed and posable figures ever produced in the 6" size. The series was an instant hit with collectors, but failed to attract the retailer interest necessary for an ongoing toy line.

		CNP	MIP	MMP
SK2001	Baron Dark	3	6	12
SK2003	Aracula	3	6	12
SK2005	Shriek	3	6	12
SK2007	Dr. Cyborn	3	6	12
SK2009	Dagger	3	6	12
SK2011	Prince Lightstar	4	8	14
SK2013	Grimskull	5	9	15
SK2015	Ursak: The Guardian	4	8	14
SK2021	Warhorse	5	10	15
SK2023	Skullcycle	5	10	15

SKY COMMANDERS (Kenner) 1987

Sky Commanders were designed to slide along cables or plastic tracks. Cliff with Battle Track Dispatch was only available by mail.

		CNP	MIP	MMP
SK9001	Ascender w/ Commander Jack Reily	3	5	8
SK9002	Search and Rescue w/ Commander Rex Kling	3	5	8
SK9003	Cable Rider w/ Raider Rath	3	5	8
SK9004	Rollerball w/General Summit	3	5	8
SK9005	Deception Raider w/General Plague	3	5	8
SK9006	Geyser Attack w/ Commander R.J. Scott	3	5	8
SK9007	Battle Track Dispatch w/Commander Cliff Baxter (mail-in)	5	7	9
SK9011	Bomb Blast vehicle w/ Commander Pete Crane	4	6	8
SK9012	Track patrol vehicle w/ Commander Cliff Baxter	4	6	8
SK9021	Flex Wing vehicle w/ Commander R.J. Scott	6	10	12
SK9022	Locust Raider vehicle w/Raider Rath	6	10	12
SK9023	Battle Track Protector w/ Commander Jack Reily	6	10	12
SK9024	Jackal Raider w/General Plague	6	10	12
SK9025	Rapid Deployment w/General Plague	6	10	12
SK9026	Outrider w/Commander Rex Kling	6	10	12
SK9027	Cable Cannon w/ Commander Pete Crane	6	10	12
SK9031	Vector Command	10	20	24

SLEEPING BEAUTY (Mattel) 1991

Two figures were produced as part of an ongoing line of 12" Disney characters. The Sleeping Beauty figure's gown is reversable — pink or blue — with the pink side showing in the package. The blue material showed through the original bodice, so Mattel made a running change to a darker pink fabric.

SL2501	Sleeping Beauty (light pink bodice)	5	15	20
SL2502	(dark pink bodice)	5	15	20
SL2503	Prince Phillip	8	20	25
SL2505	Peasant Dress	6	18	22
SL2507	Maleficent Costume	3	6	10

See also: *Bubble Princess; Musical Princess; Perfume Princess*

S.M.A.C. FIGHTING TEAMS (Blue Box Toys)

S.M.A.C. figures were a Woolworth exclusive. Each included a comb for its rooted hair, and a weapon designed to fit in the figure's headband. S.M.A.C. stands for Special Mission Action Commandos.

		CNP	MIP	MMP
Commando Assault Team SM1001-04				
SM1001	Fuse	8	15	18
SM1002	Scuba	8	15	18
SM1003	Arch	8	15	18
SM1004	Lookout	8	15	18
Martial Arts Team SM1011-14				
SM1011	Shuriken	8	15	18
SM1012	Sticks	8	15	18
SM1013	Flail	8	15	18
SM1014	Mohawk	8	15	18
Special Forces Team SM1021-24				
SM1021	Plan Man	8	15	18
SM1022	Boomarang	8	15	18
SM1023	CB	8	15	18
SM1024	Dagger	8	15	18

SMOKEY BEAR (Tonka), (R. Dakin Co.) 1976

Figures of Smokey Bear, rangers, and campers were sold in a series of playsets by Tonka. Figures had moveable arms and heads, but were otherwise non-articulate. Most were glued to a disc-shaped stand. Each set included Smokey Bear, one or more Tonka vehicles, and at least one other figure. Some sets also included Golden Books and campground accessories. The Dakin figure was also an Aim toothpaste mail-in premium (See DA2230).

BARON DARK	ARACULA	SHRIEK	DR. CYBORN	DAGGER	PRINCE LIGHTSTAR
SK2001	SK2003	SK2005	SK2007	SK2009	SK2011

GRIMSKULL	URSAK: THE GUARDIAN	SKELETON LEGION WARHORSE	SKELETON LEGION SKULLCYCLE
SK2013	SK2015	SK2021	SK2023

SL2501	SL2502	SL2503	SN6501	SN6503	SN6505

		CNP	MIP	MMP
SM5001	Patrol Kit	25	60	80
SM5002	Camping set	30	70	90
SM5003	Smokey w/Rangers	30	70	90
SM5004	Smokey w/Friends	35	80	100

See also: *Dakin and Dakin-Style Figures*

SMURFS (Bikin) 1988, (Irwin) 1996

Unlike the original PVC Smurfs, Bikin's figures are articulated flocked vinyl. They were sold individually or in sets with two to four figures. The packages were generic, but stickers were used to identify the characters included in larger sets. The packages could also be cut open and used as play scenes.

Nearly a decade later, Irwin Toys introduced a new articulated *Smurfs* line.

Bikin flocked figures, 1988		CNP	MIP	MMP
SM7001	Smurf	1	3	4
SM7002	Brainy	1	3	4
SM7003	Smurfette	1	3	4
SM7004	Grouchy	1	3	4
SM7005	Baby Smurf	1	3	4
SM7006	Papa Smurf	1	3	4
Smurflings SM7010-13				
SM7010	Snappy	1	3	4
SM7011	Sassette	1	3	4

SM7012	Nat	1	3	4
SM7013	Slouchy	1	3	4
SM7020	2 Smurf package	-	6	8
SM7030	3 Smurfs Gift Box	-	7	9
SM7041	Circus box set	-	8	12
SM7042	Seaside box set	-	8	12
SM7043	Choir box set	-	8	12
SM7044	Cleaning Up box set	-	8	12
SM7050	4 Smurflings Gift Box	-	8	15
Irwin Figures, 1996				
SM7101	Papa Smurf	1	3	5
SM7103	Smurfette	1	3	5
SM7105	Handy Smurf	1	3	5
SM7109	Artist Smurf	1	3	5
SM7111	Baby Smurf	1	3	5

SNOW WHITE AND THE SEVEN DWARFS (Mattel) 1992

These figures were produced as part of a larger series of 12" scale Disney figures. The Snow White figure featured a gown which could be transformed into a village dress. In addition to a boxed set of the seven dwarfs, a special Dopey & Sneezy set was packaged with a trenchcoat to re-create the dance sequence from the film. A carded mask and costume was produced to transform any 11½" doll into the Wicked Queen.

		CNP	MIP	MMP
SN6501	Snow White	5	15	20
SN6503	Dopey & Sneezy	8	15	20
SN6505	Seven Dwarfs Gift Set	14	28	35
SN6507	Queen Costume	3	6	9

See also: *Bubble Princess; Musical Princess; Perfume Princess*

SOUND TEAM/ FORCE (Toy Island) 1989

Each of the three members of the *Sound Team* came with two plastic guns, and had two sound effects buttons on its chest.

SO8501	Captain Adam	3	8	12
SO8502	Agent Zebra	3	8	12
SO8503	Red Top	3	8	12

SPACE: 1999 (Mattel) 1976-77

Space: 1999 figures came in two sizes. Large figures were sold on bubble cards, three small ones came with the Eagle One Transporter. Seven small action figures were originally planned to be sold separately, but the other four never made it past the prototype stage.

Large action figures SP1010-13				
SP1010	Commander Koenig	12	30	42
SP1011	Dr. Russell	12	30	42

CNP: Complete, no package, with all weapons and accessories; MIP: Mint in package; MMP: Mint item in Mint package. Values in U.S. dollars. See page 3 for details.

| SN6507 | SP1010 | SP1011 | SP1012 | SP1013 | SP1015 |

| SP1160 | SP1304 |

ny's plans for the line, creator Todd McFarlane formed his own toy company six weeks before the 1994 toy fair. A favorite among collectors for its detail and faithfulness to the comics, *Spawn* figures have often been difficult to find because of lower production runs. Numerous color variations have been produced, including both running changes and full re-decos. Only major variations which affect the value of the figure are listed below.

Early packages were marked with the company name "Todd Toys." This name was changed to "McFarlane Toys" in 1995. The original figures were sold in plastic clamshell packages with a comic book enclosed. This was soon switched to a standard bubble card with a lightning-bolt pattern in the background. The first six figures were repainted, and a paper insert covered the comic book to give the line a "family" look.

		CNP	MIP	MMP
SP1012	Professor Bergman	12	30	42
SP1013	Zython	75	125	225
SP1015	Moon Base Alpha	25	45	70
SP1160	Eagle One Transporter w/figures	45	100	150

		CNP	MIP	MMP
SP1301	Issac Gampu	15	20	28
SP1302	Chris Gentry	15	20	28
SP1303	Tee Gar Soom	15	20	28
SP1304	Loki	10	18	22

SPACE ACADEMY (Hasbro/Aviva) 1977
This series was a Woolworth exclusive.

SPAWN (Todd Toys/McFarlane Toys) 1994-96
The *Spawn* line was originally planned as a Mattel product. Unsatisfied with the compa-

First Series, clamshell w/comic SP1401-11

		CNP	MIP	MMP
SP1401	Spawn	4	8	14
SP1403	Medieval Spawn	4	8	14
SP1405	Violator	3	7	9

| SP1401 | SP1403 | SP1405 | SP1407 | SP1409 |

| SP1411 | SP1411 | SP1413 | SP1422 | SP1422 |

SP1423 · SP1425 · SP1427 · SP1429 · SP1431

SP1433 · SP1441 · SP1443 · SP1445 · SP1449

SP1461 · SP1463 · SP1465 · SP1467 · SP1469

Item	Description	CNP	MIP	MMP
SP1407	Tremor	5	10	14
SP1409	Overtkill	5	10	14
SP1411	Clown	5	10	11
SP1413	"Blue" Spawn (Diamond Comics)	15	45	75
Repainted First Series w/insert SP1422-31				
SP1422	Unmasked Spawn ("hamburger head") available with or without insert	10	20	25
SP1423	Medieval Spawn	4	8	10
SP1425	Violator	3	7	9
SP1427	Tremor	4	10	15
SP1429	Overtkill	4	10	15
SP1431	Clown	4	10	15
Second Series, blister card SP1433-52				
SP1433	Angela, first release	5	10	25
SP1434	Angela, revised release	4	12	14
SP1435	Angela, painted staff w/ribbon	4	10	15
SP1436	Angela, painted staff w/o ribbon	4	10	14
SP1441	Badrock (blue suit)	4	8	10
SP1443	Chapel (blue pants)	4	7	9
SP1445	Commando Spawn, plain gun	6	12	20
SP1447	Commando Spawn, speckled gun	4	8	10
SP1449	Pilot Spawn (black suit)	4	8	12
SP1451	Malebolgia (yellow, assorted hair colors)	15	30	50
SP1452	Malebolgia (olive and brown skin)	15	32	55
2nd Series Repaints (McFarlane logo begins) SP1461-69				
SP1461	Angela (black and silver costume)	5	8	10
SP1463	Badrock (red suit)	4	7	9
SP1465	Chapel (green pants)	4	6	8
SP1467	Commando (gold gun)	4	8	10
SP1469	Pilot Spawn (white)	5	10	15
SP1471	Red Violator (mail-in)	8	18	25
Third Series SP1481-93				
SP1481	Ninja Spawn	4	6	8
SP1483	Cosmic Angela	5	7	9
SP1485	Redeemer	4	6	8
SP1487	Spawn II	4	6	8
SP1489	Violator II	6	12	18
SP1491	Vertebreaker	6	12	18
SP1493	The Curse	4	7	9

CNP: Complete, no package, with all weapons and accessories; MIP: Mint in package; MMP: Mint item in Mint package. Values in U.S. dollars. See page 3 for details.

SP1451

SP1452

SP1471

SP1481

SP1483

SP1485

SP1487

SP1489

SP1491

SP1493

SP1511

SP1513

SP1515

SP1517

SP1519

SP1521

Vehicles, Accessories, and Playsets

SP1511	Spawn Mobile	8	10	16
SP1513	Violator Monster Rig	8	12	16
SP1515	Spawn Alley	10	20	30
SP1517	Spawn Air Cycle w/Pilot Spawn	8	14	20
SP1519	Violator Chopper w/12" Violator	8	14	20
SP1521	Battle Horse w/special Medieval Spawn	8	12	18
SP1531	Gold Spawn (Kay-Bee Exclusive)	7	15	20
SP1545	Platinum Medieval Spawn (Puzzle Zoo/ Venture Exclusive)	10	20	25

SP1546	Future Spawn, black/red	6	12	14
SP1547	SP1546, black	6	12	14
SP1551	Medieval Spawn vs. Malebolgia (K mart)	-	30	50
SP1553	Commando Spawn vs. Violator (Target)	10	30	35

Fourth Series SP1561-71

SP1561	Clown II	5	8	10
SP1563	Cy-gor	8	15	25
SP1565	Shadowhawk	4	7	9
SP1567	The Maxx (black Isz)	10	15	18
SP1568	The Maxx (white Isz)	10	15	19
SP1569	She-Spawn	5	8	10
SP1571	Exo-Skeleton Spawn	5	8	10
SP1572	SP1571, w/full mask	6	10	15

Fourth Series repaints SP1581-89

SP1581	Clown II	4	7	9
SP1583	Cy-gor	6	12	20
SP1585	Shadowhawk	5	8	10
SP1589	She-Spawn	5	8	10
SP1591	Cybernetic Violator	5	8	10
SP1595	13" Spawn	10	20	30
SP1597	13" Angela	10	20	30

Fifth Series SP1601-11

SP1601	Nuclear Spawn	not determined	
SP1603	Overtkill II	not determined	
SP1605	Tremor II	not determined	
SP1607	Vandalizer	not determined	
SP1609	Viking Spawn	not determined	
SP1611	Wildstorm	not determined	

| SP1531 | SP1545 | SP1546 | SP1551 | SP1553 |

| SP1561 | SP1563 | SP1565 | SP1567 | SP1569 |

| SP1571 | SP1583 | SP1591 | SP4001 | SP4003 |

Sixth Series SP1641-51

SP1641	Alien Spawn	not determined
SP1643	Battleclad Spawn	not determined
SP1645	The Freak	not determined
SP1647	Sansker	not determined
SP1649	Super Patriot	not determined
SP1651	Tiffany	not determined
SP1675	13" Medieval Spawn	not determined
SP1677	13" Violator	not determined

See also: *Total Chaos; Wetworks; Youngblood*

SPECLATRON (S & T Sales) 1984-85

Another *He-Man* knock-off series. These figures had transparent bodies filled with glitter and water.

SP3001	Hero	1	4	5
SP3002	Kandar	1	4	5

CNP: Complete, no package, with all weapons and accessories; MIP: Mint in package; MMP: Mint item in Mint package. Values in U.S. dollars. See page 3.

SP3003	Dethlor	1	4	5
SP3004	Adak	1	4	5
SP3005	Deemin	1	4	5
SP3006	Venum	1	4	5

SPIDER-MAN (Toy Biz) 1994-96

Toy Biz broke *Spider-Man* out of the *Marvel Super Heroes* line starting in 1994. The first assortment of figures was released in conjunction with a new animated series.

The Rhino figure was delayed, and was subsequently released in limited quantities, making it the most sought-after figure in the line. A number of Rhino figures on English/French cards were imported from Canada, but English-only U.S. packaging is preferred by collectors. Figure cards were lengthened by two inches beginning with Assortment IV. The black and red "Night Shadow" Spider-Man was created in tribute to the character's original appearance in *Amazing Fantasy #15*.

| SP1597 |

SP4005 SP4007 SP4009 SP4011 SP4013

SP4031 SP4033 SP4035 SP4037 SP4039

SP4041 SP4043 SP4021 SP4023 SP4025 SP4051

SP4053 SP4055 SP4057 SP4059 SP4061

The Toy Biz's count indicates an Assortment V, but no new figures were produced for it. This was apparently the designation used for shipments including a mix of figures from Assortments III and IV.

The 12" collector's edition figure came with cloth costumes, and could be dressed as either Spider-Man or Peter Parker. Toy Biz's market-ing research indicated a higher percentage of female viewers than originally anticipated, so a matching 12" Mary Jane was also produced.

Carnage II was originally scheduled for Assortment VI, but was delayed as a result of retailer demands for smaller case assortments.

This section includes only figures sold under the name *Spider-Man*. Figures sold under the name *The Amazing Spider-Man* and figures made as part of a larger series appear elsewhere.

		CNP	MIP	MMP
Assortment I (1994) SP4001-13				
SP4001	Spider-Man (Web Racer)	5	10	15
SP4003	Spider-Man (Web Shooter)	5	10	15

SMYTHE BATTLE CHAIR ATTACK VEHICLE

SP4071

HOBGOBLIN WING BOMBER

SP4073

TRI-SPIDER SLAYER

SP4075

DAILY BUGLE PLAYSET

SP4077

SP4065				
SP4005	Dr. Octopus	5	10	15
SP4007	Smythe	5	10	15
SP4009	Carnage	5	10	15
SP4011	Venom	5	10	15
SP4013	Hobgoblin	5	10	15
SP4021	10" Spider-Man	7	14	18
SP4023	10" Venom	7	14	18
SP4025	10" Hobgoblin	7	14	18

Assortment II (1994) SP4031-43

SP4031	Spider-Man (Web Parachute)	6	12	16
SP4033	Peter Parker	5	10	15
SP4035	Kraven	5	10	15
SP4037	Vulture	5	10	15
SP4039	Kingpin	5	10	15
SP4041	The Lizard	6	12	16
SP4043	Alien Spider-Slayer	5	10	15
SP4051	10" Spider-Man (Wall Hanging)	7	14	18
SP4053	10" Dr. Octopus	7	14	18
SP4055	10" The Lizard	7	14	18
SP4057	10" Kraven	7	14	18
SP4059	10" Vulture	7	14	18
SP4061	10" Carnage	8	16	19

Electronic Talking Figures

SP4065	Spider-Man	10	20	30
SP4067	Venom	10	20	30

Accessories and Playsets (1994)

SP4071	Smythe Battle Chair	6	12	15
SP4073	Hobgoblin Wing Bomber	10	18	25
SP4075	Tri-Spider Slayer	10	18	25
SP4077	Daily Bugle Playset	12	20	32

Assortment III (1995) SP4081-91

SP4081	Spider-Man (Multi-Jointed)	5	10	15
SP4083	Spider-Man (Spider Armor)	5	10	15
SP4085	Green Goblin	5	10	15
SP4087	Shocker	5	10	15
SP4089	Scorpion	5	10	15
SP4091	The Rhino	10	20	30
SP4101	10" Super Poseable Spider-Man	7	14	18
SP4103	10" Spider-Man (Spider Armor)	7	14	18
SP4105	10" Mysterio	7	14	18

Assortment IV (1995) SP4111-4123

SP4111	Spider-Man (Web Glider)	5	10	15
SP4113	Spider-Man (Black Costume)	5	10	15
SP4115	Mysterio	5	10	15
SP4117	The Cameleon	5	10	15
SP4119	Venom II	5	10	15
SP4121	The Prowler	5	10	15
SP4123	Night Shadow Spider-Man	5	10	15

Assortment V

No new figures were produced for Assortment V. See above for details.

Collector Heroes

SP4151	Spider-Man	15	30	40
SP4153	Mary Jane	15	30	40

SPIDER-MAN — **SP4081**

SPIDER-MAN — **SP4083**

GREEN GOBLIN — **SP4085**

SHOCKER — **SP4087**

SCORPION — **SP4089**

RHINO — **SP4091**

SP4101

SP4103

MYSTERIO — **SP4105**

SP4151

| SP4111 | SP4113 | SP4115 | SP4117 | SP4119 |

| SP4121 | SP4123 | SP4161 | SP4163 | SP4165 |

| SP4167 | SP4169 | SP4171 | SP4181 | SP4183 |

SP4153   SP4171   SP4175   SP4200

Assortment VI (1995) SP4161-71

SP4161	Battle Ravaged S-Man	5	10	15
SP4163	Six Arm Spider-Man	5	10	15
SP4165	Spider-Sense S-Man	5	10	15
SP4167	Nick Fury	5	10	15
SP4169	Morbius	5	10	15
SP4171	Punisher	5	10	15
SP4174	10" Punisher	7	14	18
SP4175	10" Spider-Sense S-Man	7	14	18

Kay-Bee Exclusives

SP4181	Web Trap Spider-Man	8	20	25
SP4183	Web Lair Spider-Man	8	20	25

Assortment VII (1996) SP4191-99

SP4191	Web Cannon S-Man	5	10	15
SP4193	Octo Spider-Man	5	10	15
SP4195	Man-Spider	5	10	15
SP4197	Tombstone	5	10	15
SP4199	Carnage II	5	10	15
SP4200	10" Sensational Spider-Man	7	14	18

Assortment VIII (1996)

SP4201	Cyborg Spider-Man	not determined
SP4203	Doppelganger S-Man	not determined
SP4205	Black Cat	not determined
SP4207	Dr. Strange	not determined
SP4209	Hydroman	not determined

Assortment IX

SP4211	New Spider-Man	not determined
SP4213	Spider-Man 2099	not determined
SP4215	Stealth Venom	not determined
SP4217	Spider-Woman	not determined
SP4219	Total Armor Rhino	not determined

Arachniphobia

SP4301	Spider-Goblin	not determined

| SP4191 | SP4193 | SP4195 | SP4197 | SP4199 |

| SP5503 | SP6001 | SP6012 | SP6025 | SP6035 |

| ST1301 | ST1402 |

| SP4303 | Man-Lizard | not determined |
| SP4305 | Vampider | not determined |

See also: *Amazing Spider-Man, The; Captain Action; Comic Action Heroes; Die-Cast Super Heroes; Marvel Super Heroes; Marvel Super Heroes Secret Wars; Maximum Carnage; Official World's Greatest Super Heroes; Pocket Super Heroes; X-Men/Spider-Man Collector's Edition*

SPIDER-MAN WEB OF STEEL (Toy Biz) 1994

A set of die-cast mini-figures, designed to tie-in with the *Spider-Man* line. Each package featured Spider-Man vs. one of his many foes.

		CNP	MIP	MMP
SP5501	vs. Carnage	2	4	8
SP5503	vs. Venom	2	4	8
SP5505	vs. Dr. Octopus	2	4	8
SP5507	vs. Hobgoblin	2	4	8
SP5509	vs. Lizard	2	4	8
SP5511	vs. Smythe	2	4	8
SP5513	vs. Kingpin	2	4	8
SP5515	vs. Vulture	2	4	8

SPIRAL ZONE (Tonka) 1987

Zone Riders SP6001-04		CNP	MIP	MMP
SP6001	Dirk Courage	6	8	10
SP6002	Tank Schmidt	6	8	10
SP6003	Max Jones	6	8	10
SP6004	Hiro Taka	6	8	10
Black Widows SP6011-15				
SP6011	Overlord	6	8	10
SP6012	Bandit	6	8	10
SP6013	Reaper	6	8	10
SP6014	Razorback	6	8	10
SP6015	Duchess Dire	6	8	10
Accessories SP6021-26				
SP6021	Zone Runner	2	4	6
SP6022	Zone Blaster	2	4	6
SP6023	Auto Grappler	2	4	6
SP6024	Spin Shot	2	4	6
SP6025	Zone Drone	2	4	6
SP6026	Snapper Claws	2	4	6
SP6031	Zone Rider Cycle	6	12	16
SP6032	Sledge Hammer Tank	6	12	16
SP6033	Rimfire Cannon	6	12	16
SP6034	Bullwhip Cannon	6	12	16
SP6035	Frogman Suit	2	4	5

STAR RAIDERS (Tomland) 1977-78

A low quality "me too" copy inspired by *Star Wars* demand. Several figure packages depict a space ship which closely resembles the *Millennium Falcon*.

Four of the figures packaged as "aliens" were also used in the *Famous Monsters of Legend* line. They are highly-sought after on the Monster cards, but are of less value loose.

		CNP	MIP	MMP
ST1201-16	Star Raiders, ea	5	15	25

See also: *Famous Monsters of Legend*

STAR SHERIFF (Jak Pak) 1987

A cheaply made set of western-style space figures. The figures all had the same body, which included a gun molded into the right hand. Figures were differentiated by slight variations in the heads and paint jobs. A logo on the package reads "Galaxy Fighters Commando Force."

		CNP	MIP	MMP
ST1301	Figure, black outfit	1	3	5
ST1302	Figure, blue outfit	1	3	5

STAR TEAM (Ideal) 1978

The *Star Team* was a few new figures combined with a rehash of *Zeroids*, designed to take advantage of the space boom created by *Star Wars*. The Zeroid robot included with the Star Hawk flying saucer has red highlights, while those sold individually have blue highlights. The Star Hawk is a re-make of the ZEM XXI, which was made by Ideal in 1970.

		CNP	MIP	MMP
ST1401	Knight of Darkness	10	25	35
ST1402	Zem 21	8	20	35
ST1403	Blue Zeroid	10	25	35
ST1405	Star Hawk vehicle			
	w/red Zeroid	15	38	50
ST1410	Kent and his Cosmic			
	Cruiser	20	30	40

See also: *Zeroids*

STAR TREK (Mego) 1974-76, 1979; (ERTL) 1984; (Galoob) 1988-89; (Playmates) 1992-96; (Enesco) 1994

Star Trek action figures were first introduced by Mego in 1974, along with the original *Enterprise* playset. A series of four aliens was made the following year. A second series of Mego aliens (ST1510-13) was produced in 1976, and is extremely rare. Smaller plastic figures were produced in conjunction with some of the films, beginning in 1979. Decker was the limited figure for the large figures.

With the demise of the Mego Corporation, the rights for the figures were subsequently

ST1500

ST1501

ST1502

ST1503

ST1504

ST1505

ST1506

ST1507

ST1508

ST1509

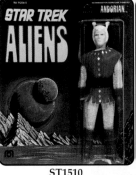
ST1510

ST1511

ST1512

ST1513

licensed to ERTL in 1984, but only four characters from *Star Trek III* were produced.

The Louis Galoob Toy Company made *Star Trek: The Next Generation* products in 1988 and 1989. Riker figures were so common that the toy stores were still trying to get rid of them on closeout as late as 1990. In addition to the usual scarcity of alien figures, only two figures of Data and Tasha Yar were included in each carton. Some Data figures had production mishaps, resulting in figures with blue-green or spotted faces. Collectors who are interested in such variations want all three, and pay higher prices for the deviations. Lieutenant Yar occasionally brings higher prices.

Galoob also made five figures for *Star Trek V: The Final Frontier*. These were more like statues than action figures, and failed to entice much retailer support. The film was also a bomb, and Galoob gave up the license.

Playmates outdid all its predecessors starting in 1992, producing a more diverse line of figures with superior sculpting. Over the years, the Playmates line branched out into numerous sub-lines, including figures for *The Next Generation*, *Star Trek: Deep Space Nine*, "Classic" *Star Trek* (the original TV series), the motion pictures, and *Voyager*.

Collector interest has always been greatest for figures of alien characters, as the values below clearly indicate. Toy companies before Playmates never seemed to understand what the market wanted. They overproduced Kirk and Spock while doing shorter runs on aliens or, as in ERTL's case, failed to produce any at all. Galoob's *Next Generation* failure was largely because no aliens were included in the first assortment. When four were later produced, many retailers had already dropped the line. As a result, three great playsets—the Enterprise Bridge, Transporter Room, and Alien Planet—were cancelled. Playmates included aliens from the beginning, and the difference—on the same license—was dramatic.

ST1750

For the 25th anniversary of *Star Trek* in 1996, Playmates planned to produce three figures limited to a run of 1,701: Picard from "Tapestry," Tasha Yar from "Yesterday's Enterprise," and Barclay from "Projections." Figures were packed randomly in the Orient. The idea sold well to retailers, but outraged fans and collectors. After numerous complaints, Playmates increased the production of Barclay to 3,000, but not before Picard and Yar had already shipped.

STAR TREK MISSION TO GAMMA VI

- IDOL OVER 18 INCHES HIGH INCLUDES:
- FOUR GAMMA CREATURES, OTHER FIGURES NOT INCLUDED
- YOU OPERATE THE CLUTCHING CAVE GLOVE CREATURE
- MOVABLE JAWS
- GLOW IN THE DARK EYES
- GAMMA PLANT TRAP
- SECRET TRAP DOOR FLOOR
- SUBTERRANEAN CAVE DWELLING

ASSEMBLY REQUIRED

ST1760

Mego Television-style figures		CNP	MIP	MMP
ST1500	Kirk	15	25	50
ST1501	Spock	15	25	50
ST1502	McCoy	20	50	90
ST1503	Scotty	25	55	100
ST1504	Uhura	20	45	90
ST1505	Klingon	20	40	80
ST1506	Gorn	80	175	250
ST1507	Cheron	75	160	200
ST1508	The Keeper	65	175	210
ST1509	Neptunian	75	175	250
ST1510	Andorian	225	450	650
ST1511	Mugato	160	300	425
ST1512	Romulan	275	500	800
ST1513	Talos	150	260	390
ST1750	Enterprise Bridge	60	125	180
ST1751	Enterprise Gift set	-	250	300

ST1760	Mission to Gamma VI	200	500	750
Mego *Star Trek: The Motion Picture* 12"				
ST1514	Kirk	20	45	75
ST1515	Spock	20	45	75
ST1516	Ilia	15	35	65
ST1517	Decker	40	100	150
ST1518	Klingon	40	90	125
ST1519	Arcturian	30	50	90
Mego *Star Trek: The Motion Picture* 3¾"				
ST1520	Kirk	8	20	35
ST1521	Spock	8	20	35
ST1522	McCoy	8	20	40
ST1523	Scotty	8	20	40
ST1524	Decker	8	20	40
ST1525	Ilia	8	15	30

ST1526	Klingon	50	100	150
ST1527	Arcturian	50	125	175
ST1528	Betelgeusian	100	200	250
ST1529	Megarite	100	210	275
ST1530	Rigellian	50	145	185
ST1531	Zaranite	75	140	80
ST1535	Set: Klingon, Arcturian & Rigellian (Penney's Exclusive, white box)	-	175	225
ST1761	Command Bridge	30	120	180

ERTL *Star Trek III: The Search For Spock*

ST1540	Kirk	10	18	35
ST1541	Spock	10	18	35
ST1542	Scotty	10	18	35
ST1543	Klingon Leader	12	22	50

Galoob *Star Trek: The Next Generation*

ST1700	Picard		5	9	15
ST1701	Riker		5	9	15
ST1702	Data		8	18	25
ST1704	La Forge		5	9	15

ST1705	Yar	8	15	25
ST1706	Worf	5	9	15
ST1707	Ferengi	22	55	80
ST1708	Antican	20	50	72
ST1709	Selay	20	50	72
ST1710	Q	25	65	98
ST1711	Data, spotted face	8	18	25
ST1712	Data, blue-green face	20	85	120
ST1713	Shuttlecraft Galileo	15	40	70
ST1714	Ferengi Fighter	15	30	50

Galoob *Star Trek V: The Final Frontier*

ST1715	Kirk	10	20	35
ST1716	Spock	10	20	35
ST1717	McCoy	10	20	35
ST1718	Klaa	10	30	55
ST1719	Sybok	10	25	45

ST1514   ST1515   ST1516   ST1517   ST1518   ST1519   ST1761

ST1520   ST1521   ST1522   ST1524   ST1525   ST1526   ST1527   ST1528   ST1529   ST1530   ST1531

ST1540   ST1541   ST1542   ST1543   ST1713   ST1714

ST1700   ST1701   ST1702   ST1704   ST1705

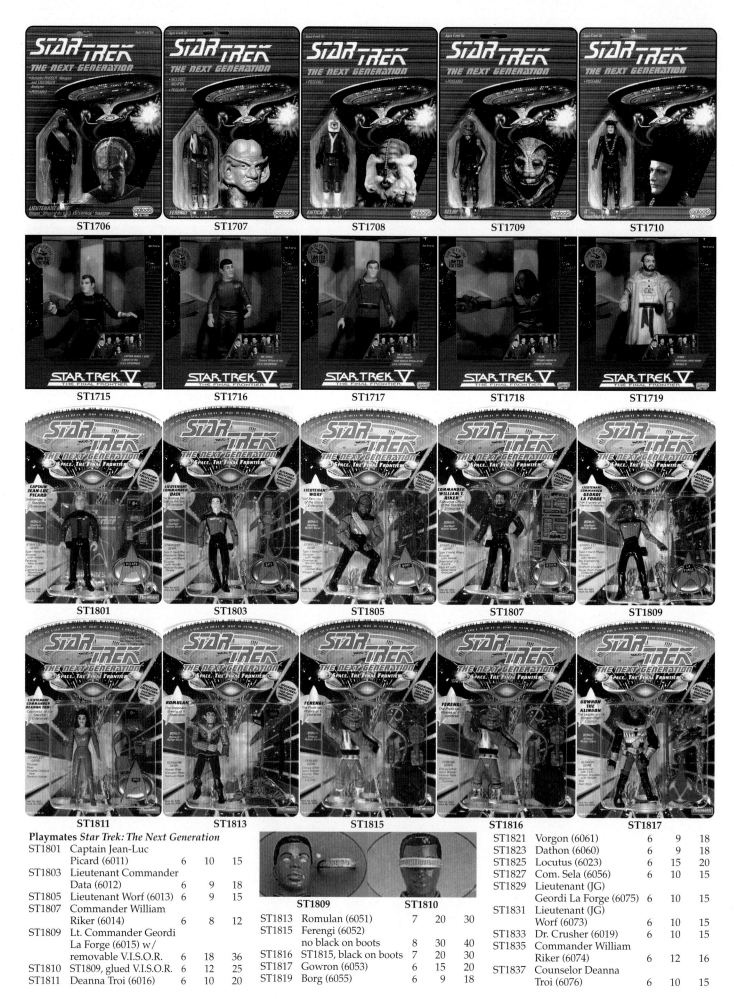

ST1706 ST1707 ST1708 ST1709 ST1710

ST1715 ST1716 ST1717 ST1718 ST1719

ST1801 ST1803 ST1805 ST1807 ST1809

ST1811 ST1813 ST1815 ST1816 ST1817

ST1809   ST1810

Playmates *Star Trek: The Next Generation*

ST1801	Captain Jean-Luc Picard (6011)	6	10	15
ST1803	Lieutenant Commander Data (6012)	6	9	18
ST1805	Lieutenant Worf (6013)	6	9	15
ST1807	Commander William Riker (6014)	6	8	12
ST1809	Lt. Commander Geordi La Forge (6015) w/ removable V.I.S.O.R.	6	18	36
ST1810	ST1809, glued V.I.S.O.R.	6	12	25
ST1811	Deanna Troi (6016)	6	10	20
ST1813	Romulan (6051)	7	20	30
ST1815	Ferengi (6052) no black on boots	8	30	40
ST1816	ST1815, black on boots	7	20	30
ST1817	Gowron (6053)	6	15	20
ST1819	Borg (6055)	6	9	18
ST1821	Vorgon (6061)	6	9	18
ST1823	Dathon (6060)	6	9	18
ST1825	Locutus (6023)	6	15	20
ST1827	Com. Sela (6056)	6	10	15
ST1829	Lieutenant (JG) Geordi La Forge (6075)	6	10	15
ST1831	Lieutenant (JG) Worf (6073)	6	10	15
ST1833	Dr. Crusher (6019)	6	10	15
ST1835	Commander William Riker (6074)	6	12	16
ST1837	Counselor Deanna Troi (6076)	6	10	15

ST1819	ST1821	ST1823	ST1825	ST1827
ST1829	ST1831	ST1833	ST1835	ST1837
ST1839	ST1841	ST1845	ST1847	ST1849
ST1851	ST1853	ST1855	ST1857	ST1859

ST1839	Guinan (6020)	6	10	15
ST1841	Lt. Com. Data (6072)	6	12	18
ST1843	Captain Jean-Luc Picard (6071)	6	9	14
ST1845	Ambassador Spock (6027)	6	8	10
ST1847	Admiral McCoy (6028)	6	8	10
ST1849	Captain Scott (6029)	6	8	10
ST1851	Thomas Riker (6946)	70	145	185
ST1853	Data, Red Uniform (6947)	80	185	255
ST1855	LaForge as Tarchannen III Alien (6033)	5	6	8
ST1857	Benzite (6057)	6	12	18
ST1859	Esoqq (6049)	15	40	50
ST1861	Captain Picard as a Romulan (6032)	5	7	9
ST1863	Lore (6022)	6	8	12
ST1865	Q (6058)	6	11	16
ST1867	Lt. Worf in Starfleet Rescue Outfit (6036)	6	10	15
ST1869	Ensign Wesley Crusher (6943)	6	10	15
ST1870	Cadet Wesley Crusher (6021)	6	11	16
ST1873	Lt. Barclay (6045)	6	10	15
ST1875	Q in Judges Robe (6042)	6	18	25
ST1877	Captain Jean-Luc Picard as Dixon Hill (6050)	6	11	15
ST1879	Klingon Warrior Worf (6024)	6	9	15

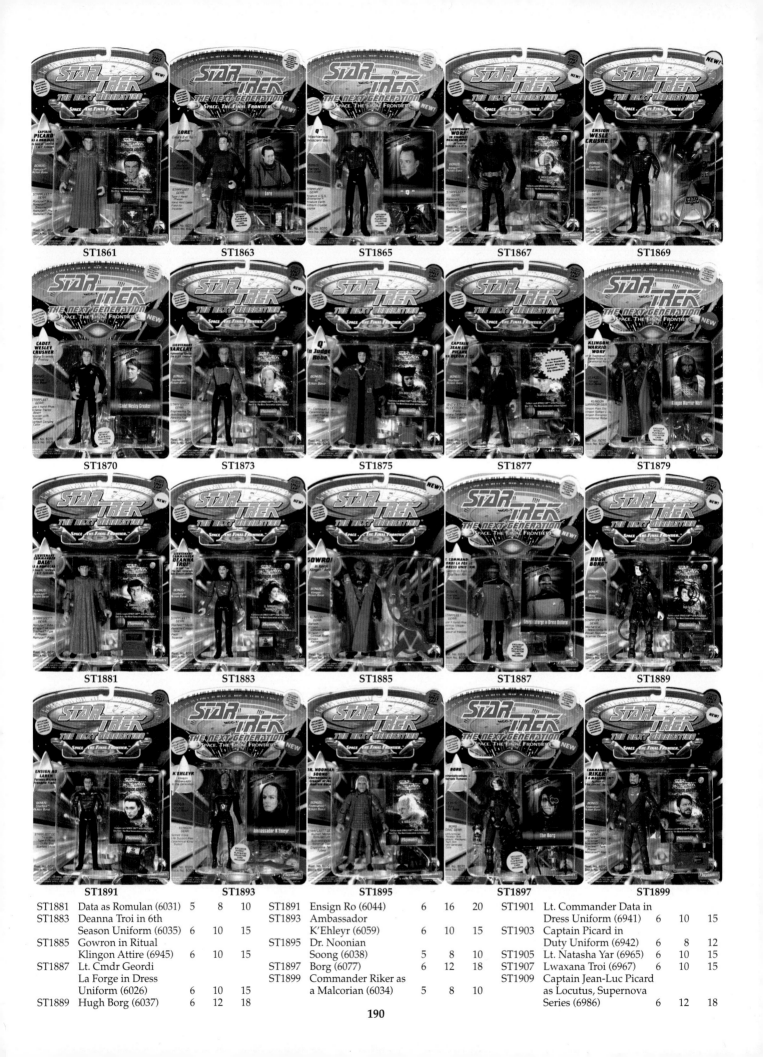

ST1861 ST1863 ST1865 ST1867 ST1869
ST1870 ST1873 ST1875 ST1877 ST1879
ST1881 ST1883 ST1885 ST1887 ST1889
ST1891 ST1893 ST1895 ST1897 ST1899

ST1881	Data as Romulan (6031)	5	8	10	ST1891	Ensign Ro (6044)	6	16	20	ST1901	Lt. Commander Data in Dress Uniform (6941)	6	10	15
ST1883	Deanna Troi in 6th Season Uniform (6035)	6	10	15	ST1893	Ambassador K'Ehleyr (6059)	6	10	15	ST1903	Captain Picard in Duty Uniform (6942)	6	8	12
ST1885	Gowron in Ritual Klingon Attire (6945)	6	10	15	ST1895	Dr. Noonian Soong (6038)	5	8	10	ST1905	Lt. Natasha Yar (6965)	6	10	15
ST1887	Lt. Cmdr Geordi La Forge in Dress Uniform (6026)	6	10	15	ST1897	Borg (6077)	6	12	18	ST1907	Lwaxana Troi (6967)	6	10	15
ST1889	Hugh Borg (6037)	6	12	18	ST1899	Commander Riker as a Malcorian (6034)	5	8	10	ST1909	Captain Jean-Luc Picard as Locutus, Supernova Series (6986)	6	12	18

ST1901	ST1903	ST1905	ST1907	ST1909
ST1911	ST1913	ST1915	ST1917	ST1919
ST1921	ST1923	ST1925	ST1927	ST1929
ST1931	ST1933	ST1935	ST1937	ST1940

ST1911	Lieutenant Worf in Ritual Klingon Attire, Supernova Series (6985)	6	12	18	ST1917	Dr. Beverly Crusher in Starfleet Duty Uniform (6961)	6	10	15	ST1921	Lieutenant Commander LaForge in Movie Uniform (6960)	5	9	12
ST1913	Lieutenant Commander Data in Movie Uniform (6962)	5	9	12	ST1919	Captain Jean-Luc Picard in "All Good Things" (6974)	6	10	15	ST1923	Data in 1940s Attire, Holodeck Series (6979)	6	10	15
ST1915	Ambassador Sarek (6968)	5	9	12						ST1925	Ensign Ro Laren (6981)	8	15	22
										ST1927	The Nausicaan (6969)	5	9	12

CNP: Complete, no package, with all weapons and accessories; MIP: Mint in package; MMP: Mint item in Mint package. Values in U.S. dollars. See page 3 for details.

| ST1941 | ST1943 | ST1945 | ST1947 | ST1949 |

| ST1961 | ST1963 | ST1965 | ST1967 | ST2003 |

| ST2005 | ST2009 | ST2011 | ST2013 |

| ST2015 | ST2017 | ST2021 |

ST1929	Dr. Noonian Soong (6982)	5	8	10
ST1931	Dr. Katherine Pulaski (6428)	5	9	12
ST1933	Dr. Beverly Crusher in 1940s Attire (6435)	6	10	15
ST1935	Captain Picard as Galen (6432)	5	6	8
ST1937	Geordi LaForge, "All Good Things" (6433)	5	8	10
ST1939	Sheriff Worf from "A Fist Full of Datas" (6434) Card over PVC figure	6	10	15
ST1940	ST1939, PVC visible	5	9	12
ST1941	Vash (6429)	5	9	12
ST1943	The Traveler (6436)	4	6	8
ST1945	Counselor Deanna Troi as Durango (6438)	5	9	12
ST1947	Interstellar Action Borg (6441)	6	10	15

ST1949	Interstellar Action LaForge (6443)	6	10	15
Space Talk Series ST1961-07				
ST1961	Commander William Riker (6082)	5	8	10
ST1963	Q (6086)	5	9	12
ST1965	Captain Picard (6081)	5	8	10
ST1967	Borg (6085)	6	15	18
ST2001	Shuttlecraft Goddard (6101)	10	22	30
ST2003	Bridge Playset (6103)	25	40	60
ST2005	Klingon Bird-of-Prey (6128)	9	20	30
ST2007	Romulan Warbird (6154)	9	20	30
ST2009	Borg Ship (6158)	10	22	32
ST2011	Starship *Enterprise* 1701-D (6102)	12	25	35
ST2013	7th Anniversary Gold Starship *Enterprise* 1701-D (6112)	15	55	75

ST2015	Transporter (6104)	15	30	45
ST2017	Klingon Attack Cruiser (6155)	9	20	30
ST2019	Space Talk Starship *Enterprise* NCC-1701-D (6106)	10	25	35
ST2021	Officers Collector Set (6190)	15	20	25

The Remainder of
Star Trek
appears in Book 3 of
*Tomart's Encyclopedia and
Price Guide to
Action Figure Collectibles.*